Hou ~~Grand A Flame~~

A

A

How Grand A Flame

A Chronicle of a Plantation Family,

1813–1947

BY CLYDE BRESEE

ALGONQUIN BOOKS
OF CHAPEL HILL
1992

Published by

ALGONQUIN BOOKS OF CHAPEL HILL

Post Office Box 2225

Chapel Hill, North Carolina 27515-2225

a division of

WORKMAN PUBLISHING COMPANY, INC.

708 Broadway

New York, New York 10003

LIBRARY OF CONGRESS

CATALOGING-IN-PUBLICATION DATA

Bresee, Clyde, 1916–

How grand a flame : a chronicle of a

plantation family, 1813–1947 / by Clyde Bresee.

p.   cm.

ISBN 0-945575-55-6

1. Charleston (S.C.) — Biography.   2. Lawton family.

3. Plantation life — South Carolina — Charleston — History.

4. Charleston (S.C.) — History.   I. Title

F279.C453A227   1992

975.7'915'00992 — dc20   91-13161

[B]   CIP

FIRST EDITION, FIRST PRINTING

2   4   6   8   10   9   7   5   3   1

For those who love and support me best:
my wife, Elizabeth,
and my children, Jerome and Catherine.

How grand a flame
    this marble watches o'er.
Their wars behind them,
    God's great peace before.

Epitaph, St. Michael's Church
Charleston, South Carolina

Contents

List of Illustrations

Acknowledgments

I AM INDEBTED to many people who have helped in the writing of this book.

My deepest gratitude goes to Dr. Louis D. Rubin, Jr., for his encouragement and masterful editorial help.

Willis J. Keith, "Skipper," of James Island is a historian by avocation, but a man who works with professional care and accuracy; his sustained help in supplying historical materials and in securing illustrations has been invaluable.

Thomas Lawton, an attorney from Allendale, South Carolina, president of the South Carolina Historical Society, president of the Huguenot Society of South Carolina, and a governing board member of the Caroliniana Library of the University of South Carolina, has provided much valuable counsel as well as access to his personal collection of genealogical materials.

The South Carolina Historical Society and the Charleston Library Society have been generous with their resources, and I am indebted to the staff members of these two institutions for their help.

I owe much to Mary S. Crockett, chief librarian of the *News and Courier — Evening Post,* and to Kathryn Gaillard of the staff of the Museum of Charleston for their help in obtaining photographs. My thanks also to Donald West for allowing me to examine materials at the Avery Research Center for African Studies, and to Angela Mack, curator of collections for the Gibbes Art Gallery.

Permission to use material from the manuscript diary of Cecilia Lawton was granted by Lavinia R. Campbell.

David Ruth, chief ranger at Fort Sumter and Fort Moultrie, graciously allowed me access to the extensive files under his supervision and offered much personal assistance.

Dr. Harry Freeman, secretary of the South Carolina Agricultural Society, offered valuable counsel and permitted me to read in the society archives.

Through conversations and bits of memorabilia I have been greatly assisted by Maggie Gardner, Bonum Wilson, Tom Waring, Thomas and Kennon Welch, and Azalie Washington.

My thanks to David May, photographer, and to Captain Buddy Ward, tugboat pilot in Charleston Harbor, for taking the picture of the Jetties.

Over innumerable breakfasts at Michels, Dr. Creighton Frampton, former superintendent of Charleston County Schools, whose parents were neighbors of the Lawtons on James Island, has given me unique and varied insights into the life and times of my characters that I could have obtained in no other way. His warm support of this undertaking has helped me immensely.

My children, Jerome and Catherine, have read the manuscript and I have gained from their penetrating, loving, and (as only from family) uninhibited criticism.

The blending of the collected information has been mine, and I beg the indulgence of the friends who have helped me if errors or distortions appear.

Athens, Pennsylvania   CLYDE BRESEE
July 1991

How Grand A Flame

A Visit to Peter Brown

THE CEMETERY WE ENTERED that morning was unlike any I had ever seen before. There were no neat rows of headstones set in clipped grass, but rather a tract of land filled with bushes, vines, and small trees that was more like a thicket than a graveyard. What my brother and I and Jamsie, our black playmate, were seeing that afternoon was a recently abandoned burial ground that extended back into slavery days. In the morning we had seen from our front porch a funeral procession wind its way across the pasture to the black cemetery at the eastern edge of the plantation. The hearse led the way, keeping just ahead of a slowly moving line of people dressed in their Sunday clothes, a line that stretched across the entire pasture. While we were playing we had heard far-off singing from the direction of the graveyard. By noon the singing had stopped and the guests began to straggle back to the public wharf on James Island Creek where they would take a boat for Charleston. Now that everyone had gone home, Jamsie, Kenneth, and I wanted to see the grave.

As we worked our way through the underbrush, we began to notice small rectangular stones, some upright and some lying flat. Many of the graves seemed to be marked with a low wooden post on which a little crosspiece was attached. These, too, were often fallen or rotten. Pushing our way through tangles of smilax vines that caught at our bare legs, we finally found the new grave, an oblong mound strewn with wilted flowers and ferns. We stood watching it silently. A fresh grave makes even little boys quiet for a moment. Then Jamsie said, "My mama say her grandpapa was buried here. He was a slave of Mr. Lawton."

"I wonder where he is," one of us said. "Let's look."

I

"I ain know he name. My mama say she look, but can't find it."

We tried to read a few names on the half-buried stones, but the writing was too eroded and moss covered to be legible. We turned to go. An abandoned cemetery cannot hold the attention of small boys for long. We had satisfied our curiosity. But I had unwittingly touched a bit of the past that I could not fathom, and would continue to probe and wonder at for the rest of my life. Only years later would I try to recreate that scene of black families slipping away from their field labor—briefly, anxiously—to this secluded corner of the plantation, there to sing and cry together over an open grave.

Such thoughts did not trouble me then. We had escaped the demands of our parents, and a sunny afternoon lay before us. We left the cemetery, detouring around a marshy inlet, and crossed the causeway leading to the pasture for dry cows that stretched in an unbroken expanse of green out to the harbor's edge. Scattered about the pasture were some fifty cows cropping grass and keeping a watchful eye on us. They were not used to people in this remote field and were backing away from us as we walked. I had come here with my father one gray, cloudy Saturday in the fall of the year when he hunted quail and doves; today there was a bowl of thin blue sky over us, and the only birds we saw were meadowlarks and cowbirds rising and falling in gentle arcs as we walked.

We came at length to the line where the pasture stopped and marsh stretched out a hundred yards to the Ashley River. Beyond the marsh and the river was the low, even skyline of Charleston with its row of fine white and red houses extending upriver until they merged into a misty line somewhere up the Ashley. We could see cars moving on Murray Boulevard and the stacks and superstructures of steamships projecting above the docks on the Cooper River. We were now at the harbor's edge, and to our right lived Peter Brown in his little cottage—quite unlike the usual black cabins—and certainly at the best location on the plantation. Behind Peter's house was his wharf that began with a long one-board walkway mounted on spindling supports, by which he could cross the marsh to a little platform where his boat was moored. The little house had several rooms and windows of glass panes instead of wooden blinds. Surrounding the front yard was a picket fence, probably built to keep the cows at a distance. Inside his yard, vegetables such as cabbage, beans, and turnips were growing, and some sunflowers were leaning against the house.

"Let's go say hello to Uncle Peter," I said.

"You know him?" Jamsie asked.

"Sure, he brings us a string of fish every Friday."

"What kind of fish?"

"Whiting and sea trout. We like the sea trout best."

We walked up to the gate, uncertain of what to do next, when Peter came to the door and invited us to sit on the steps of his little porch.

Peter was old without a doubt—a head of fuzzy white hair and a gray beard—but he stood erect and tall like a young man.

"How come you boys so far from home?"

"We've been out to the cemetery. There was a big funeral and we wanted to see where they buried him."

"That was Jim Scott's funeral. He used to work on the Bluff." Then he added, "I gonna be buried in that cemetery someday."

"Oh," we said almost in unison, not knowing what to say further.

"Emma, she my wife, she buried there, too. And my papa and my Uncle John."

Peter then settled himself in a big chair, apparently for a long talk. I had never been closely associated with elderly people and did not know of their eagerness for an audience—particularly if they lived alone.

One of us asked him why he lived "way out here" instead of down at the Bluff. He said that "everything used to be out here at this end of the plantation in the old days." The big house had once stood to the right of his cottage and the gin house and barns and all the houses for the colored people were over here. He could even show us the old bricks in the grass where the big house once stood. Had we boys heard about the War Between the States? Things were a lot different here before that.

"Massa Winborn, he was the granddaddy of the Mr. Lawton dat your father work for. He is the first Lawton I remember."

"Did you fight in the war?" my brother asked.

"No, but I go downstate with them and all the folks on the plantation when the Yankees took over James Island. Den we come back and start all over again. We build this little house. When Mistuh Wallace go to de house *you* live in, he tell Emma and me to stay here."

I can't remember why we left Uncle Peter to drift back across the pasture to our house rather than urge him to keep talking. The attention span of three little boys had apparently been exhausted.

At supper that night we told our parents of our afternoon hike and of our talk with Uncle Peter.

"Was he really a slave?" we asked. "We didn't want to ask him."

"Yes, he was," my father replied. "He says they made him a house and yard boy when he was about twelve."

"How old is he?"

"He's over eighty, but I don't know exactly. He says he has worked for the Lawtons all his life, and, as he put it, he 'stayed on' after freedom," my father replied.

"Then he must have known three generations of Lawtons," my mother said.

"Yes, he's worked under all three—Winborn, Wallace, and Alison Lawton."

IT IS SIXTY-FIVE years later. As the tour boat *General Beauregard* backs away from its pier and sets out on the cruise to Fort Sumter, the guide announces, "You are entering the Harbor of History. Straight ahead of you, against the horizon, you can see the fort where we will dock in half an hour. The Atlantic Ocean is beyond. On our right is historic James Island, scene of many struggles in the Revolutionary and Civil wars."

I think, Yes indeed. James Island. My island! And behind that hedgerow of cassena bushes and low oaks lies the Lawton plantation where I grew up. Harbor of History . . . Plantation of History. On my last cruise to Fort Sumter I could just make out the roof and dormer windows of the old Dutch Colonial house where I had lived, and where two generations of Lawtons had lived before my family came down from Pennsylvania. From my upstairs bedroom window of the Cuthbert House (such was its name then) the whole scene was spread out in reverse—the city of Charleston on its peninsula, the porticoed white houses on the Battery, and the two famous church steeples. The expanse of sky and busy water was half of our horizon then, and the harbor was literally a source of life for our plantation and much of James Island. From it the tide poured into our creeks and inlets, making little rivers and lakes for play or navigation; six hours later the water would return to the harbor to leave our boats sloping helplessly on a mud bank skimming with fiddler crabs.

The Ashley River and its twin, the Cooper, arise some miles back from the coast as two small streams heading for the same egress to the Atlantic Ocean. Flowing through the coastal lowlands, they widen into navigable rivers, and as they approach the sea leave a long, narrow peninsula between them; here rests the city of Charleston. These rivers, the Ashley and Cooper, broaden dramatically as they flow through the lowlands and meet inside the barrier islands to form Charleston Harbor. Standing on the Lawton shoreline, just opposite the tip of the peninsula, I was never able to fix the imaginary point where the two rivers meet and the harbor begins.

St. John Alison Lawton was the last of the Lawtons to live on the family plantation. When he turned from cotton production to milk production, he needed a man trained in dairy husbandry to manage his growing herd of cattle. My father was his choice. Our little Pennsylvania farm had been operational, but apparently not challenging enough to my father who was chafing for an opportunity to apply the principles that he had learned in college. The large and expanding herd of blooded cows on this plantation and its location near a good milk market seemed to be the opportunity for which he had been waiting.

When I was going over my father's papers after his death, I came upon a packet of letters from the years 1919–21 in the handwriting of St. John Alison Lawton. He was quite aware of the lure of his beautifully located plantation. In these letters, written after my father had completed an exploratory visit to James Island, Alison was trying to induce him to take the position of manager. Alison wrote:

> Have you changed your mind yet? Don't you think you might consider fixing up the old house by those live oaks? I'm sure that it is a beautiful location with the two large live oaks in the yard. The view of the city across the water is magnificent.

The Lawton plantation was not remarkable in any particular, other than for its "magnificent" location. One can easily find fault with its topography. Its seven hundred acres were scarcely six feet above sea level, and on the harbor side there were two marshy inlets that filled with water at high tide, requiring substantial earthen causeways to carry the farm roads. Other plantations had finer buildings, larger fields, and probably better-drained ones — everything except three-quarters of a mile of shoreline directly across the water from Charleston's famous Battery.

The Lawton plantation is no more. The city of Charleston has crept across the Ashley River and covered the Lawton pasture lands and cotton fields with paved streets and fine houses. To the east of the Cuthbert House where I lived, the pasture once rippled away to the woods in a succession of low green ridges because no one had bothered to flatten out the hilled cotton rows when the last crop had been picked and the grass had been allowed to take over. Dairying and truck crops had completely replaced cotton when I came to James Island, and Alison Lawton's herd of blooded Holstein cattle grazed on the pasture that nearly surrounded the house by the two live oaks.

Winborn, Wallace, and Alison had each made a living off their James Island plantation, but under vastly different conditions. We see them now against a backdrop of history that they did not fully sense. Winborn fitted most nearly the classic picture of the planter. He lived in the heyday of slavery and escaped the disaster that his generation had helped to create by dying a few weeks before the first shot was fired at Fort Sumter. His son, Wallace, felt the full force of the Civil War and led a peculiarly tortured life because of it, fleeing first the enemy forces on James Island and later

Sherman's army. His young wife, Cecilia, whom he married when she was but sixteen years old, kept a diary of those years, which she arranged as a memoir, a heavy, ledgerlike book bearing the label "Events in the Life of Cecilia Lawton." This book records with remarkable detail how the Civil War literally tore apart the lives of her large and wealthy family. And now Cecilia and Wallace's son, the gentlemanly and compassionate Alison, had brought the Bresee family to this historic plantation to live in the very house in which he had grown up.

When I discovered James Island, the plantation system was in its twilight years. We can lament its passing only with romantic and nostalgic sentiments of perhaps dubious value. The semifeudal structure of the plantation, depending as it did upon animal power and exploited labor, could not survive the advent of mechanized agriculture and a more enlightened morality. Cotton production could certainly have persisted under modern methods, however, had not an insect pest known as the boll weevil made the growing of long-staple cotton on the Sea Islands impossible after 1917. Planters along the Atlantic coast had prospered for many decades raising Sea Island cotton, but when we arrived on James Island no one was growing the prized fiber.

Even as a child I sensed that much of the talk among my elders centered around a better past that they all remembered. We were now living, it seemed to me, in a sort of afterglow of those good times. Remarks like this were common: "That was when Mr. Hinson made all his money" or "Down at Stono they cleaned up in those years." For me, the most conspicuous reminder of the Sea Island cotton days was the gin house, a square, three-storied barnlike structure with cavernous storage rooms. One could find these abandoned structures on most James Island plantations; ours stood down by the wharf on James Island Creek. Only the ground floor was used then. The giant one-cylinder gasoline engine with a six-foot flywheel that used to drive the cotton gin was now started up once a week to grind corn for the cattle. In the period I remember, the plantation owner-manager's life was not an easy one. He tilted daily with the interplay of drought and cloudburst, recalcitrant labor, killing winds that drove the sand against his fragile seedlings, insect pests, and fluctuating prices. Anxiety ran high under the live oaks and magnolias.

NOT ONLY ARE THE chief players in my story gone, but the attitudes and perceptions by which they ordered their lives are gone as well. If perception is the way a person internalizes what his eyes and ears pick up, no one today can conceptualize a black man as did Winborn and Wallace Lawton; the gap between their day and ours is unbridgeable. We can study their accomplishments and their values, we can find endless fascination in the way they met the vicissitudes of life, we can admire them and at times despise them, but we can never quite perceive the world as they did, never change places with them.

And what of my father's black friend, Peter Brown? My brother and I did not go back to his little house by the harbor. In the intervening years I have wished a thousand times that we had responded to his genial "Come back again sometime, boys." A child of ten cannot be expected to perceive those once-in-a-lifetime moments. We should have gone back on a rainy afternoon when no one could leave the house for hours, when Peter might have started a fire to remove the chill, and set a bowl of pecans before us (we cracked them with our teeth in those days), and talked and talked and talked.

We saw him periodically, of course, as when he came to the plantation store to buy supplies, or to leave his string of fish at our house. I can see him now across the pasture to the east on a Friday afternoon emerging from a grove of live oaks that now shades expensive homes, following the field road past our house and down to the store by the creek, wearing a hat—not a cap—bent slightly at the waist, his hands clasped behind his back. He was surely deep in thought. Sitting on the oats bin in the store, he would rest a while, exchange stories with the storekeeper, Mr. Knight, and with my father, who might be there to examine the books and meet the milk boat. Talk among the black boys lounging in the store was never quite as loud after Peter entered; they, like all of us, showed, quite unconsciously, respect for his age and his dignity. My father was fascinated, I know, by the aura of the past that seemed to emanate from this white-haired, quiet man, who, you sensed, harbored a dozen thoughts behind each word that he so carefully spoke. This man was inextricably linked to the Bluff, as were his children and his grandchildren.

My father's and Peter's friendship, which seemed to be based on deep admiration for each other, lasted until Peter's death about four years after we came to James Island. Thinking that a man over eighty should not have to walk a mile carrying his bags of groceries, my father would often have one of the field men deliver them to his house in a cart. Again, in late after-noon, from our house beside the two live oaks we would see Peter crossing the pasture on the way to his home at the harbor's edge, always walking slowly, hands clasped behind his back. Our family prizes one relic of this remarkable man, a musket that he brought to my father one Friday along with the string of fish. "This," he said, "is one of the first things I bought after freedom. I want you to have it, Mr. Bresee." My father was probably closer to Uncle Peter than to any other man on the plantation; I can only be glad now that he shared with us so many of the stories that Uncle Peter told him, for I can no longer ask my father questions.

Had my brother and I returned to Uncle Peter's house as he invited us to do on that long-ago afternoon, I wonder how carefully we would have listened. We should have asked him about old Winborn II, the first of the James Island Lawtons to emerge clearly from the mists of history, but we did not. We would have cared much more about Peter's advice on where to drop our lines in James Island Creek. I certainly would not have known enough history to ask him about the twenty-five years he spent in slavery. While no mortal could remain untouched by that experience, Peter gave the impression to everyone, even to me as a child, that he was free of inner warfare; there was no malevolence now, even though God knows he had reason enough for it. He had set his thoughts and his heart in order.

He might have told us about that fateful day in 1850 when Winborn and Martha Lawton, hurrying to prepare for a party, needed help in the yard and reached out for an alert ten-year-old slave boy to meet the emergency—a routine, passing decision of two busy people, but one that would lift Peter forever from the obloquy of field labor to which his brothers and sisters were doomed. His old master and his wife could not know that Peter would spend his entire life with their family, that he would outlive them and their children and be laid to rest on Lawton land. Neither could they know that when he was an old man working under their grandson he would tell my father and me much of the story that I now want to tell.

ONE

Winborn II, Master Planter

THE ATLANTIC COAST OF lower South Carolina and Georgia has been called a succession of sunken river mouths. The low hills in the Piedmont section of South Carolina grow smaller and smaller as you travel eastward, finally giving up to become sprawling, flat marshes that never seem to be quite sure whether they are land or water. This indeterminate area drifts out to the sand dunes of the barrier islands where nature suddenly makes up its mind and the sea takes over in earnest. The rivers of the low country below Charleston—the Ashley, the Stono, the Wadmalaw, running roughly from west to east—meander through the flatlands and eventually reach the Atlantic Ocean. Among these rivers is a network of connecting streams that create islands in the vast expanse of marsh—little ones the size of a house with a cluster of cassena bushes and a single water oak, or the large agricultural islands like James Island, Johns Island, and Edisto. James Island, unlike its sisters, is almost cut in half by a stream called James Island Creek, which leaves the Ashley River at a point directly across from Charleston's famous Battery and winds its way down toward the Stono River, never quite reaching it because it gets lost in the expanses of marsh.

Even in 1813 a home by Charleston Harbor had its pleasures—the small craft darting among the three-masters, the bell buoys rocking endlessly, the foghorns cutting through the morning mist. What new ships had come in over the bar during the night? Which ones were making sail? One could awake to the sounds of the city drifting across the water and still be pleasantly separated from the confusion there. The soil was fertile, yielding good crops; the South Carolina Agricultural Society had predicted that England would take all the cotton the state could produce, and was asking for more. The labor problem was easing also, now that slaves could be purchased from Virginia breeders.

By the year 1813 Winborn II, Alison's grandfather, had consolidated the lands that constituted the Lawton plantation as I knew it. He had absorbed a tract directly across from the Battery that was once owned by the Heyward family, who in 1747 had built the Cuthbert House, now renamed the Heyward House. This Dutch Colonial—style house has survived the hurricanes of two and a half centuries and played an important part in the lives of the Lawtons as well as my own. The Lawton plantation was now bounded on the west by James Island Creek and extended eastward for a mile to the Hinson plantation, then known as Stiles Point. Thus the Lawtons had navigable waters on two sides; freight and passenger boats could come directly across the harbor, or slip into the quieter waters of James Island Creek even at low tide.

The year 1813 was not the most auspicious year for this expansion because the United States had just gone to war with England. Extensive land holdings could hardly have eased Winborn's anxiety when he stared across Charleston Harbor at half a dozen motionless vessels, anchored and their sails furled. Some of those ships held that year's cotton crop, and some held the previous year's crop, bottled up by the British blockade. This plantation, with its charming picture of the city by the sea, the busy harbor, and his pride of owning this piece of land on which he stood had through the years brought Winborn II much pleasure. And now his country was engaged in a war that could destroy it all. During the American Revolution his father had seen the British men-o'-war sail up the channel in 1780 with their cannon roaring, and he had watched their big guns throw shells and incendiaries onto the city, setting great fires. And now his country was at war with Britain again. In this second war with England no enemy vessels had entered the harbor thus far, but the British were waiting out there beyond the bar, ready to pounce on any ship that attempted to pass. His cotton crop would languish in some Charleston warehouse or ship's hold where, for all he knew, it might rot. A shipper up the Santee had just lost seven thousand dollars' worth of rice in a schooner that the British captured outside the harbor. Business in Charleston had come to a standstill; hundreds of unemployed walked the streets. The ships in the harbor, loaded and floating at anchor, presented a calm and serene picture that belied the widespread distress in the city and on the plantations. The Ladies Benevolent Society, organized in 1813, was feeding hundreds in Charleston who had been reduced to poverty by the blockade. While no British ships had actually entered the harbor, the people on Sullivans Island and Morris Island had sighted them at sea and heard their occasional practice shots.

Every day Winborn walked among earthworks that had been thrown up to ward off the British not fifty years ago. Now young men in government—the press called them "War Hawks"—were springing up; they wanted a second war with Britain. With John C. Calhoun leading the way, they wanted to put England in her place for searching American ships on the high seas. "Enough of clumsy diplomacy," they said, "let us declare war at once. This growing young nation must not be patronized." But patriotic idealism ran smack into economic realities: England was now the greatest buyer of southern cotton, and this source of planter wealth that had developed so auspiciously was now threatened.

Young Winborn could only guess why his father had chosen to settle in the somewhat more limited lands at the mouth of the Ashley River, rather than stay at Edisto with the other early Lawtons; the fields were smaller on James Island and ran to wetness. Remote Edisto, an island called half seriously by its residents "The Republic of Edisto," lay a day's journey away and had larger and more feudally organized plantations than James Island. Winborn's land near the harbor could not duplicate the well-drained fields of Edisto that stretched in unbroken succession from hedgerow to hedgerow. Still, a James Island plantation had its advantages: no home was more than four or five miles away from the city, and the Lawtons' was only a half-mile away.

We may well suppose that the war dimmed everyone's spirits at the

Christmas party to which Winborn invited most of the Lawton clan. His reputation as a lover of fine parties was already established, and it would be hard to scale things down. A shipment of books and some new china was months overdue; even though Margaret Lawton had not had a new dress in two years, it appeared that they might as well forget about the order for silk. A glass of French wine was now but a dim memory. Yet, the plantation could supply enough food for a lavish dinner, and there was always room for distant guests to stay over. A man who loved entertaining as much as Winborn did would not cancel a Christmas party because of hard times. If things were not quite up to standard, people would have to understand.

THE GUEST LIST CERTAINLY included Winborn's sister, Beulah, from Charleston and at least two carriage-loads from the Beaufort area. This was the party about which Winborn is supposed to have said, "Invite brother James if you want, but after him no more Presbyterians. A few of them can spoil any party, and at Christmastime we don't want any sour faces." Three years earlier Winborn had asked to be separated from the Presbyterian church because some members had openly accosted him about his swearing and dancing. His name, so far as he knew, had not been brought before the church session; he would get out first. A story comes down to us — it's hard to see how we could know of it except through his body servant, John — that he had come home late at night, slightly inebriated, after a visit to his Black Swamp relatives in Beaufort District, and called out to John as he descended from the carriage, "Are you sure I'm home and away from those damned Baptists?" He soon joined the St. James Chapel, an outreach of St. Andrew's Parish, an Episcopal church on James Island where the strictures on social life were less exacting.

Margaret Frampton, Winborn's wife of nearly eight years, was born in Pocotaligo, South Carolina. The daughter of a distinguished planter there, she was a distant cousin to the man she married. Most of the Lawtons in the low country had married cousins; it seemed the one sure way to find a mate with the right connections, and the one sure way to keep the land and money from being dissipated. Margaret had been reared for her role as plantation mistress, and from what little we can learn of her through family lore and references in letters, she performed her duties quietly and beneficently.

Margaret's genius for management would no doubt have produced a Christmas Day nearly the equal of previous ones. The Beaufort group would like to stay overnight, and she would find beds for them. A quail and dove hunt for the young men in the morning, a standard procedure for Christmas Day, and a big dinner at three o'clock. The children would have been fed earlier and turned over to servants. After dinner a walk to the water's edge to stare at the motionless ships in the harbor, talk about the evil policies of the British navy, and make plans for the new year. Even in bad times the new year always brings hope.

The War of 1812 did not end decisively for the combatants up and down the Atlantic coast; the final days were, as everyone now knows, a disaster in communications. There was no fanfare when in the spring of 1815 the blockading ships drifted away. Small fishing craft working out near the bar began to report that they had seen no British ships. In a few days, first one vessel and then another made sail and slipped out of the harbor, and no new warships appeared on the horizon. The cotton factors and chandlers sent word that they were receiving new shipments, and slowly the life of the port returned to normal.

WE DO NOT KNOW WHEN "the big house" on the eastern edge of the plantation was built. It faced the water and from its broad piazzas on two floors commanded a view of 180 degrees—from far up the Ashley River curving to the west, the harbor and the city directly in front, and then to the tip of Sullivans Island as it disappeared in the mists of the Atlantic Ocean. There was room for this house without disturbing the trees. Long ago someone had planted a grove of pines and they now towered far above the lower growth; people called them and his plantation the "Hundred Pines," and although hurricanes and lightning may have thinned the grove, Winborn's pine trees were the most striking feature of the James Island shoreline.

Only a hint of how they looked is to be found in a painting by Augustus

Paul Trouche, a young French artist who had come to Charleston some-time after the trees had reached their full height. Born in France, he had lived in New York for a while, drifted to Charleston, and one day crossed over the harbor in a rowboat to study the trees. His attention had been drawn to them as he approached the harbor; a ship's officer had told him that the grove of tall pines on James Island was one of the sighting points he used in navigating the channel. How much artistic license Trouche took in composing his picture we do not know. His oil painting, which is called *The Hundred Pines*, is a dreamy, dark picture in the style of the times, mainly a landscape with a hint of water in the foreground. I searched the picture for traces of the big house, but found none. The painting, now being restored, is in the Gibbes Art Gallery in Charleston.

I have never been able to find a picture of Winborn Lawton's "mansion," as his daughter-in-law, Cecilia, referred to it in her memoir, although I have searched the libraries and archives of Charleston. The only person I have known who actually saw the house was Peter Brown, who must have worked in and around it until the Lawtons refugeed to Beaufort District during the war. He told my father that it had three floors, if you count the cupola at the top. It was built on the high brick piers of the period and stood not far from the Stiles Point line and near to where his own little house was built later. William McCleod, a cousin of the Lawtons who had lived on James Island all of his life and who died recently at the age of 104, told me that he had always heard that it was a "fine house—said to be the finest in the low country. This house that I am living in is a big house," he remarked, "but it's not a fine house like the Lawton house." I suppose by "fine" he meant imported wallpaper, hand-carved woodwork, some marble here and there, and rich hangings. Since it was built on land acquired from the Bennett family, it was often called "the house at Bennetts."

Long before the real estate developers took over the plantation, I stood at the harbor's edge and tried to reconstruct this building in my mind's eye. Grand piazzas facing the harbor, surely; two floors of them it must have had, with wide hallways, high ceilings, and a dozen fireplaces. Behind it and perhaps to the sides were the Hundred Pines. I came across a letter recently from a soldier of Charleston's Light Dragoons named John Strong, stationed on James Island, who wrote to his family in 1862 that "the enemy attacked us and we were harried out last night, at first stopping at the Lawton place, or the celebrated Hundred Pines opposite the Battery."

BY THE YEAR 1828 Winborn II was a well-established planter and represented St. Andrew's Parish in the state legislature. He had served for several years as free school commissioner for the parish, a job that permitted little opportunity for leadership or influence. The planters in the Charleston area were in need of representation in Columbia to counteract the lawyers and businessmen in the city who were always seeking election, and Winborn seemed the right man for the post. He won easily.

THE NEED FOR PLANTERS in the halls of government seemed imperative to Winborn and his colleagues; South Carolina, with its large plantations with many slaves, and the seaports, created problems that upstate men did not see. Winborn took public office in the same year that two other South Carolinians were elected to high public office: Andrew Jackson to become president and John C. Calhoun his vice president.

Margaret fell ill and died sometime in 1830, while Winborn was in the legislature. We can probably never know the nature of her illness, diagnostic methods being what they were at that time. Peter, of course, did not remember her, and we do not know exactly where she was buried. She left six children who grew to maturity, all of whom made careers and marriages in keeping with their economic and social station. She seems to have played well the role of mistress of the plantation, supporting her husband in his public life as well as quietly assisting in the many duties of managing her household and its large contingent of slaves.

We do not know much about Winborn Lawton as a planter. We know much more about his son, Wallace, because he remained on the plantation and "planted" there for the majority of his life. I have conversed with several of his relatives who knew him personally. His father, Winborn, in addition to being a planter, held posts both in local and state government and we have a little information about his role in these positions. Certainly he was a wealthy man by the standards of his day. James Osker writes that "to own twenty slaves in 1860 was to be among the wealthiest men in America, easily within the top five per cent of the southern white families . . . only a small fraction of slaveholders, less than two and a half per cent, ever owned fifty slaves or more." While Winborn was in the state legislature he probably passed the direction of the plantation to managers and overseers. The well-to-do low-country families frequently went north and inland to avoid malaria and yellow fever. His will mentions a body servant, John, who was to be given to his eldest son, William. It is hard to see Winborn whole, for as a man recedes into history there is a tendency to view him more and more in generalizations and stereotypes, unless one determines to engage in muckraking or to present a preconceived picture. I have no such intention, and could do neither with the facts available.

Slavery on the plantation was a system for enforced gang labor. Like livestock, slaves were owned. But they were *not* livestock; they were human beings: men and women. The relationship between owner and property, therefore, was a complex matter, with far-reaching economic, social, and moral ramifications. All slaves suffered a subtle but deeply damaging wrong that their masters never dreamed of. In the state of complete dependence upon and servitude to the master, slaves were never permitted to learn a fundamental principle of responsible adulthood, the principle of delayed gratification. Their labors could produce nothing but the immediate satisfaction of bodily needs; they learned early in life never to set goals, for goals would never be reached, and unrealized desire could only intensify their misery. Their masters, with characteristic lack of insight, summed up the situation with the words "they are just naturally lazy."

The basic family ties were always threatened by disruption; fathers or mothers could never be authority figures to their children because they possessed no authority. All authority was vested in the owner, who could heap abuse and humiliation on parents in the presence of their children. Some charitable masters would refuse to break up slave families, but this concern could not reach out from the grave; when estates were settled at death, economic interests subjugated all others. One of the abiding fears of slaves in even the more humanitarian plantations was "what will happen to us when old Marsa dies?"

The facts are that the plantation prospered, and this prosperity was fueled by slave labor, a labor that was controlled and directed by the threat of punishment. One has only to ask what would induce men and women to work from dawn till dark on a weekly ration of three pecks of meal and a piece of salt pork, sleep on ground that was softened only by straw or hay, return at dawn to an unending succession of days to a labor that was dignified by no reward whatever, only the promise of sustenance and of ultimate deliverance by death. Will men and women be persuaded to follow this deadening routine all the days of their lives by gentle words of pleading? The Charleston novelist and poet, DuBose Heyward, confronted the fact in his contribution to *The Carolina Low-Country* published in 1931 by the Society for the Preservation of Spirituals: "Slaves were punished. The lash was employed." He adds, however, that "we must not forget that during the period of slavery the cat-o'-nine-tails was used in the United States Navy, and in the City of Charleston, as well as in New England, the public whipping post was commonly employed as a disciplinary measure for white petty offenders." There were many in the South who, as incontrovertible evidence shows, refused to own slaves for moral reasons, or if they did, treated them humanely, but the critical factor in any discussion of the institution of slavery is that the punishment I have mentioned was permissible and legally sanctioned.

We must conclude that if Winborn's cotton crops produced his wealth then he, like all planters, relied upon coercion expressed in violence to the human body. In defense of the slavery system, elaborate, overintellectualized justifications poured from the legislative halls, the press, and the pulpits of the South. The idea needed continual reinforcement, for slavery imposed an enormous emotional strain not only on the slaves themselves, but also upon their white masters who were supposed to be the benefactors of the system. To be seen by the world as supporting an institution that most civilized nations abjured created a frantic defensiveness in the South.

Clyde Bresee

IN THE EARLY EIGHTEEN-TWENTIES three people with powerful personalities appeared in the city across the Ashley River. They were the sisters Sarah and Angelina Grimké and the mulatto Denmark Vesey. These three personified the coiled spring that lay just below the surface of the South's "peculiar institution."

Vesey first attracted attention when he was twelve years old, on a slave ship headed for Santo Domingo. The ship's officers were impressed by this bright, handsome youth, tall for his age, and they dressed him up in fine clothes. He became a ward of the captain and was later sold for a good price. The buyer found fault with the boy for reasons unknown, returned him to the captain, and got his money back. Denmark landed in Charleston, took the name of his owner, and was a faithful slave for twenty years, becoming an active member of the African Methodist Episcopal church. Then one day he entered a lottery, won fifteen hundred dollars, purchased his freedom, and set himself up as a carpenter. He apparently took trips north where he came under the influence of the abolitionists and, according to Charlestonians, where he picked up his evil doctrines. He was said to be a fluent and convincing talker and a man of high energy.

From here on, Denmark Vesey's role in the aborted "insurrection" is far from clear. A complete account of what actually did happen may never be known, but what is important to us is knowing what the people of Charleston *believed* to have happened. Indeed, Vesey may not have been the prime instigator, for a number of others up and down the coast were involved. What follows is the popularly believed account of the event and those responsible; it was believed by enough of the people of Charleston for them to conduct a public hanging of Denmark Vesey and thirty-five slaves.

The plan—Vesey's plan—was for all the slaves in the Charleston low country, beginning with those on the plantations, to march on the arsenal in the city, kill the officials, and take over the town. There is evidence that organizers did work among some of the slaves on the low country plantations, particularly among the field-workers, on whom the cruelties of slavery fell most painfully. From this distance we can only speculate about the involvement of the slaves on James Island; it is not hard to believe that there was a cell of the insurrectionists among the field-workers on a plantation so close to Charleston.

Vesey's chief colleague was Gullah Jack, said to be a conjurer and to have a large following among the slaves. He traveled to plantations as far south as Beaufort and up to the Santee River, winning followers for the insurrection by his necromantic skills. The slaves on the islands were to converge on Charleston on the night of June 12, 1822, capture the armory—it was not well secured—execute the white officers, and take over the city. Mrs. Ravenel in her book *Charleston* (1906) writes: "The Intendant and the Governor were to be instantly killed; the town fired in many places; all white men to be massacred; the women kept; all booty to be secured. There was much talk of St. Domingo, to which place they were to go with their plunder."

But a few days before the appointed night, some house servants revealed the plan to their master. The authorities spread the word at once, the guards around the armory were doubled, and the militia placed on the alert. Mrs. Ravenel continues: "There was horrible anxiety, and few people slept on the night of the 12th of June." Hearing of the leak, Denmark Vesey immediately called off the raid. The authorities closed in upon him, and neither he nor his leaders escaped.

OVER THE NEXT TWENTY YEARS the effect of the abortive Vesey revolt on master-slave relationships, however, was electric. The planters throughout the South saw at once that education was the greatest threat to servility. Vesey and his lieutenants were educated and no doubt read abolitionist literature—stuff such as Charleston's banished Grimké sisters were putting out. The solution was obvious. South Carolina and ten other states passed laws making it a crime to teach slaves to read or write. Slaves were forbidden to talk in groups of more than two on the street and were required to be in their cabins after dark. The convivial gathering of field hands around a bonfire at night to sing and pray—the only emotional and spiritual release they had after a day of meaningless labor—was forbidden.

The whole frightening episode unified the planters as nothing had done before; this threat to white supremacy came at a time when all believed that the burgeoning cotton economy would collapse without slave labor. The day of King Cotton had come, and in the decades from 1820 to 1860 the slavery system in the South reached its most entrenched state.

THE "MAD" GRIMKÉ SISTERS, who were blamed for much unrest among the slaves, had left town some years earlier and were stirring things up in the North with their speeches and books. (Winborn was a little older than Sarah Grimké and could easily have attended parties with her in the city.) The two sisters had rebelled against slavery from childhood. The town was stunned when the two daughters of old Judge Grimké—rising belles in Charleston society—became raving abolitionists, left Charleston, joined the Quakers and antislavery groups, and, as their friends said, "lost their reason completely." Fragments of the story of their fame and speeches drifted back to Charleston, although no one professed to know much about them. On the plantations of the South their teaching served only to draw the lines tighter around slavery, and in intellectual and educational circles to elicit a flood of books and pamphlets in defense of the slavery system.

TOWARD THE END OF Winborn's fourth year in Columbia, he was deep into the matter of nullification. In popular history books today the word gets only passing attention, as it probably should, but to Winborn and his fellow planters it was a monumental principle that critically affected their livelihoods. The merchants and foreign traders of the industrial North were taking unfair advantage of the agricultural South. Stated in its simplest form, that was the problem. If ever a man might battle in the legislature for the rights of his constituents, this was his opportunity. Nullification came close to producing the Civil War thirty years ahead of time.

The agitation over slavery triggered by the Missouri Compromise debates, the fear of servile insurrection that followed the Vesey conspiracy, and the rise of Abolitionist sentiment in the Northeast coincided during the 1820s with a profound economic decline that left the state of South

How Grand A Flame

Carolina and Charleston in a more than ordinarily distressed condition. One of the results of the War of 1812–1814 was the stimulation of manufactures in New England and the Middle Atlantic states. Despite several abortive tries, South Carolina failed to follow suit; the extremely high prices being paid for Sea Island cotton immediately after the war encouraged investment in land and slaves rather than manufacturing. The prosperity of the city of Charleston was greatly dependent upon its role as a seaport. But where in the previous century it had grown wealthy as the central port for the exporting of rice, it was able to maintain no such hegemony in the export of cotton. To do so, as George C. Rogers, Jr., declares in *Charleston in the Age of the Pinckneys,* it would have had to develop canal and then railroad access to the interior and the Deep South, and to do so required a merchandizing expertise that the city failed to display. As the rich lands of the newly opened Alabama and Mississippi country began to eclipse the depleted soil of the East in the profitable growing of cotton for the market, the importance of Charleston and South Carolina in the nation's economy dwindled.

As Rogers points out, the development of steam power for ship propulsion was fraught with consequence for city and state. For as long as goods from Europe arrived by sail, the most efficient and direct route was by way of the West Indies and over to the American mainland along the Carolina coast. Steam power, however, meant that westbound ships could move directly to the Northeast across the North Atlantic, so that Charleston was now far from the east-west shipping routes and no longer an important port in transoceanic commerce.

With the rise of manufactures, the North no longer needed southern economic support. I quote George Rogers: "What was revealed was a bitter rivalry between the ports, with New York winning at the expense of Charleston, among others." While the Charlestonians invested their money in cotton, New York and New England sent their buyers down to purchase the crops and their steam packets to transport it either directly to England or else to the spinning mills of Massachusetts and Rhode Island, where it was made into cloth. What economists refer to as "value added" to raw materials and natural products through manufacturing processes remained no important part of the South Carolina economy; the Northeast and England were allowed to reap the revenues from converting cotton into cloth.

The political provisions for representation in the Congress of the United States had been framed for thirteen seaboard states, and had reflected a balance of power between New England, the Middle Atlantic states, and the South. Had the national boundaries stayed more or less as they were in 1789, the sectional schism might have been held in check. But instead of stasis, what swiftly developed was a dynamic situation whereby, as population crowded westward, the old balance was destroyed. In the competition for control of the new territories being opened up for statehood, almost all the advantage in westward expansion lay with New York and the Northeast, and against South Carolina and Charleston. Geographically, the rivers that tapped the southern interior flowed north-south, not eastward to South Carolina and the port of Charleston. The entrepreneurs of New York, by constructing the Erie Canal, were able to effect a link to the Great Lakes, thus giving the port of New York direct access to the upper Midwest. Moreover, where competition with slave labor discouraged immigration into the southern states, population poured into the old Northwest Territory and beyond.

Economically, socially, and politically the canals and railroads — the Pennsylvania Railroad, the New York Central, the Baltimore and Ohio — were binding the interior of the continent ever more powerfully to the Northeastern and Middle Atlantic cities. Charleston and South Carolina were losing out. Efforts to build a railroad that would link the state's port city to Cincinnati and the Midwest failed, both for lack of capital and because Charleston itself was of two minds on the matter. To quote from Rogers's excellent book yet again:

> The attitude of the city is best expressed in the fact, as the building of the railroad drew near the city, the city would not let the company lay tracks to the wharves. The railroad must stop at Line Street, the 1814 fortifications and the city limits of those days. All freight must

be transshipped to wagons and hauled to the docks. The advantage of bypassing Savannah was thus lost in the city of Charleston itself. And so Charleston held up her hand to the smoking engines and said, "Do not enter."

Even in the slave states the preponderance of political power was shifting from the old seaboard centers to the Deep South. The result of all this was that Charleston and South Carolina developed a siege mentality — a cherished way of life was in danger. A united front must be presented to the enemy; internal dissent must be suppressed. John C. Calhoun, the state's leading spokesman, who in the 1810s and early 1820s was no foe to the federal government's role in furthering internal improvements while fostering domestic manufactures by protecting them from cheaper European imports through a tariff, and who was an ardent nationalist and a critic of sectionalism, was the bellwether. By the mid-1820s he began drawing back, changing his position, and, as vice president of the United States under Andrew Jackson, emerging as the spokesman for strict construction of the provisions of the Constitution and the placing of all powers not clearly granted to the federal government in the hands of the individual states themselves. As the nullification crisis arose, Calhoun moved to become its leader.

In Columbia, Winborn no doubt had heard Thomas Cooper in a public address ask, "Is it worthwhile to continue the union of the states when the North demands to be our masters and we are required to be their tributaries?" A radical idea was spreading through the legislature, and toward the end of Winborn's fourth year a word with ominous implications was being heard. The trouble had been brewing ever since his first days in the legislature. The northern industrialists wanted protection for their products from British imports and had recently gotten a law through Congress that trebled the duty on wool, iron, textiles, and salt — the basic necessities of a large plantation, goods for which the planter could naturally exchange his cotton. The majority rule in Congress was leading the South to slow ruin. South Carolina now had two sons in Washington's top posts, the president and vice president; why had they done nothing? They had split on the issue of states' rights, Jackson maintaining that the United States government made the supreme laws of the land, whereupon Calhoun came up with the doctrine of nullification—a state may nullify a federal law if the state's own courts find the law to be unconstitutional. Calhoun's idea held the seeds of catastrophe, for if one state could place itself above the federal constitution, the Union was doomed. Well, so be it. The states might have to reassert themselves, the argument ran. They had done it once, against England—and won.

WINBORN HAD MADE HIS contribution to the southern cause when he first went to the legislature and helped pass the "Exposition of 1828," an act that set up a state convention whose purpose was to determine the constitutionality of legislation. And now the convention had met and delivered its verdict: the tariff act is "unauthorized by the constitution of the United States, null, and void, and not binding upon this state, its officers or its citizens." Furthermore, the ordinance threatened that South Carolina would immediately secede if the federal government attempted to blockade Charleston or to use force. President Jackson, a South Carolinian who was now proving shockingly disloyal to his state, promised to stop and search every ship that entered the harbor if South Carolina persisted in resisting the tariff. And he had done just that! Winborn could see warships lying at anchor.

The gravity of the situation was not lost on the man whose plantation bordered Charleston Harbor. No one wants cannon firing within a half-mile of his house. Among the planters there was the knee-jerk reaction of responding with force—against whom was always unclear. Southern honor was threatened and must be defended. Immediately rifle clubs began to form along the coast and appeals went out for funds to train troops. In the city of Charleston, feeling on nullification was divided, although a local militia was already drilling and using arms supplied by the state. While everyone found the tariff obnoxious, opinion was split on defying the federal government to the point of secession. Men were still living who had fought in the Revolutionary War, and their pride in the nation was high. South Carolina had done its share and more to create the

How Grand A Flame

United States of America. To many of Winborn's friends this threat to the precious Union was unthinkable, and for Winborn there was also a purely selfish consideration. If violence exploded in the harbor, less than a mile from his house and lands, what protection could he offer to his family, his buildings, his slaves? His friends who opposed the nullification ordinance called themselves Unionists, but that was not the word they heard as they walked the streets. They were called cringing Submissionists! A genuine South Carolinian with any manhood and pride in his state was a Nullifier. We don't know what Winborn called himself, but there is little to suggest that he deserted the ranks of the planters.

Now there were federal warships out there in the water, loaded with troops, greatly disturbing the social and business life of Charleston and the surrounding islands. Their baleful presence brought out of hiding questions that had long been put to rest and intensified troublesome ideas like sectionalism, slavery, and the future of the South. The ships' officers, Commander Elliot and General Scott, who were said not to have been wholeheartedly pleased with their assignment, spent little time on the ships and tried hard to be civil. They had taken rooms in the city, where the ladies fell over one another inviting them to dinners and receptions.

The Civil War did not begin then. The lawmakers in Washington were at last aroused to the seriousness of the situation. President Jackson's proclamation and the intransigence of the South had at last produced action; a flurry of compromise efforts began. The effect of troops drilling on the islands had not been lost on the nation. At first neither side showed any sign of giving in; when it appeared that South Carolina would act out its violent rhetoric and secede, the congressional committees grew more and more alarmed. Each side finally relented somewhat, and by working night and day the men produced a compromise. The import duties would be scaled down over a ten-year period. Jackson maintained the principle of constitutional law, however, by signing a bill that permitted him to use the army and navy against any violators of the new regulation.

When word of the compromise drifted back to the plantations everyone gave thanks. We may suspect that Winborn, now a vestryman in St. James Chapel, was particularly grateful and, kneeling on the hard boards of the chapel, attended with fervency to Father Trapier reading from the prayer book:

> Save us from violence, discord and confusion; from pride and arrogancy and from every evil way. Defend our liberties and fashion into one united people the multitudes brought hither out of many kindreds and tongues.

WINBORN BECAME ONE OF THE founding vestrymen in St. James Episcopal Church in 1831. The Beaufort District Lawtons had produced a number of Baptist and Presbyterian preachers; the James Island Lawtons, not regarded as a religious branch of the family, had produced none. Family tradition has it that neither Winborn nor his father liked the many social restrictions imposed by Baptists, Presbyterians, and Methodists. Why have a good house, good food, good wine, and a little prosperity if you can't enjoy them? Winborn, like most large planters, welcomed the itinerant preachers who came by periodically to preach to the slaves. The Methodists were especially strong on sobriety; indeed, a number of planters had standing arrangements with itinerant Methodist circuit riders to visit their plantations. Drunkenness and stealing among the slaves were distinctly reduced after the Methodists preached. These men were welcomed on plantations as long as they confined their preachings to the Christian doctrines of personal salvation. Moreover, in accepting these preachers the slave owners were endorsing one of the most frequently advanced arguments for slavery: the Africans in America could find salvation here that would be forever denied their unfortunate brothers on the Dark Continent.

With the nullification problem settled, Winborn could turn his full attention to managing the plantation and living a responsible life on the island. There had been risks these recent months, but in the end it had paid to stand up for states' rights. Besides, politics was in his blood now, and he was considering running for the state senate in the fall. Both the Sea Island planters and friends in the city said they would back him because the low country now needed a man in the senate.

It is not an overstatement to say that the planter class ruled the South— at least they did in the section where Winborn lived. Below the class of large plantation owners was a much more numerous group—the farmers, or "crackers" as they were deprecatingly called—whose influence on government was slight. South Carolina political life was also marked by an upstate-downstate schism. The state constitution of 1790, which required that all members of the legislature own property or possess wealth, and conferred great power upon the slave-owning low-country aristocracy, was not revised to reflect the growth of the upstate counties in wealth and population during the decades before the Civil War. Charleston and Colleton Counties, with a white population of 26,795 in 1840, had thirteen times as many state senators and four and a half times the number of representatives as Pickens and Anderson Counties, with a white population of 24,295.

We know little about Winborn's demeanor as a family head and slave owner, and we must beware of overgeneralizing about the southern gentleman. We do know that he had many slaves and unbounded time for leisure and the pleasures of the period that affluence afforded. We know that he lived well, liked parties, had the most beautiful house in the area, while being at the same time, apparently, the wise and prudent manager. By 1830 he had six children, the oldest, William, being twenty-five, and his daughter, Margaret, about to be married.

The decade of the thirties, then, saw Winborn II approaching his prime. It was a decade of sadness and special joys, but a period that pushed his family and his influence forward into the golden age of the low country. The southern economy was coming to rest unequivocally on the foundation of slavery, flawed though it was. Beginning in the thirties and extending until the system's downfall, the overriding concern of Winborn and his friends would be to make that foundation secure.

THE ONLY CLOUD OVER the festivities of daughter Margaret's marriage to Dr. Eneas Mikell in 1834 was that her mother did not live to see the wedding. She had left three boys and three girls between the ages of five and twenty-five, a grieving husband, and a plantation without a mistress. It was now the eldest daughter who supervised the seamstresses day after day as they made and repaired clothes for the slaves, gave out medicine, bandaged cut hands, carried food to sick old Aunt Betsy and the brood of grandchildren who lived with her, tended in childbirth, and saw that unruly children were punished. Safeguarding the plantation property from a hundred pilfering hands was her responsibility. She carried keys to the food pantry, the silver chest, the linen closet, the wine chests, the smokehouse. The master of the plantation usually held the keys to the stables, lest he find his horses hagridden in the morning. Behind the facade of ease and the famous hospitality, the mistress of the plantation had to put up with dawdling house girls, forgotten orders, blundering kitchen help, tasks left unfinished, and she had to wage perpetual warfare against cockroaches, ants, centipedes, flies, and mice.

Winborn's plantation, enlarged and more intensively cultivated now, was producing bigger cotton crops, almost doubling the output of the discouraging years of the second war with Britain. Like other planters in the low country who raised long-staple cotton, he could relax comfortably in the assurance that England was crying for more cotton with every passing year. A ship loaded with his cotton could now make its way safely past Fort Sumter and down the Morris Island channel and, if the sea did not claim it, reach England. Once a year he entertained cotton brokers from England who came over to inspect his long-staple cotton and tell him how much they appreciated buying his unsanded bales. Up-country farmers would sometimes ship bales with as much as 20 percent of their weight sand and stones. There was one warehouse in Liverpool, the brokers told him, full of cotton so sanded that no buyer would touch it.

The wedding of his eldest daughter provided Winborn with an occasion that all successful planters looked forward to—an excuse to throw a big party and to show off his plantation to admiring guests. By the time all the cousins, uncles, and aunts among the Lawtons, Framptons, Mikells, and McCleods were invited, the house would be full. The date was set for the first week in November; the days then would be mild and sunny and none of the guests who stayed over would have to spend a hot, sleepless night.

A party such as this required money and a good supply of servants. We are told that his wife had run her house with a moderate number of servants. Margaret's requests had been small compared to the ostentatious demands of some women—women whose houses were so full of servants that you bumped into one wherever you turned. The size of the household's retinue was a status symbol, and many mistresses could not resist using it to the utmost. We may well believe that Winborn's wife and daughter were not given to such pretensions. The staff of servants for a home the size of Winborn's usually consisted of a majordomo, two or three chambermaids, two seamstresses—one who made clothes exclusively for the slaves—a cook and a helper, a carriage driver, two gardeners, a maid for the mistress and each of her daughters, a man for each male member, a fisherman, and a miscellany of youngsters to sweep, scrub, brush flies, and run errands. Winborn Lawton's plantation, with nearly a hundred slaves, was not the largest on James Island, that place being held by W. B. Seabrook of Secessionville, but it was of respectable size indeed.

An entry in a family genealogy states that Margaret Lawton was married to Dr. Eneas Mikell in 1834 "at her father's home on James Island in the presence of a large company." Daughter Margaret's wedding, if one examined it thoughtfully in the spirit of the times, was surely a beautiful statement of the master-servant relationship, for it embodied so many of the "finer qualities" of the system. The excitement over the approaching wedding would spread like a contagion among the inner circle at the big house; everyone tried harder, the dawdlers became prompt, the forgetful ones remembered, the bunglers became more careful. "Master-servant" was the wording that cultured people were using then, a much more agreeable expression than "owner-slave." A wedding in the master's house would bring a degree of satisfaction to field hands, would it not? Everyone would want Miss Margaret to have a "nice weddin'." A few might wonder at the opulence of the affair and the grinding labor required to produce it, but communication of such sentiments up the chain of command was not encouraged. Although the wedding meant additional work for everyone from yard boy to majordomo, there were spillovers, particularly from the kitchen, for nearly everyone. Moving among the household of servants bent on pleasing their superiors must have been a deeply reassuring experience. At moments like this, Winborn could scarcely have escaped a sense of the fundamental rightness of things.

In cotton, of course, lay the secret of this good life. In far-off Europe the rough linens and woolens were giving way to the soft, comfortable, manageable cotton, and the southern planters knew how to produce it. Southern planters saw it as almost providential; God was taking care of two needs at the same time. Cotton required vast amounts of field and hand labor, even with the miraculous new gins, and that labor was now available. At this propitious moment when the world so much needed better clothing, the South was ready. There was a kind of rightness in this juxtaposition of the demand for comfortable, warm clothing and the means to produce it. And how could this enormous demand be met, if not by a large and dependable supply of labor? The keeping of slaves caused problems; no one doubted that. It was a system that could be abused, but surely there was a greater good. The Negroes, only recently released from godless savagery, were now members of a civilized society, incalculably advanced over their African tribal brothers and sisters. For the first time, they were hearing the gospel. In fact, the more one considered the matter, it was the way God ordered the world. One saw it everywhere. Master-servant, teacher-pupil, parent-child. The able and the strong must discharge these obligations as accountable to God — indeed, as God's servants themselves. To question this assumption was to invite political and moral ostracism.

EARLY IN 1852 WINBORN read one of the most exciting reports of the South Carolina Agricultural Society that had ever been published: "The United States cotton crop of 1851 exceeded one billion pounds and the total should reach ten billion pounds by 1855." The Lawton plantation had done its part — good land, healthy Negroes, strong, well-fed mules, competent overseers, the new cotton gins, and, above all, sound management. He had lived long enough to see his life falling into periods. Up until his first marriage at age twenty-three he had been almost an apprentice planter to his father, a man who had managed with a strong hand.

How Grand A Flame

Then the first family with Margaret and the six children and the years in the state legislature had been good.

Five years after his wife died, Martha Waring Hughes crossed his path and the world changed. She was the age of his oldest daughter when he married her, and people had smiled a bit. Well, let them smile. Now his second family was half grown—Wallace, sixteen, and Juliet and Powell thirteen and six. The record on Winborn is silent for a number of years after his marriage to Martha Hughes. This we do know: he grew prosperous, his slaves numbered just under a hundred, he gave a big party—probably in the year 1852, and he was slowly going blind.

Since he left the legislature we do not know how much he was caught up in the political debates of the times. He may have sought comfort in President Tyler's incredible statement, "The slavery issue is now at rest." The forties and fifties gave him a breathing spell. The ninety-five slaves who worked for him had doubled his cotton production and quadrupled his income. The Fugitive Slave Law of 1850, despite the outcry against it in the North, could only strengthen one's convictions in the rightness of the southern position. The uproar that the abolitionists were creating in New England hardly touched the Lawton plantation in the prosperous fifties.

WINBORN HAD LATELY GOTTEN his hands on some pieces by John C. Calhoun and other men who set the matter in right perspective. Thank God for some southern writers and thinkers who were ably disposing of this heretical outpouring from the northern press and were producing an intellectual buttressing for a system of labor "peculiar to the South." John C. Calhoun had said it perfectly: "Many in the South once believed that slavery was once a moral and political evil. That folly and delusion are gone. We see it now in its true light, and regard it as the most safe and stable basis for free institutions in the world." Doubtless Winborn, like most southern gentlemen, reached hungrily for such statements. In the words of the historian Samuel Eliot Morison, "This nonsense became orthodox in the South by 1850."

Winborn had a good reason for slowly backing away from Charleston in the fateful decade of the eighteen-fifties—he was going blind from cataracts. Doctors understood the disorder then, for they were performing operations to correct the condition. Family tradition has it that Winborn agreed to the operation with one proviso—that the bandages could be removed by the time of the "big party," which was probably his seventieth birthday celebration. The operation was thought to be successful, but the doctor wanted him to retain the bandages a week longer than he had promised. Winborn disobeyed him, tore off the bandages the night of his party, vowing that he would see his family on his birthday. In a few days he was permanently blind.

The decade of the fifties began with the funeral of John C. Calhoun, which was said to be the most elaborate of any funeral in the city up to that time. There were two days of mourning, a parade, a military guard; many distinguished guests appeared, and Jefferson Davis served as one of the pallbearers. The seeds of secession that Calhoun had sown were germinating in 1851 when the Southern Rights Association convened in Charleston to advocate secession provided other states would join. Not enough states chose to follow South Carolina, and the proposal failed for lack of supporters. The efforts to justify slavery intensified in sermons, lectures, and editorials.

The "Positive Good" school had its adherents, although whether most low-country planters really believed it is another matter. As the historian David Duncan Wallace points out in *South Carolina: A Short History*, barely a year before the secession convention, for example, the *Southern Episcopalian*, published in Charleston, noted that earlier generations had regarded slavery as an evil, but had found no practical way to end it, and had come to see that under existing conditions it was necessary. Now, however, "there has been manifested a disposition to break from our entrenchments and assume the offensive." The sentiment of the South, the diocesan organ lamented, "and especially of South Carolina, seems verging toward the opposite end of a natural oscillation, passing from morbid sensitiveness into aggressive assertion."

How Grand A Flame

In Charleston the Reverend James Henley Thornwell, a leading Presbyterian divine, in an hour-long address at the dedication of a black orphanage sponsored by the Second Presbyterian Church, asserted that the Golden Rule "simply requires, in the case of slavery, that we should treat our slaves as we should feel that we had a right to be treated if we were slaves ourselves." As for the institution of slavery, it was, he said, founded upon "the principle that captivity in war-time gives a right to the life of the prisoner for which his bondage is accepted in exchange." This rationale, he conceded, was no longer acceptable, but "it was recognized as true for ages and generations—it was a step in the moral development of nations, and has laid the foundation of institutions and usages, which cannot now be disturbed with impunity."

The polyglot of peoples in Charleston—slaves, unskilled poor whites, freedmen, artisans and traders, mulattoes who owned slaves, immigrants and drifters from the ships in port, and the elite at the top—created a steady crescendo of problems. One historian noted that 3 percent of the heads of free households owned half of the wealth of Charleston.

Unionists such as James L. Petigru and William J. Grayson, both of them distinguished attorneys and slave owners, dreaded the advent of secession. If the South were to lose the resulting war, they contended, it would be occupied and ruled as a conquered province. If it succeeded in winning its independence, the division between slaveholders and nonslaveholders would swiftly intensify; there would be growing economic rivalry between white laborers and blacks. The southern states would fall to wrangling between themselves, Grayson warned, and the southern people become, to quote David Duncan Wallace again, "the tolls and prey of military rulers, wretches at home and contemptible abroad." When the secession ordinance was passed in 1860, Petigru declared that "they have this day set a blazing torch to the temple of constitutional liberty, and please God, we shall have no more peace forever."

Winborn, on his plantation, was mercifully spared much of this. If there was ever a period in American history from which one could wish to make a gentle exit, it was the decade of the eighteen-fifties. Across the

Ashley, Winborn was not forced to deal with a restless and often criminal lower class, or foul streets, or open sewers, or contaminated wells, or the two outbreaks of yellow fever that took fourteen hundred lives. From much of this, his plantation was a self-contained haven. If the overseers and foremen kept nearly a hundred slaves working submissively at their tasks, his little world was safe, whatever happened across the harbor. Blindness was an affliction that Winborn probably did not bear graciously, but by it he was permitted a gentle withdrawal from the turmoil that would erupt in war a few weeks after his death.

UNCLE PETER BROWN, in one of his many visits with my father, said that he first came to the big house at about the time of "Marse Winborn's birthday party." He was a little vague about his age, and my father sensed that this uncertainty embarrassed Peter. "Everyone told me that I came to the big house when I was about twelve and I believe that. I know I was two or three years younger than Mr. Wallace."

My father, who as I have said earlier became a close friend of Peter Brown and spent hours in conversation with him, loved history enough to realize at once that here was a rare opportunity to learn about it from an original source. His own father had won the Congressional Medal of Honor at Spotsylvania Courthouse, although I never heard that this figured in his conversations with Uncle Peter. He was, however, an excellent raconteur, and in the days before radio and television there was little for our family to do, as we sat around the Rochester Burner lamp after supper, but read or talk. We children did a great deal of listening. My father is no longer alive to help me on details, but he was so fascinated with Uncle Peter and the rich lore behind him — I heard the stories so many times — that I am able to give what, I think, is a fairly accurate account of Peter's life with the Lawtons.

We should know at the outset that Peter had "inside help" in landing his job as house boy, or yard boy, in the person of Winborn Lawton's servant, John. John was Peter's uncle. Martha probably felt overwhelmed as the preparations for the party thickened and was casting about for more help. Peter was working with his father, the carriage driver, when word came down from the big house that Peter was to report to the cook house. "Uncle John was there," Peter told my father, "and he said to get busy with the rake. He said, 'Do a very good job and you won't be sorry.' He had heard Miss Martha talking about bringing me to the house. The first work I did for Miz Lawton was to rake up all those little leaves that fall off the oaks in the spring."

Peter had seen his mistress many times when he had accompanied his father as he drove Martha in the carriage. She had taken a fancy to this alert, polite boy who rode in the rear and jumped out and opened the door for her, and she told John to try him out as a yard boy. We will never know what subtle influences John brought to bear on the decision to bring Peter to the house. For a slave it was a decision of enormous magnitude, with scarcely a parallel in the white man's world. It would lift Peter from a lifetime of dawn-to-dusk field labor to one of dignity and responsibility and even education. If he behaved himself he was there for life — or until his owners decided to sell him.

In Martha's house, Peter would not have to endure the hardships of the field, although the women servants would not hesitate to give him a cuff when no one was looking. Unless he was quick at adapting to the demands of a dozen men and women, he could at any moment fall from his high estate. He must be all things to all people. First there was Wallace, Martha's eldest son and only three years his senior, who was instinctively and unabashedly tyrannical; then there was old Winborn, easily irritated and always in need of another person's eyes and feet; and Martha, who wanted propriety at all times; to say nothing of the watchful eye of Uncle John, the person who knew the price of a slip from grace.

Peter's judgment was put to the test soon after he arrived. The Edisto Lawtons were coming for a visit, and Winborn had wanted all his family to be on hand when they arrived. Wallace thought otherwise. He was not looking forward, apparently, to a boring day talking to aunts, uncles, and cousins whom he hardly knew. The city of Charleston was beckoning. He ordered Peter to get the rowboat ready for a quick departure before the Edisto family arrived. Uncle John had told Peter to do as Wallace said, and he gave him a tin pail of food to hide in the stern of the boat. Before their absence was discovered that morning, Peter was tying up at a wharf on East Bay. He spent the day on or near the boat, talking to an occasional fisherman, watching the harbor traffic, eating from his tin pail, and throwing scraps of food to the seagulls swirling and swooping above him.

It was late afternoon when Wallace returned and took his seat in the stern. He told Peter to listen hard and "get this straight. If anyone ask you, tell 'em you took me fishing—all day. If they ask why you so late, say we went to Stiles Point for a while." Then he said, "If you change that story, you get ten cuts." Peter was scared when that night he went to the big house to see Uncle John. Either Winborn or Wallace could send him back to the field, and both could assign a beating if they got angry at him. Uncle John's advice was instant. "My Uncle John said, 'You gonna live with Marse Wallace a long time, you hope, and his daddy is old and can't do so much to you. If he *do* find out he will be madder at he son dan at you, and maybe you get off. Better say you fished all day.'" Uncle John's advice was good, because the matter never came up again.

This episode greatly impressed my father, for he had a tenderness for children and saw the helplessness of a slave in a new light. Peter could be punished whether he told a lie or told the truth; there was no way to extricate himself from any network of falsehoods that Wallace might devise. Appeal to Uncle John? He was powerless to do anything but secretly whisper advice to the boy, at the risk of a punishment himself. Peter's own parents were utterly helpless. How does a twelve-year-old boy deal with helpless parents? In my father's world one could say, "Well, as a last resort I can appeal to—." But there was no higher court on an antebellum plantation.

Martha apparently liked Peter and took a genuine interest in seeing that he was properly trained. She came to his rescue when he was trying to round up a mother hen and chicks that had strayed into her flower garden. As he lunged for the fleeing chickens, he fell flat on his face in a bed of canna lilies. Ned, the yardman, yelled at him and cooks screamed from the cook house. Not everyone on the staff welcomed this bright young intruder, who they knew was on probation. From an upstairs window Martha saw the whole episode and came to his defense. She called out, "The rest of you get back to work. That was an accident. Those plants will stand up again."

In a few weeks Peter, with Ned to help him, would be catching more chickens—this time for the party. He would also help Ned butcher two suckling pigs and half a dozen ducks and lay the big sheets of iron for the oyster roast. Sam, who was the plantation fisherman, would take a couple of men to the inner reaches of Morris Island sound to gather oysters.

Peter told my father that he had always heard that this was the day when Winborn got so angry because he could not see his relatives that he simply yanked the bandages off his eyes, confirming the story that I had heard from family sources. The children had protested and his son-in-law, Dr. Eneas Mikell, tried to persuade him to put them back on immediately. No, he was enjoying the day immensely, and he expected to keep on doing that.

Uncle John told Peter, when it was all over, exactly what had happened. On Sunday morning, the third day of his gala celebration, Winborn left his bed thinking that he must have awakened very early to find the room so dark. In a few minutes John came to the door to ask him if he would like some coffee. Winborn called out to him, "You're too early, John." "No," John said to him, "it's 'most nine o'clock." Winborn then knew he was in trouble but decided not to let his family know. He asked John to bring him some bandages before he went down to breakfast. He would tell them that his eyes smarted a little and he had put the bandages back on. When all the company had left, Dr. Gelding came over from the city and examined Winborn. Uncle John heard a lot of angry shouting, but the doctor said the damage had been done and that "Marse Winborn wouldn't ever see again."

"Prepare to Evacuate"

Secession Day — December 20, 1860.

The bells, the cannon, the bands, the fireworks, the jubilation in the streets swept across the Ashley River to reach everyone on the north shore of James Island, including Winborn Lawton, sightless now, on his second-floor piazza. The Convention of the People of South Carolina had voted, 169 to 0, "that the union now subsisting between South Carolina and other states under the name of United States of America is hereby dissolved."

The rejoicing continued throughout the day of December 20 in anticipation of the formal signing at 6:30 P.M. in Institute Hall. Nearly 3,000 people watched that night as the 169 delegates signed their names. Respectful silence prevailed as one by one the delegates made the fateful decision official, but when James Davidson, president of the Convention, proclaimed the state of South Carolina to be "an independent commonwealth," the crowd exploded. Thousands rushed into the streets singing and parading, lighting rockets and bonfires, until Mayor Macbeth had to announce an ordinance that forbade the shooting of fireworks — a law, we are told, that few obeyed.

Whoever lived in the Old Dutch Colonial Cuthbert House of my childhood had a ringside seat for the celebration that night. From my second-story bedroom window, I used to see the whole Charleston peninsula — the Battery, White Point Gardens, the juncture of the two rivers — as clearly as a painted picture. The view from Winborn's house was even grander, because his house was closer to the harbor's edge. Peter Brown told my father that he remembered the racket and commotion, although he of course did not cross over to the city. But surely Wallace, a young bachelor of twenty-three, did not remain calmly on his father's piazza that night when a fifteen-minute boat trip would place him in the middle of the noisemaking.

The first Christmas under the new dispensation was probably celebrated on the Lawton plantation as it had been in previous years, with the family gathering for the morning quail and dove hunt and the three o'clock dinner. Martha was no longer there. She had died nearly five years earlier after a long bout with an unnamed disease. Wallace and Powell were at home; daughter Juliet had married Asa Lawton, son of the Reverend Winborn Asa Lawton, her father's cousin from St. Peter's Parish. Alison Lawton told my father of a "charming Christmas custom" that the family had observed for years. The servants first dumped several cartloads of white sand in the yard in front of the piazza. While the Lawtons ate dinner, the slave children gathered outside the house waiting for the big moment. When the big dinner was over, and Winborn and his guests had gathered on the piazza, and the children were prancing about in the sand, Winborn threw handfuls of copper coins into the pile. The children would scream and thrash about while Winborn threw more coins and the family on the piazza sipped their after-dinner drinks and chuckled. No one, it seemed, not even the sensitive Alison of two generations later, saw the distressing side of this "charming custom."

Christmas week, however, was not like the old days for anyone in Charleston, or anyone in the low country. Two days after the Christmas festivities the city woke up in a state of shock. Major Robert Anderson, commander of the federal forces in the harbor, had pulled off a maneuver the night after Christmas that the local authorities could hardly believe. He had withdrawn from Fort Moultrie on the north side of the harbor, vulnerable to land attack from the rear, loaded his men in boats the night of December 26, and landed them at Fort Sumter, slipping past all the harbor guards.

"Right under our very noses," the chagrined harbor officials had said. "Brilliant," some of the officers grudgingly admitted. Not a person in the city or in the neighboring forts was aware of the move until the next morning, when the people awoke to see the Stars and Stripes flying over Fort Sumter.

How Grand A Flame

Charleston was stunned. Rumors spread that Major Anderson had turned his guns on the city and that bombardment would begin at any moment. Major Anderson's position was not enviable; he was supposed to defend his fort and repulse any attack, but in doing so he must not start a war.

Between the two main channels of the harbor, and directly in front of Winborn's house, lay a small U.S. fortification known as Castle Pinckney. If Winborn had been watching, he might have seen what, according to E. Milby Burton, was the first overt act of war. Governor Pickens ordered three companies to seize the little federal fortification. The attackers approached the fortress in the guard boat *Nina,* threw up scaling ladders, and entered the fort, only to find a small work party that could offer no resistance. The invaders pulled down the Stars and Stripes and ran up the *Nina*'s flag, a white star on a red background. No one had thought to bring a South Carolina flag. In this little fracas no one was killed or hurt, but the new nation had won a tiny victory: it had wrested from the United States a piece of land and raised upon it a Confederate flag.

In a few days another anxious crowd would assemble on the Battery. Rumor had it that a coastal steamer, the *Star of the West*, was on its way to bring provisions for the beleaguered garrison on Fort Sumter—a fort that was running out of ammunition and food. Word of the ship's imminent sailing from New York had reached Charleston even while the vessel was loading. With so many southern sympathizers in New York City, a secret departure was out of the question, and before the ship had been two days at sea the *New York Times* announced that the *Star of the West* was without doubt on her way to Charleston. Major Anderson at Fort Sumter decided against using his guns to protect the incoming *Star of the West*, although he had received instruction to do so if the vessel was attacked. He decided only to run out his guns as a show of force, fearing that if he actually fired he would be accused of starting a war. No such reticence characterized the young Citadel cadets stationed on Cummings Point at the tip of Morris Island, who had been told to defend the harbor. They opened fire with their small howitzers as soon as they sighted the ship coming up the channel. The "battle" lasted only a few hours, and Charlestonians gathered at the

Battery to try to discern through the smoke from far down the bay which side was winning. The *Star of the West* was an unarmed passenger vessel taken from the New Orleans run, and as she approached the harbor the officers had placed her two hundred soldiers below deck for safety. She moved steadily up the channel until the guns on Cummings Point got her range. When shells from the cadet's battery hit the ship's rudder and mast, she turned around and headed back to sea. This was the second episode of hysteria that was visible from Winborn's piazza—for all who had their eyesight.

The *Charleston Mercury* published the following "editorialized" report:

> Yesterday, the ninth of January, will be remembered in history. The expulsion of *The Star of the West* from Charleston Harbor yesterday morning was the opening ball of Revolution. We are proud that our harbor has been so honored. We are proud that South Carolina, so long, so bitterly, so contemptuously reviled and scoffed at above all others should thus have thrown back the scoff of her enemies . . . she has not hesitated to strike the first blow, full in the face of her insulter. . . . We would not recall or exchange that blow for millions! Upon each acre of the peaceful soil of the South armed men will spring up . . . and it will be found that every word of our insolent foe has been, indeed, a dragon's tooth sown for their destruction.

WINBORN LAWTON II's last will and testament is dated January 11, 1861. Had the rush of events in the previous three weeks prodded him into action? There was enough, surely, to induce him to prepare for the end. He was seventy-nine years old, blind, and his world was threatening to collapse. Whatever his motivation, he sent for attorney Joseph Dill.

"In the name of God, Amen. I, Winborn Lawton of James Island, planter, being of sound and disposing mind, memory and understanding, although afflicted with blindness, make and ordain this my last will and testament, after it shall have been read to me and approved by me in the presence of the subscribing witnesses . . . "

The first item in the will is the gift of "my house servant named John, to my son, William M. Lawton, his executors, administrator and assigns forever." Daughter Maria Juliet, then living in Beaufort District, was to receive $5,000 and certain named slaves. His many grandchildren were given $500 each. Then follows a statement: "And having hitherto made advances to all of my children by my first marriage . . . I have endeavored to place all of my children upon an equality and believe that I have accomplished that object." Margaret, his eldest daughter, who had lost five babies and for whom he seems to have felt a special tenderness, received $2,000 and certain slaves. Powell, youngest son by the second marriage, was to receive $15,000.

Now for the disposition of the plantation: Wallace would purchase it for $65,000, and for his share of the inheritance Winborn gave him a signed receipt for $10,000. The balance Wallace was to repay within a specified time, out of which sum the other heirs were to receive their allocations. Court records of a lawsuit among the heirs ten years later reveal that Winborn had ninety-eight slaves at the time, which he valued at $45,000, and land valued at $20,000.

On January 11, Messrs. Dill and Rivers, accompanied by three gentlemen to serve as witnesses, returned with the completed will of Winborn Lawton, which "after being read to him and approved by him in our presence, who in the presence of each other and in the presence of the Testator and at his request have hereunto subscribed our names as Witnesses. John E. Rivers, W. D. Rivers, P. M. Pepper."

Winborn Lawton died two months later, on March 24, 1861.

PETER AND WALLACE WOULD go over the night of April 12, 1861, for the rest of their lives—as would everyone who lived on the edges of Charleston Harbor. Dr. Lebby saw the first shot fired from Captain James's battery on the beach, Lieutenant Barnwell remembers being on the hill, Colonel Farley asserted that he pulled the lanyard, and Captain James gave the order to fire. Peter remembers Wallace saying, "Wake me at four in the morning. We're going to see some action." Together he and Wallace climbed to the cupola on the top of the big house and fixed their eyes on Fort Sumter. They saw a ruby sun rise above the horizon, burn its way through a smoky haze on the water to illuminate a wildly waving crowd on the Battery and a hoard of small boats collecting on the Ashley. Then the bursting shell. This was war, the long desired, the long feared, the ultimate test of southern honor—here at last, and only a mile from the plantation.

After enduring continuous bombardment for thirty-four hours, Major Anderson, commander of the Union garrison on Fort Sumter, surrendered. On Sunday, April 14, the United States flag came down and two flags—the Confederate flag and the palmetto flag of South Carolina—rose over the smoldering fort. Exultant crowds on the Battery cheered themselves hoarse and spilled over into sailboats, rowboats, and even rafts that suddenly swarmed into the harbor. Everyone, it seemed, wanted to set foot on this smoking prize at the mouth of the harbor. It is easy to believe that Wallace took a boat and joined the throng; a twenty-four-year-old man living at the water's edge, unmarried and in good health, would hardly miss such a Sunday-afternoon outing.

Both North and South were galvanized into action, the North in outrage and shock that a United States fort should be captured, and the South jubilant that it had won the first battle. President Lincoln immediately issued a call for 75,000 volunteers and a little later for 500,000 more. President Jefferson Davis called for 100,000 volunteers for twelve months in addition to the 60,000 men that composed the militias and scores of local units that had already been formed. The Confederacy rode the crest of euphoria when they routed the Yankees at Manassas on July 21, a victory so close to Washington that it must clearly show the North that continuing the struggle would be useless.

But the United States Navy was having its own successes. First, the fortifications at Hatteras Inlet in North Carolina fell easily to Union attack. A powerful fleet of warships, working its way down the Atlantic coast, brought new fears to towns like Charleston, Port Royal, and Savannah. There were now thirty-six blockading ships patrolling the waters outside these cities, with more being added every day. Needing a base for these operations, the North targeted for capture the deep harbor at Port Royal. In a series of running attacks by steam-powered ships, the Union fleet quickly reduced the several forts guarding the harbor; the garrisons as well as civilians retreated inland, leaving Port Royal and the surrounding fertile islands federal territory. Charleston was now alarmed. Here was an enemy enclave not fifty miles away that could mount an attack at any moment against a city that was nearly defenseless. The route of such an army would cut directly across Wallace's plantation on James Island. The presence of Union forces at Port Royal would plague the Confederacy for the next four years.

By the coming of the first winter, the euphoria on both sides had subsided. A long war lay ahead.

Military decisions were soon to affect Wallace directly. In November, President Jefferson Davis announced the formation of a new department consisting of South Carolina, Georgia, and East Florida with a little-known officer named Robert E. Lee in command. The new general, like his predecessor, General Beauregard, who had been transferred to Virginia in time to lead at Manassas, believed that the sprawling islands around Charleston were indefensible and ordered that defense lines be drawn in closer to the city. An almost unbelievable order then came from the commanding general: Evacuate James Island. No planter in his wildest imaginings could have anticipated this moment—being ordered to evacuate his own land. Evacuate to where? Inland, or possibly to the city. How he did it was not the concern of the military. There was an unreal, uncanny quality about it—like something from history books or the Bible, fleeing for your life from an approaching army.

"Prepare to evacuate." The order had refrained from stating a specific time, but danger was imminent, for federal gunboats were now cruising on the Stono River. The military situation was clear. The Confederacy could not allocate sufficient troops and weapons to defend the jagged, indented edges of the Sea Islands from landing parties. The evacuation order was really inevitable. It said in effect: Your lives and property are at peril, so prepare to move out; go southward, westward, wherever you wish; take what you can, leave what you can't carry with you. Events since

Christmas a year before should have alerted the people on James Island to expect the worst, but clearly they had not. Complying with such an order even in peacetime would have been a staggering task. But now? It was just another one of the impossibilities that war demanded. Up to now everyone, or nearly everyone, was preparing for the best—the establishment of a new and successful nation, the Confederate States of America. In a few months, or a year at most, it would all be over, because those northerners in the cities didn't know how to fight, and things would soon return to normal. But the "return to normal" was stretching out to a distressingly long period.

The most recent and most preposterous move from Washington, so the Charlestonians thought, was to send a fleet of ships loaded with granite to be sunk in the channel entrance. It was unbelievably foolish, but it happened. There was a cry of outrage from the capitals of Europe indicating, so the South felt, a ground swell of sympathy for the southern cause, more evidence that England would fly to their aid. There hadn't been enough rocks in the first ships to do the job well, so the Federals sent out a second "stone fleet," which the muck on the floor of Charleston Harbor also gladly received and swallowed. Swift tides and a storm did their work quickly, and the channel was soon ready for traffic again. The people of Charleston saw these moves as the desperate expedients that the North would take to humiliate the city where secession was born. The real disaster had been the loss of Port Royal, only fifty miles away, to the Union forces in the first months of the war. Those planters on large islands like Hilton Head had faced a crisis worse than Wallace Lawton or his neighbors; they had fled for their very lives, leaving their houses, livestock, and thousands of wandering slaves to do as they pleased. James Island was at least being allowed a little time to prepare. In December 1862, Wallace watched "the great fire" in Charleston burn over five hundred acres on the end of the peninsula. Along with other James Island planters, he sent his slaves over to help the fire fighters. Northern papers were jubilant—this was God's retribution on the cradle of secession.

Even before General Robert E. Lee took command of the Southeast Department, General Ripley had ordered the throwing up of breastworks at strategic points on James Island. One fortification, Battery Glover, was built where Wallace's land touched Stiles Point, and two more were being started farther east. All the planters had sent help. Wallace lost two good slaves in the process. In the haste and confusion, two young men saw their opportunity; Wallace believed they escaped to the blockading fleet, for so he reported to the state on a form headed "Request for Reimbursement." This document, signed by W. Wallace Lawton on March 8, 1862, reports that Paris, age eighteen, and William, age seventeen, "absconded" while on a work detail and "escaped on one of the blockading vessels off the bar." The form does not state the monetary value he placed on the two young men; whether the strained Confederate treasury found funds to reimburse Wallace for his loss is doubtful.

Over on the Stono River another row of batteries was being prepared—the Western Line. James Islanders felt they were ready. But not really ready; Generals Lee and Beauregard had said that the island defenses could not withstand an assault like the one at Port Royal. Citizens should be prepared to evacuate, because the army could not guarantee their safety.

Now that Wallace was owner of the plantation, he, and he alone, had to decide how to comply with that order. Big, irreversible decisions lay ahead, and there was no one else to involve or to blame. At this point Wallace apparently decided to wait for clarification, to make plans but stay on until there was more definite word.

James Island was becoming almost unrecognizable, with batteries of fresh earth appearing along the water courses, trees being cut for fire lanes, and temporary roads being built in abandoned fields. The wide, navigable Stono River to the west was the threat. Its mouth was thirty miles north of Port Royal, the perfect jumping-off place for the six thousand Union soldiers encamped there. Cole's Island at the mouth of the Stono was only weakly fortified. Given these facts, the question was how best to defend Charleston: whether to strengthen the outer defenses such as Cole's Island at the mouth of the Stono, or withdraw to a smaller perimeter. The matter was debated at all levels of command.

The general in charge of the Southeast District, Robert E. Lee, made his headquarters at Coosawhatchie, a stop on the Savannah-Charleston Railroad between Charleston and Beaufort, the better to keep an eye on these two vulnerable towns. From this vantage point he saw that the ragged coastline of the Sea Islands, with its many inlets and sounds, would be difficult if not impossible to defend. Recognizing the importance of the railroad, Lee ordered an expanded effort to defend it, and selected for the task the Rutledge Mounted Riflemen. A light mobile force — not a whole army — was needed to ward off attacks of raiding guerrilla forces who could reduce railroad track to tangled iron in a few hours. The Rutledge Mounted Riflemen had received their mission.

Here was the military unit made to order for the planter. Wallace could work in an area not too far from home and keep an eye on his plantation. There was little likelihood of full-scale battles, presumably no vanishing into the anonymity of the big armies in Virginia or Mississippi; nevertheless, there would be real military duty on horseback, a service where one could bring one's man, an elite unit which had fine uniforms, good mounts, and their own tested weapons. Working in small companies only a day's travel from home, it was altogether the perfect way for planters to go to war. So Wallace joined up. He brought Peter as his man, to care for the horses and the leather, clean the weapons, prepare the meals, set up and break camp, and help with personal needs. Peter had a good mount, too, and although he never assisted directly in patrol duty, he was valuable as a courier and errand boy because he could now read and write enough to be useful. A day before his own departure, Wallace loaned Peter to the advance team of wagons bearing tents, food, and ammunition. By nightfall they would have the new circular tents erected in a wooded area not far from the railroad, and a meal prepared for the mounted riflemen when they arrived at dusk.

While Wallace was patrolling the railroad he did not know that a few miles to the east of his camp, his brother, Powell, age fourteen, was training with the Beaufort Volunteer Artillery. Powell was supposed to be in school where Wallace had sent him, a pupil of Dr. Henry Holcomb in Lawtonville, a small South Carolina town six miles from the Savannah River. One Sunday morning Powell decided to call on his big brother.

Wallace responded to Powell with the protective concern that a man feels for a brother who is ten years younger than himself.

First, why was he not in school? Dr. Holcomb, who may have been teaching to avoid the draft, finally signed on with the army, and the school had closed. The boys were all glad of that, for most of them felt they should enlist instead of studying Latin and algebra. Wallace, Powell, and Peter no doubt enjoyed a pleasant reunion, but even before Powell left for his camp, it appears that Wallace was making plans to get his brother out of the service.

The day after Powell left, Wallace obtained permission to visit Powell's commanding officer, Captain Elliot, and told him of the illegal enlistment of his fourteen-year-old brother. The captain was not deeply moved by the request, but sent for Powell and asked him if he wanted to be relieved of his duties. "Upon my telling him no," wrote Powell years later, "he would not sanction my discharge." Captain Elliot doubtless expected Powell would do what most boys did under similar circumstances—enlist in another outfit.

Wallace was not easily thwarted. A few days later he received another leave of absence. "He went immediately to the commanding general, presumably General Lee," Powell writes, "who ordered my release because I had joined before I was fifteen years old. Captain Elliot then had to grant my discharge." Wallace assured the authorities that his brother would be sent to the South Carolina Military College.

WALLACE'S TOUR OF DUTY with the Rutledge Mounted Riflemen lasted four months. The enemy attacks against the railroad appear to have been minimal, and it is doubtful if the mounted riflemen sought out the enemy. The experience gave Wallace a kind of veteran's status that he and his wife would use thirty years later to seek membership for their son in the Camp Moultrie Chapter of the Sons of Confederate Veterans.

The official word for the demise of the elite mounted riflemen was "reorganization," but above the heads of the volunteers a battle over command was raging. Who was giving the orders? Was it ambitious and combative

Francis Pickens, whose position as governor of the state made him commander in chief of the militia and the Rutledge Mounted Riflemen, or was it the generals of the Confederate army, who felt bypassed? At the outbreak of the war, and even before then, southern patriots had formed dozens of elite volunteer companies for local defense under the auspices of their state militias. Cavalry units were the most popular—a uniformed man on horseback was unmatched for parade and display purposes, and he was a world removed from the infantryman on foot. The soldiers in volunteer units elected their own officers, a feature that the planters all liked, but one that many historians concede was a serious flaw in the Confederate army. Moreover, soldiers under the command of Governor Pickens were not subject to the insistent calls from Virginia for replacements. There must be "states' rights" in the military command—even if it wrecked the war effort. The "reorganization" was inevitable, and in the end the Confederacy prevailed, a change that gave Wallace an opportunity to resign and return to the plantation that badly needed him.

Wallace was faced with two conflicting demands: the pressure on all young men to do some sort of military duty and the order to evacuate his plantation. As for reenlisting, there was already much agitation for national conscription, a law opposed by the planter class but one that would probably pass if the "twenty-slave" rule was attached. The big planters insisted that they required a white man to keep twenty slaves working, and should therefore be granted an exemption from the draft for themselves and their overseers; otherwise their plantations would fail. The obvious unfairness of this provision to other farmers with fewer than twenty slaves was apparently lost on the advocates of the legislation.

Another quite unexpected turn of events would settle the "refugeeing" problem for a while. One afternoon in late January Wallace fell seriously ill of a disease that was called "malarial-typhoid"; at least that was what he told his future wife. The disease laid him up for a year, he said. His physician was Dr. Robert Lebby, a man who divided his practice between the civilians and soldiers. His diagnosis hardly makes sense to us today, but we must remember that even though physicians of the period were knowledgeable in anatomy and were respected as surgeons, they knew very little about human physiology. So futile were the treatments for blood ailments and abdominal infections—what is now called internal medicine—that people were beginning to notice that the ill who went to doctors died sooner than those who did not. Indeed, a young South Carolina physician was one of the first to discover that the body healed best when left alone, unhindered by such "heroic" measures as purging and bloodletting. The names of the doctors Lebby, for they were a father-and-son team, figure largely in James Island lore. Such physicians were "comforters and consolers of the ailing and even though their attentions were frequently lethal, they themselves were appreciated and admired by the general run of the citizenry," writes the historian Page Smith.

Impressive fortifications, called batteries, were now in place along the Stono River, and large companies of Confederate soldiers were setting up defenses on Johns Island. The consensus was that there would be an attack from the south and west via the Stono River. Although Wallace probably did not suspect it, the stage was being set for a battle.

The Battle of Secessionville saved the day for Wallace—and for the city of Charleston. When I lived on James Island, everyone talked about that battle. A few old men whom I knew had seen the fighting, and my school-teacher's family plantation had been destroyed by it. Peter Brown had watched the battle at a safe distance, and the United Daughters of the Confederacy, who met over the Agricultural Hall on our school-ground, named their chapter after the Battle of Secessionville. It was the island's chief claim to fame, exceeding perhaps that of "the first shot" fired down at Fort Johnson. I was present at a ceremony one spring afternoon, along with other children of the James Island school, when we gathered to sing Confederate songs around a new monument that was about to be dedicated to the men who had died there. The local chapter of the United Daughters of the Confederacy never let us forget the victory at Secessionville.

Secessionville was actually the name of a large plantation, owned by W. B. Seabrook, that bordered Clark's Sound and extended well toward the Stono River. Here a set of earthworks, given the name of Fort Lamar, was built to guard against gunboats that might enter the sound. It was also the key defense against the enemy who might enter by the Stono River. General John C. Pemberton had asked the railroad officials to have trains in readiness to rush troops to Charleston because "the enemy in large force is preparing to attack Charleston—probably through James and Johns Island." The Confederates were fully determined that the attack fail. General Robert E. Lee wrote to General Pemberton that the city of Charleston must be defended at all costs; if necessary, the battle was to be fought "street by street and house by house as long as we have a foot of ground to stand upon." The victory at Secessionville made that desperate expedient unnecessary.

In early June, federal troops from Port Royal came up the Edisto, began landing on Johns Island, and marched northward toward the Stono River and James Island. It was a jaunt that the survivors would long remember. Stretched out in a dreary procession across Johns Island, the largest of the Sea Islands, the men suffered mightily from fatigue and heat exhaustion as they cut their way through tangled undergrowth and waded through boggy, brackish swamps. If the Confederates had attacked en route, they might have defeated the invaders much more easily than they did two days later at Secessionville. For reasons that are still a mystery, however, the Confederates did not do so.

On that memorable day, June 16, 1862, Wallace's fever flared up again, and he called Peter to his room and told him to go out and reconnoiter. There was a big battle in progress—they could hear the cannons booming to the south and west. Peter would go by horseback—taking Duke, Wallace's own horse—to the other side of the island to find out what was going on. He should take his pass, tell anyone who asked that he belonged to Wallace Lawton, and ask questions of anyone who would talk; he probably couldn't get too close, but he should try to find out what was happening. He was to go on the King's Highway as far as Drake's Causeway and turn left. He would probably run into medical and supply posts; he was just to ask questions and keep his eyes open. How long should Peter stay away? As long as he was "finding out something." This would be Peter's first and only brush with actual warfare.

It was the worst of days for the impatient and impulsive Wallace to be incapacitated. Peter might return with a little news—anything to break this waiting. His black skin and slave status might get him into places where a white man couldn't go. Peter was as dependable as salt.

Dusk had fallen when Peter galloped up to the big house at the Hundred Pines. Yes, he had seen a hospital tent and a man being carried in on a stretcher. No one would talk much, but one man said to him, "We winnin'." Every time a cannon went off, Duke would jump and nearly throw him. Just as he started to return home a soldier accosted him and told him to get off that horse and start digging where a gang of men were working on a causeway over the marsh. Peter told the man he had a very sick master back home, then turned and dug his heels into Duke's sides and galloped off.

The decisive little Battle of Secessionville lasted less than a day. Colonel Lamar, fearing a Union attack, had hastily fortified a peninsula only 125 yards wide, with marsh on both sides. The breastworks were incomplete when his men fell asleep exhausted at about 3.00 A.M. At 2.00 A.M. the federal troops to the southwest had begun forming into two columns of over three thousand men each. The attack came at daybreak, and the garrison of five hundred, augmented by reinforcements, repelled the much larger Union force. There was intensive hand-to-hand fighting, and for such a short battle the losses were high. Over seven hundred Union soldiers were killed or missing, compared to Confederate losses of slightly over two hundred.

After the Battle of Secessionville the Union forces lost interest in James Island. The commanding general received orders to "withdraw to some more healthy location," and by July 9 the evacuation of James Island was complete. The assault aimed at Charleston had failed. Had the Union forces been able to push to the Ashley River and attack from the rear, as the British had done successfully nearly a century before . . . well, no one wanted to think about that. James Island could easily serve as the site for launching another attack on Charleston. Lincoln and his War Department had announced publicly that Charleston must be taken. But no one would have to evacuate if the Confederates won before that time and a treaty was signed—always a clear possibility. The generals were adamant. "Evacuate the island" the planters were being told again and again, and it appears that now Wallace was sending out feelers to the Lawtons in Beaufort District.

There were two pieces of good news at the moment: federal forces had left James Island, and Powell was back on the plantation to help carry the load. Nearly a year had passed since Wallace had first come down with malarial-typhoid fever, along with internal complications that Dr. Lebby couldn't figure out. Unlike the farmers, planters could survive long illnesses economically because they had a support system—the slaves, and overseers to keep them working. As long as these two basics were firmly in place, Wallace could run the plantation from his bed. In peacetime many planters in the low country, particularly rice growers, were often absent for most of the summer months. One of Wallace's friends in the Santee area said that he would as soon stay on his plantation during the season when malaria and yellow fever raged as face a Kentucky rifleman at a hundred yards. Plantations bordered by salt marshes or tidal inlets, for reasons then unknown, were spared the more serious outbreaks of malaria. Indeed, the James Island planters who could not go away to the mountains summered at Fort Johnson and Secessionville, areas on peninsulas of land largely surrounded by salt water. Still, despite all precautions, a white person who by middle age had not suffered at least one attack of malaria was a rarity.

The cooler weather of October brought a pleasant relief both from the heat and the threat of disease, but it also brought a startling bit of intelligence from Confederate officials: Admiral DuPont's fleet had left Hilton Head and was planning to attack Charleston in three weeks. The coastal defenses from Georgetown to Edisto Inlet tightened like the muscles of a boxer on guard. Pressure on the planters was mounting to supply more and more slaves to work on the fortifications both on James Island and on the barrier islands. Presumably, Wallace did his share. Many years later when he and his wife were seeking membership for their son, Alison, in the Sons of Confederate Veterans, he claimed to have done so. Applicants were required to describe fully their fathers' military activities. There was actually little to write about. The application, in his mother's handwriting, describes Wallace's service in the Rutledge Mounted Riflemen and adds that during his long convalescence Wallace had "loaned men and carts to the local defense effort on James Island and had fed many soldiers." Under "Remarks," Cecilia wrote that "he was arrested at the close of the war for not swearing allegiance to the United States," a sentence designed, apparently, to show that the enemy had considered her husband dangerous.

The military authorities thought that Admiral DuPont, whose big fleet was even then in Beaufort, would try for Charleston again. The engineers at Fort Moultrie were making booms of heavy logs chained together to float across the channel openings. Everyone predicted that they "would raise hell" with the paddle wheels. General Beauregard, who didn't have much faith in the booms because he thought the tides would carry them out to sea, nevertheless gave his permission to go ahead with the attempt. In coming up the harbor the Union ships would have to pass through the firepower of Fort Moultrie and Fort Sumter. If they got past Castle Pinckney, the guns on the Battery would finish them off.

The harbor fortifications were prepared for an attack that did not come, for Admiral DuPont's fleet did not then enter the harbor. True, it had left Port Royal ahead of schedule, but its destination was Wilmington on the North Carolina coast; the intelligence had erred. Charleston was spared, but only for the moment. Everyone knew quite well that the Federals would never weaken in their resolve to capture the city. "Doom hangs over wicked Charleston," wrote the *New York Tribune*, "that viper's nest and breeding place of rebellion. If there is any city deserving of holocaustic infamy, it is Charleston. Should the inhabitants choose to make it a desert blasted by fire, we do not think many tears would be shed." General Beauregard, back in charge now, stated publicly that James Island was the key to the defense of Charleston, and that the residents must recognize that they lived in a potential war zone. On Edisto Island Wallace's friend, Jenkins Mikell, had left months ago, but not before he had burned his entire crop of baled cotton to keep it from the enemy.

DURING THIS LULL IN military activities, Wallace attended to a provision of his father's will—the regular payments on the $65,000 note that he had given for the plantation. He had made the payments on schedule so far, give or take a few weeks, and now an installment of $8,000 was due. Wallace must have kept a reserve of cash either in his own safe or in the bank vaults in Charleston. Surely he converted it to Confederate money if he was paying bills. Inflation was running then at 14 percent a day, but Confederate money was legal tender—provided you could get someone to accept it. He would send a letter of instructions to the bank. Peter was the messenger for the occasion. Peter would row over to the city in Wallace's boat, a craft so slim and devoid of accoutrements that he dubbed it the *Stark Naked*, deliver the letter to the manager of Wallace's bank, and wait for a reply. He should wear his black broadcloth, take his pass, and if he was stopped say that he was Mr. Lawton's servant, on business for him.

There were at least three kinds of currency in circulation—Confederate issue, United States currency, and bills issued by local banks. In 1861 Wallace had bought a few Confederate bonds, but he had stopped abruptly when he saw what inflation was doing to the economy. The government was printing new money at a furious rate to finance the war, since bonds and taxes were not producing sufficient revenue. Counterfeiters were now getting into the game, turning out notes that looked more genuine than the official ones. Could this flood of new currency be used to pay off old debts? was the legal question everyone was asking. The government was intentionally silent on the matter, fearing that a statement would do more harm than good. Obviously Wallace believed that his little transaction—transferring funds under his control from one account to another—would be immune to criticism.

Wallace may have endured a boringly routine day, but Peter spent a day that he remembered for the rest of his life. He returned to the plantation well after dusk had fallen; he did not have the letter, and he had not lost it. This is the story that he told my father. He delivered the envelope to Mr. Pinckney, who told Peter to return to the bank in a few hours. To pass the time, he had gone around the corner to State Street to talk to a cook who worked in one of the big houses. They sat outside the cook house and talked too long, he was to discover. When he returned to pick up the letter the bank was closed. Try as he might, he could find no one who could help him. He had even tried to find Mr. Pinckney's house, which was why he was so late getting home. Wallace would hardly hear him out. He shouted that he hadn't sent him over to the city to hell around, to which Peter replied that they had just sat and talked.

"Did he punish you?" my father asked.

Peter nodded. Mr. Wallace sent for Miles, the overseer, and told him to take Peter out and give him twenty cuts. He was so angry that he ordered Peter to take off his shirt while he stood there. If he hadn't felt so weak, he would have taken care of Peter himself. Peter told Wallace he was sorry and would never do such a thing again. Miles, a white man, said he was sorry Mr. Lawton was sick and would take care of the problem. "Mr. Wallace say again to 'give him twenty cuts' and for me to get my black ass in that boat tomorrow and be at the bank at nine o'clock."

Peter, Wallace, and Miles—almost a bizarre triangle, one that could exist only under the shadow of slavery. Peter, with probably the most native intelligence of the three, and often the seeming victim, was the most skillful in manipulating the affection, distrust, and dependency that flowed among them. He was not always successful.

Peter followed Miles abjectly from the room. He had been through this many times before: Wallace venting an outburst of apparent hatred, bristling with threats and oaths that ended in a promised beating. Tomorrow "Marse Wallace would be real kind and laugh and carry on."

Then Peter said, "He didn't beat me."

As Peter reminisced about the whole episode, my father came to see what he thought were the forces that played below the surface of the conflicted relationship between the two men. Peter knew—and Miles knew that Peter knew—of the cotton brokers who came on secret visits to confer with Miles down by the gin house. Peter knew of the special shipping labels that these men left to be fastened to certain bales of cotton. He wasn't sure what happened to these bales, but he was told to be "damn sure" that Marse Wallace didn't see them. Peter, in fact, attached some of the labels himself. He was only following orders. Peter said that he did not know how Miles was rewarded in this transaction, but "he sure got somthin' out of it." Miles must have known that Peter spent a lot of time with Wallace, almost as much time as he did with any white man. Sometimes Wallace treated him as if he were not a slave. Very unpleasant to think about. Very unpleasant, indeed. To put the matter plainly, Miles was afraid Peter would talk too much. It would be Miles's word against Peter's, and if Peter really decided to plead his case—tell all he knew, the conversations he had overheard, the phony labels—Miles would come off badly.

And there was one more thing to worry about. Wallace had a strange way with Peter, a way that Miles surely must have noticed. When Wallace would roar and shout at him, it was as if he was just going through the motions, treating him the way a master was automatically supposed to treat a slave—what he was expected to do, what you're supposed to do—but they always made up quickly. Everyone knew that underneath, Wallace liked Peter. Indeed, this realization may be why Peter, a man who could have had his pick of jobs, told my father that he had stayed with the Lawtons even after emancipation.

In any event, Miles could find peace of mind only in the assurance that Peter wouldn't tell anything he had decided not to tell, no matter how Wallace tried to "work" him. Miles's job was simple; he must see that Peter kept on deciding not to tell all he knew. One could hardly whip such a man—not very hard, at least.

IN THE SPRING OF 1863 a third attack on Charleston was imminent. This time Confederate intelligence was correct. The Federals had just completed four heavily armored ships of the monitor type, and the word was out that these ships and the *New Ironsides* were planning to sail up the Charleston channel and demand surrender of all defenses, "or suffer the consequences." There were, moreover, ten thousand soldiers in Port Royal waiting to march northward. General Beauregard still maintained that

James Island was the key to the city's defenses, and ordered the strengthening of all island batteries.

We can only speculate about Wallace's fear for his own land, bordered as it was by the harbor on the north and navigable James Island Creek on the west. Sizable craft could move in from the Ashley and penetrate the heart of his plantation. His response may have been the creation of the hemispherical pit in which we played as children, located at "the Point," our name for a little projection of land at the mouth of the creek. I discovered the Point one Sunday afternoon soon after we came to James Island, when our family went there for our Sunday-afternoon walk. In the Methodist family in which I was brought up, Sunday activities were severely restricted, as indeed they were for most of my James Island Presbyterian friends at the time: no picnics, no ball games, no "loud stuff." Along with writing letters and reading, however, a stroll in the fields and woods was highly approved. My parents often took us on walks to the less frequented parts of the plantation on Sunday afternoons, and it was on such a journey that I first visited the Point. We brought our binoculars along to scan a view that encompassed three-fourths of a circle—marshland to our left, then the mouth of the creek, the city, the harbor. At the end of this projection of land was a perfect circle of a hole, possibly thirty feet across (although a child's estimate of size is suspect) with sides steep enough for us to run down. A big bowl, it was. When my parents suggested that it might have been used in the Civil War, it suddenly seemed to us the perfect place to station men with rifles to fire on anyone entering James Island Creek. In the exact center of the circle grew a palmetto tree whose top soared far above the shrubs in the pasture. I have found no record of this pit on any of the maps of the period, causing me to think that it did not have a name and might not have been officially positioned. But it was there, clearly a man-made depression, and at the exact location for posting soldiers with rifles. With no evidence to the contrary, I like to think that Wallace Lawton made this little fortification to protect his plantation. Bulldozers have long since filled in the hole, and a new home is now at the Point.

When General Beauregard learned that Admiral DuPont had lifted anchor at Port Royal and was heading northward, he issued an order for all women and children to leave Charleston. Most of them ignored it, however, having complete confidence in their general's plan for defense. The Union fleet waited outside the harbor, perhaps regrouping or waiting for tides, but early on the morning of April 7 a watcher in St. Michael's steeple noticed that the fleet had begun to stir. Powell and Wallace could not have seen this movement from their plantation even if they had been watching, but at three in the afternoon the boom of cannon at Fort Moultrie would have brought them running to the water's edge. At the same time Charlestonians flocked to the Battery.

Eight ships were steaming up the channel toward Fort Sumter, with the monitor *Weehawken* in the lead. These were the latest warships, many of them carrying eleven- and fifteen-inch guns. Five more ships remained outside the harbor and did not enter the action. Surely these powerful guns, firing point-blank across a glassy harbor, could reduce any fortifications to rubble and sail straight to the tip of the Charleston peninsula.

Then while the Lawtons and the crowd on the Battery watched, the shore batteries suddenly opened fire on the line of the ships, scoring hits with unbelievable accuracy. General Beauregard had ordered buoys placed at specified points along the route up the harbor; in passing near them, a ship came into the known range of some Confederate gunner. Twenty-six guns were trained on the invading fleet. Shells from the land batteries might not sink an ironclad, but they could disable its revolving turrets. The *New Ironsides* ran aground on the bar and later collided with the *Catskill* and the *Nantucket*. Shells struck Fort Moultrie and Fort Sumter, but many more struck the ships. Guns in the big ironclad turrets could not reload and fix the range as fast as shore batteries, making some of the ships look helpless as they turned crazily in the cross fire. By late afternoon the ships were making awkward movements in the harbor. Could those ships actually be turning around? They were! Surely they must be backing away to regroup.

But the fleet did not regroup. Five of the eight Union ships were either wholly or partially disabled. A few days later, while Washington was still trying to fix blame for the defeat, Major General David Hunter had written to Admiral DuPont congratulating him and "all the gallant men under your command who sailed so calmly and fearlessly into and under and through a concentric fire which has never heretofore had a parallel in the history of warfare." By night all firing had ceased, and the ships limped back to sea, three of them so badly damaged that they had to be towed. The Lawtons had indeed witnessed an important victory—one that caused Admiral DuPont to state that Charleston could not, he believed, "be taken by purely naval attack."

Other alarming facts, however, were bearing in on the few planters who chose to remain on James Island. Their land lay squarely between a large army forty miles south of them and its objective, Charleston. Would not the attackers need a foothold on James Island from which to silence the deadly batteries on Morris Island and at Fort Sumter; then, a march straight through the Lawton plantation to the city itself? The capture of Fort Sumter and Charleston had now become an obsession in the North— crush the city where the rebellion began. Washington longed for a newspaper headline that read "Fort Sumter taken—Charleston next." Nothing could so strengthen northern morale.

Wallace at last yielded to the growing pressure to move, and he chose Beaufort District in the lower corner of South Carolina, not far from the Savannah River. His new plantation would be six miles from the town of Lawtonville. Sister Juliet had married a man from that area, Asa Lawton, who we may suppose helped Wallace locate a property that was for sale. We know that it was a plantation of some three thousand acres, with a fine, large house and many outbuildings. We do not know how he financed the purchase of it unless while on James Island he had acquired funds of his own apart from the plantation earnings. He seems always to have had money when he lived in Beaufort District.

BEAUFORT DISTRICT LIES south of James Island, but the road Wallace would take made a westward crescent to avoid the deep indentations of marshlands and ran roughly parallel to the Savannah-Charleston Railroad. Wallace was undoubtedly familiar with much of this land from his duty with the Rutledge Mounted Riflemen; the road was decently maintained and patrolled because of its importance to the war effort. We do not know the exact date when Wallace got his procession of wagons, cattle, and slaves underway. The whole venture must have been a logistical nightmare—no doubt he wished for a dozen more wagons and mule teams to carry his farm tools, enough food for the journey and for sustenance after his arrival, seeds, beds, surely some cookware, basic furniture. The very old and the very young would ride; the others would walk and help keep the cattle in line. The cattle and mules could browse and graze at night, but he must plan to feed a hundred people at least once a day. He might have borrowed a circular tent from the military, or perhaps they slept under the wagons as he would do on a return trip three years later. As for family treasures in the big house, most of them had to stay. We know that he did take his cut glass scent bottle in a morocco case, because a year later when the Lawtons had fled to the Beaufort area, his wife watched one of Sherman's "bummers" pocket it as he rummaged through their house. There is no record of his having sold any slaves before leaving; he probably kept them all, because the market price at that time must have been low.

Peter Brown told my father that at the time of this move Powell helped him through one of the worst periods of his life. He had been hearing for days that they might leave James Island, and he finally told Powell of his fear. He was seeing Emma, who lived on the next plantation, and they were planning to be married. Emma belonged to Mr. Hinson. The Hinsons were going to refugee, too—maybe to faraway Aiken. If this happened, Peter would never see Emma again. "Unless I ran away," he told my father, "but what good would that do? We couldn't both run away." Powell served as the intermediary. One can only speculate about the interchange between the two brothers. Both knew that Peter was the most useful slave on the plantation, that if he was grieving and depressed he would be of little help in the huge undertaking ahead of them. And one likes to think that Wallace was motivated by his own honest concern. A few days later Wallace came down to the harness room where Peter was working and said that Emma was going to work for the Lawtons from now on.

"That's how Mr. Wallace was," Peter said. "Sometimes he was so mean I never wanted to see him again, and then—kind like that."

He sent Powell, Peter, and two others ten days in advance of the departure date. Their job was to locate stopping places with water and good cover. They were to go at once to the new farm, examine fences—repair them, if possible—and discover what the vacating owner had left that might be usable. Much of the operating paraphernalia of a household was in place—the ham and bacon in the smokehouse, blacksmith tools, molasses, and even some freshly dug sweet potatoes stored in conical piles of sand and cornstalks. Peter said that they located a good cabin for him and Emma, one not far from the communal outhouse and the water pump, and that they spent a day repairing fences.

WALLACE HAD CHOSEN a plantation that lay six miles from the home of his future wife, but a year would pass before they would discover each other—a year in which Wallace prospered on the new plantation beyond his wildest expectations. It is fair to assume, I think, that he was actively looking for a wife. A few months earlier he had fallen in love—or was seeking to become acquainted with a cousin, Mary Lawton, and had written her father, Benjamin Lawton, asking to call upon her. The answer was no, without explanation. Wallace then wrote a rather formal protest to Benjamin, "hoping, if you give me a fair hearing, to satisfy by referring you to some of our oldest and most esteemed citizens as regards the character I have borne while living among them; and I shall not shrink the closest scrutiny. I acknowledge to have been guilty in a large measure of the follies and imprudencies of young men, raised amidst the circumstances which have surrounded me. Being early taught to believe that honesty, integrity, and strict attention to business made up the sum total of a man's character, that the former faults vanish as we grow older, have perhaps paid too little attention to these important particulars." His indiscretions, he seems to suggest, may have been common knowledge, but he had to point out that they were not as bad as his prospective father-in-law might imagine. He goes on to clarify his meaning: "Do not however understand that I have gone to excesses in these vices, for I believe in being able to show the light hold which they have taken on me, by proving that without reference to your favor, had quit them altogether. As you do not specify to what part of my antecedents you object, it is impossible to make a defense."

Benjamin Lawton was not satisfied, apparently, with Wallace's easy dismissal of the "vices" and "imprudencies" of young men who were reared "amidst the circumstances which have surrounded me," for he did not answer this letter. He may have demanded more than "honesty, integrity, and strict attention to business" as the "sum total" of character for the man who was to marry his daughter. She later married a young doctor in Screven County, Georgia.

As THE IMMENSE responsibilities of moving were now falling on Wallace's shoulders, we would like to know how he dealt with them in the daily round. He seems to have possessed genuine managerial ability. A plantation the size of his was an exceedingly complex organization, and nearly self-sustaining in its multifaceted activities. Wallace must have learned well the skills required to keep the plantation functioning successfully. Although imperious by nature, he nevertheless succeeded in keeping the loyalty of a number of slaves who stayed with him throughout the war and returned to James Island after emancipation.

What would Wallace's life have been like had the coming of war, invasion, defeat, and straitened circumstances not intervened so catastrophically, and had he not been forced to move his entourage away from one likely battleground and, as it happened, straight into the path of Sherman's army? He possessed land, slaves, and wealth. One assumes that he would have been able to pay off the indebtedness he had taken on in order to secure complete ownership of the plantation. He would have married reasonably well, though probably not to another Lawton — although there were so many branches of that extensive family throughout South Carolina that although he and Cecilia were cousins, the kinship was so distant as scarcely to involve more than a common surname. In and about James Island and the Charleston area there were numerous eligible plantation daughters available for courtship. There would have been children. He might well have engaged a town house in Charleston for the winter social season, and during the malarial summer months either sent his family or journeyed with them to the North Carolina mountains, as so many planter families did. The attractions of hunting and fishing in the low-country field and marshes would have been his to enjoy and savor.

Yet it seems unlikely that a life of idle pleasure and dissipation, however as a youth he might and from all accounts did involve himself, would have sufficed him. He was self-indulgent, and would continue to be, but also energetic, ambitious—and it is probable that those qualities would have been applied to making the plantation produce great profits, extending his holdings in land and slaves, and studying and making maximum use of any and all scientific advancements in agricultural technology. It is probable, too, that he would have been none too fastidious or scrupulous in the way he went about increasing his holdings and maximizing his profits. When he wanted something, he went straight after it.

Wallace was a man of high energy, able to direct it powerfully to attain almost any ends he valued, as we shall see clearly in his survival of the war and its aftermath. In day-to-day dealings with his family and servants, and in his business decisions, we see him as arbitrary, whimsical, and overbearing, as if it had never occurred to him to be otherwise. And why should he pause? Who was there in his formative years to "put a foot down" on this imperious youth? Wallace's mother, who comes down to us as a compassionate woman, could know and correct only the behavior that she saw, and on a large plantation there was very little that she could see. Among his father's ninety-eight slaves he had, even as a boy, instant and absolute authority. There was only his father to correct him—and then only the behavior that he saw.

His future wife, Cecilia, suggests in her diary that Wallace's erratic and unpredictable behavior caused her much emotional stress. She writes that shortly after his slaves were freed, "Wallace beat a black man today for impertinence." Cecilia's interpretation of this was that "Wallace found it hard to give up the habit of command." But to further confound us, she writes that when she was suffering from her many bouts with malaria, "Wallace went to town [which would have been by rowboat] to get me a bowl of ice, lemons, biscuits and tea . . . and was very kind in going out on the island and hunting up chickens, fresh tomatoes or anything I fancied."

The ideal life for Wallace in his formative years was one of leisure—that of the country gentleman. The large planter in the decades before the war did no physical labor whatever; the basic work of the world—hewing, lifting, polishing, hoeing, harvesting, cooking—was accomplished by underlings. Give the order and then retire to a place of rest—the piazza, the fireplace, the gaming table, the dining room. Out of all this leisure, writes Page Smith, came an inordinate devotion to manners and the serving of fine food. Accounts exist of homes with "dazzling displays of crystal, bone china, chafing dishes, urns, platters, and of eating utensils of infinite variety and refinement—fish forks and meat forks, salad forks, teaspoons, sugar spoons, nut spoons, and coffee spoons." And then there was the food itself, of sumptuous variety and abundance, to be served by a platoon of liveried servants. Mary Chestnut wrote of one home as "resembling a watering place where one does not pay, where one day is curiously like another . . . with people coming and going, carriages driving up and carriages driving off." She also tells of a household of servants so carefully trained that they anticipated every need: "men and women who think for you; they know your ways and wants; they save you all responsibility even in matters of your own ease and well doing." She writes of a butler who would feel himself "a ridiculous failure were I ever forced to ask him for anything."

The Winborn Lawtons may not have lived at the very apex of the social pyramid, but with nearly a hundred slaves on the plantation, they lived well indeed. Alison Lawton told my father that he was instructed by his father, Wallace, "never to do anything about the plantation that you can hire someone else to do," a piece of advice that my practical farmer father thought unwise. Do we not see the influence of Alison's father who could in earlier days order a servant to do any task?

How Grand A Flame

OF THE THREE LAWTON MALES IN THIS STORY, Wallace was the only one to endure the full weight of the war and its aftermath, although he, I am sure, never saw himself as "enduring" anything. He would be up and attacking long before he would have to produce something called endurance. "Hard-driving Wallace" are the words that come to my mind when I think of this man. Although his youth prepared him for a life of leisure and even indolence, I am struck by his transformation, under the exigencies of the times, into a man of purpose and action.

For all his faults, it is not right to see him anywhere but in the turbulent and anguished niche in time to which fate had assigned him. His father, Winborn II, had been lucky. He entered the stage and left it at just the right time. His life on that favored plantation by the harbor had spanned the years between the Constitutional Convention and the Civil War—a period for him and his family of steady growth in power, prestige, and influence. Wallace had not been so fortunate. He was to preside over—or watch in dismay—the steady dissolution of almost all that his prudent ancestors had acquired.

Would anyone, given his wishes, choose to come of age in the year 1860? The question, of course, is foolish, for we are all captives of time. A better question is would anyone choose to be born and reared on a plantation totally supported by the labors of a hundred slaves? A young man, even if he had fleeting misgivings about the moral tangle in which he was enmeshed, would soon sense how futile would be his efforts to extricate himself. Simple charity bids us to see Wallace, his wife, and their whole generation as trapped in a system not of their own making. While all their responses do not please us, they were trapped nevertheless.

Peter, Wallace, and Wallace's wife, Cecilia—these are the people of that troubled era whom I came to know best. Thrown together by history, as indeed are all of us at the start—no man can request a bed to be born in—the wonder is that Peter, Wallace, and Cecilia stayed together until death took them off, one by one.

I have always wondered why Uncle Peter spent all his life with the Lawtons. During the war we can find a partial answer to the question—

survival. A man does not go experimenting with new relationships when a rampaging army is at the door. As I have said earlier, I think Peter was uncommonly intelligent, as shown by his ability to see to the heart of a matter and to learn from experience. Somehow he learned to read and write, and though he had experienced none of the so-called discipline of education, I think that in reasoning and perceptual skills he surpassed most of the white men with whom he worked. With the coming of freedom and prosperity a few years later, Peter could have worked on any plantation of his choosing, but he chose to stay with the Lawtons. In this decision we learn something of Peter's values, although that term was not in use then. Slaves were seen as tractable or resistant, hardworking or dilatory, honest or thieving. Some slaves fought to the end against powers that they could not possibly overcome, despite all the varieties of punishment this might incur. Peter seems to have been a man of peace—study your master, learn how to please him, and enjoy a modicum of calm. He was, fortunately, not cast against a hideous slave master. Wallace comes down to us now as often harsh and capricious, but he was not cruel or vicious in principle. He had to maintain status and control and would employ means totally unacceptable to us now to achieve those objectives. Peter seems to have understood this and to have made up his mind not to strike out against his master and the system, a move that would only destroy himself and his family.

He and Emma lapsed once, in the first summer of freedom when they were living on the plantation near Lawtonville. When black soldiers in blue coats roamed the fields searching for followers, he and Emma yielded to the call of airy, heady freedom, marching off with a happy throng of slaves who had dropped their hoes to wander in the woods searching for Uncle Sam's bacon, sugar, and coffee. Peter perceived what none of the others in that intoxicated crowd perceived—this was a hoax, and starvation lay ahead. Two nights later he and Emma, humbled and repentant, returned to what safety Cecilia and Wallace could offer.

Cecilia writes in her diary in 1865, "Some of Wallace's slaves are homesick for their old plantation on James Island." I find it easy to place Peter in that group, and I often wonder when he discovered that he was bound to the land at the harbor's edge by bonds as strong as those that held the Lawtons. Did there come a time or a season when he knew beyond any doubt that for the remaining years allotted to him, the Lawton plantation would be his home? The land can belong to a man in a sense not conveyed by titles and deeds, and surely Peter knew the plantation more intimately than did its legal owners. I like to think that memories of his own boyhood surfaced when he told us of good places to play and fish, as he did on his brief visits to the store, or when he lingered at our house watching Kenneth and me clean the whiting he had just brought. He knew the hiding places of mud cooters and the dangerous water moccasins. He knew the best places where we might let down our dip nets for shrimp, where we could find a little grove of wild persimmons and a pecan tree. When high tide flooded the marshlands, he told my father where to push his flat-bottomed boat through the thin grass in search of shy game birds called "marsh hens," where in the Bennetts pasture he might find a covey of partridges, or the best place to wait for a flight of doves. As unthinkable for Peter to leave this world as for Winborn or Wallace or Alison to sell it!

If there was ever a period in history when the strengths and weaknesses of men and women were thrown into sharp relief, it was in the last half of the nineteenth century in the war-torn counties of South Carolina and Georgia. From the distance of 125 years it is easy to see that some of their values and achievements were misguided, but we cannot rob them of one prime quality—strength of purpose. Their system collapsed, but they did not.

To Wallace, then, fell the role of commander in chief in the flight from James Island in 1863. He had to plan and execute the whole venture himself—the uncertain journey, establishing his business on a new plantation in Beaufort District, deciding how to sidestep the marauding units of Sherman's army. To Cecilia and Peter fell the greater task of living with him. Peter's assignment was perhaps more difficult than Cecilia's. While she was always wife and mistress—and white—he was at one moment Wallace's coworker and confidant, and the next moment his slave who "damn well better know how to keep his place."

As the captain of the family enterprise in that patriarchal system, Wallace carried a heavy burden: he was steadily in the public view. Everyone, from servants to envious neighbors, saw the outcome of his decisions, and a great many people had to live by them. His successes, if there were any, brought praise for their courage or vision; his mistakes, derision. He was not offered the luxury of private failure.

Recently Creighton Frampton, who grew up on James Island and became superintendent of Charleston County schools, accompanied me on an exploratory trip to Beaufort, South Carolina. As U.S. Highway 17 bent its way westward in a gentle arc to avoid the deep coastal inlets and marshes, I said to Creighton, "This is the route that Wallace took with his entourage of wagons, mules, sheep, cattle, and a hundred slaves when he fled James Island in 1863." There were carts for the black people who were very old or very young, a wagonload of squealing hogs, one of chickens and geese, food for the journey and for survival on the plantation until the seeds they carried could produce beans and corn and sweet potatoes. Tucked under the seat of the safest wagon was their most precious cargo — a bag of cotton seed.

"How did they do it?" I asked Creighton. Neither of us could answer.

As we skimmed over the flat land and water on causeways and bridges, now over yawning marshes that stretched eastward to the horizon, now in woods of pines and water oaks, I imagined Wallace on horseback marshaling his teams of wheezing mules, jouncing buggies, and stray animals; I saw black boys running in the underbrush waving their sticks to prod the straggling cows, a throng of foot-weary slaves bringing up the rear, and last, the drivers carrying whips.

A few miles farther down the road I even located a half-acre of dry ground under tall pines where Wallace might have ordered his company to bed down for the night on the clean, agreeable pine straw.

THREE

Cecilia Lawton of Lawtonville

ROBERT THEMISTOCLES LAWTON, who owned plantations on both sides of the Savannah River, was the archetype of the southern planter, a man whose duty and privilege it was to administer rightly the affairs of his family, his slaves, his material possessions, as well as his intangible but equally important standing in the community. The community did not include the farmers and day laborers clustered at the edges of his big plantations, earning a marginal existence with few slaves or none. These people were "crackers," but he might be willing to refer to them as farmers if the word was used in its purely technical sense. Indeed, Robert hardly knew these people, and he strictly forbade his wife and children to associate with them. Both parents did honestly fear that their daughters would acquire the "twangy brogue," as his wife called it, of the "crackers'" children. He therefore built a schoolhouse and imported his own teachers.

One winter Robert engaged a young man fresh from Oglethorpe College to teach his children and a few of their cousins. The teacher, to increase his income, admitted two bright boys, sons of farmers, to his class. In passing the school one day, Robert saw two new faces among the children on the playground. Puzzled, he stopped to inquire. The teacher explained that the children's parents, who lived on a nearby farm, were paying tuition and that the boys were "quick learners." Robert ordered his girls home at once and dismissed the teacher. Who knows what subtle charms his daughters might have found behind the smiles of two bright farm boys?

Harriet Singleton, of Beaufort District and Screven County, Georgia, the descendent of the distinguished Huguenot Roberts family and the St. Johns of England, "owned a valuable plantation with many slaves in her own right," as her daughter would later record. She had married Robert Themistocles Dion Lawton (he later dropped the Dion) in 1831, thus creating a formidable estate with lands on both sides of the Savannah River. The Lawton-Singleton marriage produced nine children, five of whom died in childhood. Two of the daughters were to marry men who would figure largely in the social and economic life of James Island after the war—Wallace Lawton and Robert Oswald.

Robert Themistocles Lawton had certain qualities like those of the man who would seek his daughter's hand—high energy, a gift for management, and a willingness to seize any opportunity for making money. Neither man could turn away from a new enterprise if there was a chance for profit. Robert's entrepreneurial skill, however, was infused with a social sensitivity that was alien to Wallace. For Robert, lands and position, yes, but to him the index of his worldly success would always be the status and welfare of his family. He might be away for weeks building a railroad, but his wife wanted for nothing—servants in abundance and the best teachers for his children. Back home again from one of his work stints, he would take his family on a week's outing or accompany his daughter, Danda, three years older than Cecilia, on innumerable trips to eye specialists in Savannah and Charleston. His authority over his slaves and his family was complete, to be sure, and no doubt the corrupting effects of this power were present in Robert Lawton, but they were not in the ascendancy. His boundless and diversified energy, according to his daughter, was for the most part expended beneficently.

Cecilia writes vividly of her childhood in a home where she was surrounded by brothers and sisters and loving parents in what has come down to us as an affluent and happy childhood. Her mother, Harriet, was a deeply religious woman who "regularly spent a half hour in her room in private devotions with her Bible and prayer book."

"I was always told," Cecilia writes, "that I was a remarkably healthy, good natured baby — too fat and rosy to be considered pretty. I never had any illness during my childhood, and a physician was never called to attend me from my birth until after my marriage. . . . I recall with delight my first being presented with a maid, whom I was told would always be mine — Eleanor, a little negro girl who was a few months my junior. I was only four years old at the time; and went about the house and yard hand in hand with Eleanor, proclaiming to everyone, 'I b'longs to Eleanor.' The laughter this speech caused made a profound impression on me. Eleanor and I were always devoted friends until emancipation separated us. She fell heir to all my cast-off dresses; and I was ever her champion and defense in domestic troubles with the other slaves or the white children of the family.

"During 1852–53 — (in December, I think), we moved over to Screven County, Ga. to a plantation afterward known as 'Blockade Place' . . . My mother was sorry to leave her lovely home, whose surroundings she had beautified by many trees, and flowers, etc.; but Papa said he got tired of the constant gossiping and news of the neighborhood . . . to which he was often called to be judge, or arbitrator.

"My youngest sister, Janie, was born in Screven County when I was five and a half years old. My mother never became reconciled to living in Screven County. She had no associates; and always wished to move to a more congenial community. Poor, dear heart! Her wish was never gratified.

"She did a great deal of charity work among her neighbors, being an active, cheerful Christian; but in the nature of events, could find no social pleasure in the companionship of unlettered folks. She was raised in the midst of a charming and refined circle."

The move across the Savannah River went off smoothly. When a family takes trained servants back to a house they once lived in, and there are many hands to do the work, life soon returns to normal. It was there that Colonel W. J. Lawton, "Uncle Jo," came to visit them and presented Robert with a scheme for building a railroad from Americus to Albany. Both men had capital to invest and a surplus of young, healthy slaves. Uncle Jo had just finished building a line to Albany and was eager to extend what was called the Southwestern Railroad up to Americus. Robert was not hard to persuade. He would move his family and servants to Albany and buy a house for them where they might resume life as usual while he went railroading. They would take the new governess, Miss Minnie, put up a little house for her to use as a school, and Cecilia's and Danda's education would progress normally. Miss Minnie might supplement her pay by taking other pupils if Robert first approved them.

Building railroads was now in Robert's blood. He and his gang of young black slaves were laying rails farther and farther into the Georgia pinelands, and he housed his men in makeshift dormitories as he went. He did not leave his wife and children in Albany, but built log cabins for them, which Cecilia reports were fairly comfortable. En route to the work-stations, the procession of wagons and buggies forded streams and stayed overnight in lodgings hired from farmers well below them in station; on arrival at the work site, they first lived in a big circular tent until a house could be built. "We thought the large, log house with the clay chimneys an ideal place to live. The country was wild," Cecilia states, "and un-civilized—much more so than Screven County. We took our own trained house servants with us and furniture enough to make us comfortable. The only visitors we had were two young surveyors who were glad to have a home with us and with whom my parents enjoyed conversation. Even now I recall overhearing Mamma giving motherly counsel to one of these young men who was inclined to be wild." A teacher for the children always accompanied them, and Robert built a schoolhouse at each stop.

The family later moved back to Albany, where Robert became president of the bank, and so agreeable was the town and its people that, after one more stint of railroad building, he resolved to settle there permanently. Harriet found friends of her caliber and there were teachers for the children. But Robert first had to go to "the end of the line" for one last burst of railroad building, and he took his family with him. As the railroad progressed into the wilderness, he built more encampments of log cabins for his family and slaves, and always the schoolhouse. In all their moving about, Cecilia says, "Our parents kept us strictly away from our neighbors."

At the third settlement in the wilderness, which the family called "Station

3," Cecilia met her first great sorrow. Little sister Janie strayed too close to a spot where men were burning grass and her dress caught fire. Cecilia looked up from her desk at school and through the open window saw Janie's dress and petticoats ablaze and flames swirling about her face. She rushed to help and arrived just as Mauma, the maid, was beating out the flames. Mauma carried the screaming child to the house, the skin on Janie's arms hanging in shreds and her long yellow hair burned off. Janie died six weeks later.

Thereafter Harriet was no longer the willing partner in railroad-building expeditions, and the day of Janie's burial Harriet presented her husband with one of the few flat refusals of their married life. She would no longer live in this wilderness; if all persuasion failed, she would return to her own plantation on the Savannah River. And as for this land they were now on, he must place a stone over Janie's grave, and when the land was sold—as it surely would be—he must write a stipulation in the deed that the plot where Janie was buried should remain undisturbed. We do not know how long this little grave site far out in the Georgia back-country of that day was kept inviolate, as Harriet Lawton requested. Robert took on no new contracts, and in a few months his family and slaves were back in Screven County.

THE GIRLS' EDUCATION was now uppermost in everyone's mind. The intermittent schooling during the family's sojourn in the wilderness was not adequate for a planter's daughters who were now entering "young ladyhood." They did not have long to wait, for Robert Lawton soon made up his mind. In Bethlehem, a town north of Philadelphia, the Moravians had established a school that had excellent standing among the South Carolina planters—the Bethlehem Female Seminary. The school offered all the "status" a southern planter could desire; moreover it would keep his daughters out of the malaria season. He could enroll Cecilia and Danda for the summer session, which would begin in about a month, thus giving them ample time to make the journey as well as time for a little sightseeing of his own before he came home.

Harriet refused to make the trip north, and in that decision she was firm. A southern woman might not be a mover or a shaker in the big events, and her opinions might be consistently ignored at decision time, but she could say "I won't move" and usually prevail. Robert probably expected this response all along and began making plans for himself and the girls to spend a few days in Philadelphia, to install them in the seminary, and then to take a trip to New York State and Canada. They traveled by carriage to Savannah, by steamship to Wilmington, then by another ship to Baltimore, and then by train to Philadelphia. There were three days of sightseeing in the city, and then off to Bethlehem.

Cecilia and Danda had heard the usual stories about the strictness of life in a boarding school and had expected a severe routine of classes, study hours, supervised recreation, Spartan meals, and religious instruction. The Reverend Wahl and his wife ran a gentler school than the two South Carolina girls could have imagined. But Cecilia writes that she suffered deep pangs of homesickness. How else, she asks, could a twelve-year-old girl feel who is suddenly transported to a boarding school nearly a thousand miles from home? She saw in this move to Bethlehem, her memoir suggests, a masked parental rejection. Her mother, still grieving over the death of Janie, would hardly stir from the house, and her active father, preoccupied with his business, "simply had to do something about the girls." In sending his daughters to the best northern school he was doing the socially correct thing, and at the same time sparing them the danger of the summer fevers. Much of this splendid reasoning was lost on Cecilia and Danda, who longed for family intimacies, old friends, and a warm climate.

IN OCTOBER 1859, WHEN John Brown raided the arsenal at Harpers Ferry, the sisters had their first brush with hostility that was growing between the North and South. Nearly a third of the students were from below the Mason-Dixon line and the raid itself, as well as the false rumors, stirred the school deeply. Sectionalism suddenly reared its head. Not only had John Brown raided the arsenal, but "did you southern girls know that he had caused all the slaves in the South to revolt and now the rich planters have lost all their wealth?" A deputation of twelve northern girls came to

Danda and Cecilia's room to bring the great news. "It serves the cruel slave owners right!" For a few hours the Lawton sisters were in a state of panic. Then in desperation they went to Mrs. Wahl, who quickly told them that all the rumors about a slave revolt were false.

In December, Danda's eye trouble flared up again. None of the many treatments she had undergone had given her any lasting help and now she could not see well enough to prepare her lessons. Robert asked the Wahls to take her to Philadelphia where she might board a ship to Savannah. Cecilia, who "wept bitterly when my sister left," would remain until spring.

Early in May, Robert again booked passage on the *State of Georgia* for Cecilia, as he had for Danda. The Wahls sent a trusted employee to accompany Cecilia to Philadelphia by stage. When they arrived at the dock to embark, there was no ship. Had they not heard? The steamer had run aground on a sandbar in the Savannah inlet and would be delayed for several weeks. "How would we in Bethlehem have heard the news? Couldn't you have notified us?" was the girls' question. Philadelphians had known about it, it was in the papers, but probably word had not reached so far inland. The pair returned to the school and awaited a letter from her father. No, he could not possibly come for Cecilia at this time and she should plan to remain for the summer session. He could find comfort in his decision with one thought—she would miss the malaria season.

This was now her second summer away from home. There were always such good reasons why she should be separated from her father and mother. Father away building railroads; Mother sick or grieving and not able to leave home; Cecilia's "good education," always in some far-off place; and then, like a refrain, "you must miss the malaria season." Danda's poor eyes were really a terrible affliction, but at least they got her a great many trips and a lot of attention. Maybe being three years older made the difference. It was hard not to think that Danda was Papa's favorite. Had it been the same, she wondered, with her older sisters Rosa and Anna, now married and in their own homes? Were they always being put off for some important reason? When she got home that fall, she'd never leave home again. Mamma was right to put her foot down on all the traveling about.

Robert finally did arrange to bring Cecilia home in July and she writes in detail of their meeting: "I was so overjoyed at seeing him that I burst into a flood of hysterical weeping and clung to him. It was a long time before I could control myself—an hour or more. I was very much surprised at myself when I afterward recalled what an exhibition I had made of myself before everyone. I was so very fat at this time that Papa said he scarcely recognized me. We were fed five times a day, German style, on plain food."

Her father wanted to take her to see the steamship *Great Eastern* in New York, but she pleaded with him. "All I want to do is go home. I haven't seen Mamma in over a year—or anyone from down there. I hate this North and the cold!"

Robert yielded reluctantly and booked passage back to Savannah.

AS THEY TRAVELED back to Savannah by various boats and trains, Cecilia surely had time for long talks with her father. From several entries in the diary, it is not difficult to construct a bit of conversation that might have occurred as they rode along. Robert, of course, was becoming more and more preoccupied with the Southern Cause and politics, although he had an aversion to personal involvement in government. There must be some escape from the intolerable burden that the North was inflicting on the southern states. And the solution, of course, was secession. I suspect that Robert was glad to be taking his daughter out of a northern school. There were good schools in the South now, and he would find them. What was she telling him about her Fourth of July celebration?

"We had a big picnic on the lawn. It wasn't really a picnic but a big dinner out of doors."

"And why did Dr. Wahl have this big party?"

"I guess he wanted to do something nice for the National Guard. I thought it was fun. We all had a good time."

"And you said the National Guard was from Philadelphia? Why were those men there?"

"They were having a summer encampment a few miles away. I think Dr. Wahl wanted to do something patriotic and help the men celebrate the Fourth of July. A lot of the men were a long way from home and I think he wanted to do something nice for them. They came all dressed up in their best blue uniforms and were very handsome."

"Did you girls eat with them? I hope not. I don't think you girls should be mingling with those Union soldiers."

"Oh, no. Dr. Wahl had us wear dresses with red, white, and blue and we waited on table. They were very nice to us."

"What are you telling me? That you waited table for Union soldiers? Didn't he have any servants for that kind of work?"

"We didn't think it was work, it was fun. And up north there aren't as many servants as we have. And there are no slaves at all."

"If I had known that my daughter would be ordered to serve Union soldiers I'd have taken you out of that school a year ago when you wanted to come home. Now don't tell me any more. I don't want to hear it."

WHEN CECILIA RETURNED TO Screven County, Georgia, in the fall of 1860, secession talk filled the air. Her father, like most of the large slave owners, had been an ardent follower of John C. Calhoun, whose public utterances proved an acceptable rationale for slavery. Robert Themistocles Lawton entertained no doubts that the South would prevail, or that his plantation would prosper despite all the ominous and threatening talk of the abolitionists. He would not let this war interfere with a lifelong dream. He would immediately build the new house he had longed for on his Georgia plantation—one in keeping with the size of his family and his expanding business. Who could be more secure than a man with two hundred slaves, three plantations that produced sugar, corn, peas, sweet potatoes, hogs, sheep, cattle, and the big cash crop, cotton? The new house would have fourteen rooms, most of them twenty by twenty, twelve fireplaces, and big piazzas on both floors, front and back. The house would be large enough for the family parties that Robert enjoyed. "It was the custom," Cecilia tells us, "for sisters Anna and Rosa, with their families, to spend the month of December with us at our home in Screven County. Papa would 'bank' his sugarcane and keep it until they arrived, as the children enjoyed seeing the grinding and boiling. It was a frolic for us and we never tired of watching the process and of drinking the sweet juice of the cane, and eating the delightful new syrup." There was no time to lose. He would select the lumber and saw it at his own mill. He had overseers and trained slaves fully competent to do the work.

The house was only half finished when the Ordinance of Secession was passed in Charleston. This news, even with its far-reaching economic implications, cast no restraints over Robert's plans for the new house; construction continued unabated. Aunt Phoebe Lawton, who lived in a spacious home on a plantation nearby, hosted a house party to celebrate secession, to which Cecilia, Danda, and all the Lawton cousins for miles around were invited. Cecilia and Danda spent a delightful evening, and she writes of it in some detail. Aunt Phoebe engaged a group of string players to gather around her piano and entertain during dinner. The guests sang southern songs, played charades, and flirted when no one was looking. "Who has been the farthest from home?" someone asked.

"We have," Cecilia and Danda said. "We've been to Pennsylvania." No one could better that claim.

"Who has been to a foreign country?" There was a short silence.

Then one handsome cousin came up with, "We've all been to a foreign country. We are in one now! We're all outside of the United States."

"The next time I write my aunt in Lawtonville," Cecilia announced, "I'm going to address it—Lawtonville, The Independent Republic of Carolina."

All of Robert Lawton's entrenched power on four plantations was no shield for his family against the war's creeping inroads on their privileged existence. Education was an early casualty. Cecilia and Danda were enrolled in a good private school a few miles away to which they drove daily in a buggy. Dr. and Mrs. Bridgeman, a young couple from Ohio who had been married only a year, were the teachers, and they ran the little school quite effectively until sectionalism intruded. The small farmers—the "crackers" as Cecilia called them — began harassing him and his wife, calling them "enemies of the people" and demanding that Dr. Bridgeman enlist in the Confederate army. The farmers became steadily bolder, threatening to raid his house if he did not enlist. When Robert Lawton heard of these threats he moved the Bridgemans to one of his plantation houses, where they might be better protected. Robert Lawton was angry — this was typical "cracker" behavior. The attacks continued, demanding that the teacher "sign up like a man" or "get out of the country," until Dr. Bridgeman finally enlisted in the Confederate army. When he left for camp, Robert Lawton brought Mrs. Bridgeman to his home, giving his promise to care for her until the war was over.

Cecilia continues the story: "As soon as Mrs. Bridgeman came with us, several of the well-to-do neighbors begged Papa to allow her to take their children also. He finally consented for her to take a few only of them *subject to his approval.* The arrangement increased her income. We went to school at 'The Mill' for a while and afterward in a small schoolhouse that Papa erected at the head of our avenue. Driving by one day, he thought he saw me playing with another child whom he did not know, and removed me from the school that afternoon. He made a mistake as two of us were dressed alike, but he would not allow me to return, saying that I had already come into contact too much with country children, and he would send me to a boarding school."

The fall of Port Royal in November of 1861 brought the war even closer to the Lawtons of the Beaufort area. Sister Anna, married to Robert Oswald, a big planter on a Sea Island near Port Royal, experienced the war early and bitterly. In November 1861, the North, unable to capture Fort Sumter, decided as part of the blockade strategy to seize the deep-water harbor at Port Royal, fifty miles south of Charleston. During the summer the Confederates built two strong forts, one on each side of the channel, Fort Walker and Fort Beauregard. Unable to withstand the poundings of fifteen men-of-war and the ground attack of twelve thousand troops, the garrisons abandoned the forts. The defeat terrified the citizens of Beaufort and the planters on the surrounding plantations, some of the richest in the

South. An immense exodus of white people fled inland, leaving some ten thousand slaves without owners or directions of any kind to wander the islands and despoil the fine houses.

Some months before this crisis, Robert Oswald had joined the Beaufort Volunteer Artillery, leaving his plantation for his wife Anna to manage. Before the threatened attack, Anna's parents sprang into action. Robert Themistocles Lawton invited the Oswalds to use one of his several plantations near Lawtonville; Oswald's family would be safe and he could resume planting while also serving with his artillery group. But Robert Oswald had decided to remain on the island; others were still planting and so would he. Cecilia wrote, "This was a disastrous decision." The Lawtons, fearful that hostilities would break out at any moment, then decided to protect their grandchildren. Harriet wrote to her daughter that she might choose to risk her life if she wished, but that she would not allow her grandchildren to be endangered. If daughter Anna would not send her children to safety, then Harriet would come and get them. This she did. Cecilia concludes the episode: "Sister Anna then brought her four oldest children with their nurses to live with their grandparents. She kept the youngest with her."

Then the Union attack came. Robert Oswald, at the scene of the fighting, somehow got word to Anna, who was in their town house in Beaufort, to pack up what she could in a buggy, take the baby and his nurse, and head for her parents' house. Piling her clothing and a few keepsakes of silver and china into a buggy, she drove all one rainy night to her father's unfinished new home at Blockade Place. She had been there but a few hours when her husband stumbled through the door and fell on the floor exhausted. When the forts fell, the defenders had no recourse but to retreat inland. Robert had struggled all night through the mud and water of the tidal marshes, having even to abandon his weapon.

The Oswalds never regained any of their property, for their houses and lands were absorbed into the great Port Royal Experiment and divided among the newly freed slaves. The islands around Port Royal and Beaufort were held by the North throughout the war, a pocket of Yankees deep in southern territory. The philanthropists in the North saw the situation at Port Royal as the supreme opportunity to bring the ignorant slaves into productive citizenship. Teachers, preachers, and social workers poured in, and Congress appointed officials to govern and teach the rudiments of agriculture to the freed slaves, now called contrabands. But here the story slips beyond the bounds of this narrative.

Back at Blockade Place the work on the new house had stopped. The expensive finishing materials—wallpapers, moldings, carpets—that were to come from Europe never made it through the federal blockade. Idle workmen dubbed the building "the blockade house"; the name stuck, and finally the entire plantation became known as Blockade Place. Though incomplete, the house was quite fit for occupancy, and here the family held their last big Christmas party before the fall.

THE WAR WAS SLOWLY closing its grip on the girl who would become Wallace Lawton's wife, threatening not only her physical safety but creating forces that would alienate her from her family. Most wars produce victims far back from, and on both sides of, the hostility line; up to this point prosperity and an affluent family had spared Cecilia and Danda from direct experience with war's cruelty. But no longer. She was now entering a period when the encroaching war would disturb almost every aspect of her daily life.

Cecilia and Danda had somehow to continue their education, and Robert, true to his traditions, would see that they did it. Since all the good young teachers and tutors were in the army, Papa decided to send them to Orangeburg Female Seminary, located nearby and thought to be safe. They stayed only a few weeks, because Robert decided that the reduced militia there was not adequate defense for his daughters. He then transferred them to Augusta, Georgia, a place they would soon leave because the town was too exposed to the enemy. Papa would not give up, and he eventually found a school for them in McPhersonville, South Carolina, where after a few weeks they were brought home by the illness of their mother.

All we know about Harriet Singleton Lawton is found in three pages of her daughter's memoir. Cecilia brings her to life not by a series of glowing adjectives, but by telling simply how she lived. Her day began always with private religious devotions. When she closed her bedroom door each morning, she was not to be disturbed for half an hour. Turning away in recent years from the active social life of her husband, she was devoting more and more time to the destitute on the poor farms about her. She did not share her husband's disdain for farmers, and as wartime shortages developed, she took clothes and food almost daily to families where the husband or father had gone to war. "Even now I can recall how she looked with tears streaming down her sweet sympathetic face, as she listened to some tale of distress from these poor people; or as she came to us asking each one to share our purses or our wardrobes (made very scant by the war) with some destitute family." Nearly every afternoon Harriet could be seen in her buggy, loaded with food or clothing, on her way to some remote little farm where there was genuine deprivation. She provided clothing for many beyond her plantation by weaving the cloth herself; in an upstairs bedroom, she set up four looms and engaged a skilled weaver to teach four slave women how to operate them. At that time her husband was not planting cotton for sale, in the mistaken belief that a shortage of cotton would bring England to the aid of the South.

Harriet's health began to fail in the summer of 1863. Cecilia writes of a "stomach inflammation that occurred after heavy exertion," from which she never recovered. Cecilia and Danda were able to get to her bedside only one day before she died. As word of her approaching death spread on the plantation, "the slaves stopped work in the fields and hastened from every part of the plantation to gather in the yard by the big house." At the announcement of her death on August 13, 1863, "their sobs and wails became louder and several of the older women entered her room where we all stood around her bed. On the day of the funeral, the plantation slaves followed the body to the grave, and I remember that all whom we passed on the road thither four miles off—white or black folks stood respectfully beside the road with uncovered heads until the funeral procession had passed."

Cecilia's concluding entry is: "Her death seemed the beginning of disasters to our family, making as it did a step-mother possible."

A MONTH AFTER HARRIET DIED, the two sisters returned to school at McPhersonville; Cecilia wrote that they cried every night for weeks for their mother. The town seemed doubly safe because it had a local militia and sister Rosa's husband, a Confederate medical officer, was stationed there. This happy situation suddenly ended when the doctor was transferred to North Carolina and Rosa returned to Columbus. In the afternoons Cecilia and Danda would go down to the railroad station to wave to soldiers on their way to join the Army of Virginia.

Robert Themistocles Lawton was lonely in his big house at Blockade Place—true enough, no doubt—but his daughters thought a rich and clever woman tricked him into his second marriage. Was his sudden lapse of good judgment and good form also a casualty of the war, like so many of the disturbing things that were happening to his children? The gentle and compliant Harriet Lawton had not been dead nine months when Robert married Ellen Livingston of New York and Charleston. The bride was forty-seven years old and a spinster; Robert was a well-preserved man of fifty-seven, his black hair hardly graying. They were a striking pair, everyone said. His shocked daughters went into mourning at the announcement of his engagement, wrote fierce letters to one another, and resolved not to attend the wedding. As the day drew near, Cecilia and Danda, after a night of weeping, finally relented, rose early, hired a driver, and began the ten-hour trip "through drenching rain" to Blockade Place. They arrived thirty minutes before the ceremony began.

A throng of daughters and sons with their children, their new "in-laws," the nephews, nieces, and grandchildren filled the house—"literally taking over the place," as Robert's new wife Ellen said later. Robert's emotional outpouring—his bestowing of hugs and kisses in a manner that left her a mere spectator—was an event for which Ellen was not prepared and did not enjoy. And, she resolved, it would not happen again. She would see that Blockade Place from now on would no longer be a "hotel" or stopping-off place for the family, although this had been her husband's chief reason for building the house. She bluntly told the children and grandchildren after the wedding that they should now go to their own homes and await invitations to return. Cecilia and Danda could hardly believe that Papa would be so docile in all this—this man who had managed four plantations, built railroads, and had been president of a bank! Cecilia and Danda were dazed to hear him quietly asking Sister Anna if the girls might live with her at Sylvan Home, a plantation four miles from Lawtonville. Was Papa really sending his two daughters out to room and board? Yes, it was best that way, he had said. They dutifully packed their clothing and books and moved in with Anna, who lived at Sylvan Home.

LITTLE TIME WAS TO PASS before Wallace Lawton discovered that two unmarried daughters of Robert Themistocles Lawton had moved into a plantation six miles away. Indeed, was there anyone in Wallace's circle who had not heard of the pretty youngest daughter—the vivacious one with the long brown hair—who had come to live with the Oswalds at Sylvan Home?

It seems never to have occurred to Wallace to wait for an introduction, or to ask a relative to devise a picnic or party at which he might meet the new girl. Wallace never sought his objectives by indirection or circumlocution. He wrote, Cecilia reports, requesting the honor of calling upon her. He would like to bring his younger brother, Powell, with him.

Thus Cecilia learned of the existence of Wallace Lawton of James Island. Her account of the courtship and marriage contains some of the most vivid pages of the diary. She records actual conversations and the substance of many others. She does not always mention events in their correct sequence, and they are often interposed with feelings of the moment as well as reflections from many years later when she compiled and edited the book. In order to bring out the richness of her account, I shall present this portion of the story in narrative form, introducing no material not specified or implied. Peter Brown, we must remember, is now an ancillary figure in this exciting event.

How Grand A Flame

Wallace's letter sent the three sisters into a frenzy of speculation. "It's addressed to you, Cecilia, and you must write the reply," said Anna. Cecilia writes that she longed to consult her father; the letter should properly have gone to him. Wallace may have remembered his recent experience in writing to a girl's father and decided to dispense with that formality this time. This also was a courtship in wartime, when many social formalities are telescoped or omitted altogether. And, as Anna reminded her, "He may be a cousin." Even the passive Danda, who had never had a beau in her life, thought that he should be allowed to come.

Cecilia wrote a note as plain and devoid of emotion as she could make it, stating that Wallace might call with his brother Thursday afternoon at four, and asked Eleanor to find a servant to deliver it.

Thursday afternoon Wallace and Powell, riding in a carriage drawn by two bay horses, arrived promptly at four o'clock. Cecilia writes, "He used to come courting in style, driving a very handsome pair of bays, which with characteristic humor he had named for two former sweethearts of his. His body servant was always with him dressed in a full suit of black broadcloth, for few affected liveries in those days." The brothers jumped from the carriage and cautiously opened the gate to Anna's yard and flower garden. Wallace, hat in hand, climbed the flight of steps to the piazza and bowed. He introduced himself and his brother Powell, whereupon Anna, as mistress of the plantation, introduced herself and her two sisters and led them into the parlor.

Wallace should have known that his first visit on an afternoon would hardly provide an opportunity for conversation with Cecilia alone. Cecilia reports that he talked almost incessantly. First there was the war. Wallace led off with an account of his service in the Rutledge Mounted Riflemen. And what had the ladies been hearing? Only last week Cecilia and Danda had left McPhersonville because the Confederate soldiers had been ordered to Virginia, leaving the town defenseless against Yankee raiders who might come up from Beaufort. Yes, the Federals in Beaufort were a constant worry. Sister Rosa lived in Columbus, now. Poor Rosa had trailed her husband from camp to camp for three years; she, too, might have to return to Blockade Place. Sister Anna was married to Robert Oswald, who used to plant near Hilton Head. Had Wallace any news from the Charleston area? Things were certainly not going well in the West. In Virginia General Lee was now getting reinforcements and he would never yield Richmond, would he? When the Yankees were attacking Charleston by sea, we who lived farther inland were feeling fairly safe. Was it not quite terrible during the attack? Now with all those soldiers in the Beaufort area, we feel almost trapped. But the patrols had done a good job protecting the railroads. The Rutledge Mounted Riflemen had done their job well. As a member, he had participated in a number of sharp struggles. He would have joined up again if he had not been so ill—sick for almost two years. Now that his planting was well under way, he would like to join a local patrol.

And what of Mr. Lawton's family? Wallace led off again. Both of his parents were gone and he missed them sorely. But, thank God, they had been spared the agony of refugeeing. There were six half-brothers and sisters, most of whom had fled up-country. He had left one white man in charge of his property, but God only knows what could happen. General Beauregard expected a land attack from the south against Charleston any time now.

What of Mr. Lawton's full brothers and sisters? Wallace was loosening up now. "Bad news. Powell and I are the only marriageable ones left." Everyone laughed appropriately. "I brought him along for a chaperon." Powell had said hardly a word since they arrived.

Wallace was trying too hard. As Cecilia said to Danda later, "He came off a little silly at times." Three polite, attentively listening ladies made him talk too fast and too much. He told Cecilia later that he had spotted the girl he intended to marry; she would soon learn that when Wallace chose an objective he drove directly for it.

Anna did not invite them to supper. As she said later, "Two hours of talk at the rate we were going was all I could stand for one evening."

Cecilia writes that all her impressions were negative. "He talked much nonsense and I told my sister, after he left, that I could not decide if he was silly himself, or if he took me to be so." Anna and Danda both thought he was intelligent enough, but just trying too hard to make an impression. To Anna it was quite plain that this twenty-eight-year-old bachelor was looking for a wife, and she said so.

Wallace must have called or made some overture daily, occasionally bringing Peter with him. One day Cecilia visited Wallace's home, "a large comfortable house surrounded by trees and well-kept grounds and a set of excellent out-buildings." Cecilia's account of these days is not in strict chronological order. Wallace's first proposal of marriage—and there seems to have been one every day for weeks—took her completely by surprise. "I supposed it was one of his many jokes."

"I had not seen him for about ten days, having excused myself several times when he called. In fact, I had been furious at him because of an attempted impertinence on his part. While driving with him a pool of water caused him to turn out of the road. The buggy jolted a little over rough ground and he jokingly passed his arm behind my waist saying that he was afraid I would fall out. This I resented indignantly and forthwith took a great dislike to him. His profuse apologies and explanations did not appease me and I resolved never to see him again. He had wounded my maidenly pride greatly."

Did she really find his physical touch so repugnant? is the question the reader asks 150 years later. If she did, what are we to make of the statement that she was engaged six weeks after they first met? Her next entry is: "I treated him coldly and was on my dignity; barely being civil enough to avoid attracting the notice of others."

When did the magic moment come in their relationship? A number of entries in subsequent pages of her memoir suggest that it never came. "The night was one of the most perfect that I had ever seen, the moon making it bright as day. We sat upon the high piazza of a noble country residence overlooking beautiful grounds. We remained so late that I was sleepy; but he did not persuade me to give him the answer he wished. Three days afterward, he came by appointment to receive my answer, which was a refusal."

That was a Sunday. Wallace would not be stopped. He came again Monday, Tuesday, Wednesday . . . for six days, with no admission to Sylvan Home. He now set to work in earnest to win the favor of Anna, although Cecilia had asked him not to speak to her about the matter. Cecilia mentions several times how she missed the counsel of her father, whom she did not dare approach since his marriage to Ellen. "I would never have married against his will." A well-brought-up girl did not marry a man eleven years older than herself without her father's consent. Since her father was inaccessible, her sister Anna's opinion became of enormous importance to Cecilia. Anna leaned toward Wallace.

Her father, we learn years later, was deeply troubled about this break with his children. Shortly before he died, he wrote a letter addressed to his daughters, which they were to pass among themselves. He longed to see them personally, but it was impossible now for him to travel. In the letter he tells them of the deep affection he has always held for each of them, and of his regret that he did not make the effort to see them more often. He had been troubled for years. His failure to support them, they must realize, was not from lack of love, but because he was "prevented." He felt that they would understand the situation in which he found himself.

After a week of fruitless calls, Wallace met Cecilia at a party given by one of their numerous cousins and managed to have a conversation with her. She named a time, some days in the future, when she would see him and give him her answer. Her diary records: "He came a second time by appointment to receive my answer, which again was a refusal." Determined to marry her, Wallace seems to have ignored these rebuffs and proceeded on the assumption that they were engaged, or soon would be.

TO EVERYONE'S SURPRISE, Robert Themistocles Lawton and his new wife appeared early in September for a short visit to Anna's home and other relatives in the neighborhood. Wallace was elated, because he could now properly ask Robert for his daughter's hand in marriage. Cecilia begged him not to approach her father, for she was still unpersuaded. "But in spite of my entreaties, Wallace would ask his consent for our engagement."

After the interview, Cecilia writes, "Papa told me that he wished me to break off the engagement"—which in her mind seems not to have existed—"at least for the time being. He gave me no reason and, as he did not like to be questioned, I dared not ask him. Sometime after my marriage he told me that Wallace was such a perfect stranger to him, and I was so very young, that he denied it for these reasons and that he had told Wallace and that he would let him know later what his views were."

Cecilia herself wanted more time, and longed to be free for a moment from Wallace's unrelenting pressure to marry him, "to have time to think." Then relief seemed suddenly in sight! She and Danda would ask Papa and his wife to take them back to Blockade Place for a short visit when they returned the next day. Only for a few days—to collect their thoughts and see the old home again. "But our step mother would not permit it. Thus we were both cast off. We both wept when Papa and his wife went off without us, and I have often since thought how different my life would probably have been had we returned home with them."

Cecilia sees this episode in later years as being a pivotal experience in her life. She was not yet ready to marry, and not at all sure she wanted to marry Wallace. A few days away from the pressures of Anna and Wallace, she believed, would have completely changed the course of her life. Had she gone to Blockade Place and remained only a few weeks—this she does not add—she would have encountered Sherman's army sooner and might never have returned.

"But I did as Papa had requested, and wrote to Wallace breaking off the engagement. He sent an answer—a note—by my messenger, refusing to allow it to be broken. (I have always kept this) and followed his note in person in the course of an hour. I refused to see him when he called; but he remained and persisted, until, through Sister Anna's intercession, he succeeded in seeing me."

He called again that evening and by the *"most persistent and continued persuasion"*—these words are underlined—"finally got sister Anna (and me) to consent to our marriage the next week.

"As for me, I have never been able to comprehend how I was persuaded into it. I expected to marry him at some time in the future, but not then; and certainly not without my father's consent. . . . Yet I did both, and greatly offended my father, whom, however, I cannot exempt altogether from blame in the affair. Had he not so utterly cast his children off—had he allowed us to return home, I should never have married without his full consent. His unnatural conduct, his complete subservience to his wife's wishes, were the chief arguments used by Wallace with sister Anna and me."

One can understand the power of Wallace's arguments. Cecilia needed security, and she was going to need a lot more of it, with Sherman already in Atlanta and heading for Savannah. What Cecilia and Danda needed was protection—"Danda should certainly stay with us in this crisis," Wallace had said. Had they not heard of the sixty-mile swath that the Yankees were cutting through the South? Anna's experience only strengthened his argument. She had never forgotten the night of rain and wind when her husband, Robert, after the fall of Port Royal, had waded across miles of marshlands to be with her in her hour of need. And he had made it! And, she had told Cecilia privately, she should keep in mind that Wallace was an excellent manager and businessman. Look what he had accomplished as a refugee, coming all this distance from James Island with his slaves and starting all over again. True, he was eleven years older than she was, but that had a bright side, too. He was an established planter and not a dreamy boy who might be called off to Virginia any day. And as for herself, she was awfully glad to have Wallace only six miles away, with Robert being gone so much of the time.

Cecilia concludes, "Moreover, the unsettled conditions of the country (Gen. Sherman had just captured Atlanta, Ga., and was threatening to overrun the whole country), sister Anna being a refugee, etc., etc., were all adroitly used as arguments in favor of a speedy marriage by this ardent lover. . . . I was only 16 years and 9 months old; and he was nearing 28 years."

The next entry in her book: "We were married Tuesday, September 24, 1864, in the evening."

How Grand A Flame

SEPTEMBER 20, 1864, though officially autumn, was a warm summer's day, and it did not begin happily. Papa's letter to Cecilia arrived that morning stating simply that "your mother and I will be unable to attend your wedding." The sisters had presumably entertained hope of his coming until the last moment.

Great Uncle Winborn—the Reverend Winborn A. Lawton, who was to perform the ceremony, and his wife, who were the first to arrive—probably made the remark that has circulated in the family for over a century, and came down even to my ears: a Lawton was married to a Lawton by a preacher named Lawton in the town of Lawtonville. Anna had given her parlor a semiformal air for the wedding by placing a large bouquet of zinnias and asters on a low table in the far corner of the room and arranging chairs for the guests in a gentle arc. The couple would stand before the flowers as they faced the minister. The bride would wear a full-skirted dress of white India cotton, with a low-cut neck and tight waist, and carry a bouquet of pink asters. "I had worn this dress twice before," Cecilia said, "but I didn't think anyone attending had seen it. This was the nearest I could come to looking like a bride." Then there was the matter of a trousseau. "Having hurried me into the marriage, my husband wished me to accept a trousseau from him afterwards; but I was too independent for this . . ." Then she adds philosophically, "but as the war time made clothing very scarce for all, such impromptu weddings were quite in vogue. And the knowledge of this made me better satisfied."

From Wallace's side of the family came sister Juliet, her husband, Asa Lawton, and Powell. Anna, Danda, and little brother Aleck, who traveled over dangerous roads all the way from his school in Barnwell, rounded out Cecilia's family. Sister Rosa from Columbus did not attend; indeed, she may not have received the invitation, so disturbed was the mail service. Wallace, accompanied by Peter in his best black suit, was the last to arrive.

Peter was present at the wedding ceremony but could not tell my father of any details. When Wallace jumped out of the carriage, he told Peter, "Come to the cook house and get your supper; the servants will look after you. You may have to sleep in the straw because we won't be going back to my place tonight." Then, as an afterthought, he said, "If Miss Anna invites the servants to watch the marriage you can come, too." Anna, following the custom of many in the planter class, did signal the servants to stand in the rear of the parlor and watch the ceremony.

With the minister's words, "This concludes our service"—an obvious cue for the servants to file out—the Lawtons moved into the dining room. Anna had produced a miracle in the wedding supper, which she served formally. There were plates of pressed chicken, ham, turkey, sweet potatoes in brown sugar, yeast breads, and candied figs. Her desserts captivated the guests. The *pièce de résistance*, I like to think, was a huge floating island in a silver bowl, which a servant proudly placed in the center of the table. Surprise cups of coffee—thought by all to be nonexistent—concluded the meal. There was no honeymoon trip. Only a madman would attempt to go to Charleston or Savannah, and subsequent entries in the journal indicate that the couple stayed a few days at Sylvan Home.

CECILIA HERE WRITES some of the most touching and revealing passages in her memoir. These lines, composed in her later years, cannot but serve as an emotional backdrop against which we read the remainder of her story.

> With self pity I look back upon my utter unfitness to enter the marriage estate. Even now I weep to recall the girlish figure as it knelt beside her bed that night, the innocent, pure, young heart that prayed God to make her a good and faithful wife to the man who had just led her to the altar. Oh! the pity of it all! the pity of it all!
>
> And yet God has answered her prayer—has given her strength through all to keep the vows registered that night. For this much I must be thankful!

Two days after the wedding, a large carriage drove up to the gate at Sylvan Home and out stepped sister Rosa, who had come all the way from Columbus, Georgia, by private conveyance. She had taken a long, circuitous route, detouring many times to avoid Sherman's men. She had come planning to take her two sisters back to a school in Columbus and was stunned to learn of Cecilia's marriage. Wallace "danced a jig" when Rosa made her proposal to return with her sisters, and announced gleefully, "Too late—too late!"

Rosa's husband, Dr. George Douglas, was the surgeon in charge of the Confederate hospitals in Columbus and was "terribly discouraged." There were not enough doctors or supplies, and the promised victories ("the tide will turn soon"), the shipments of medicine—none of these materialized. Their son, George, Jr., was now in a northern prison. Dreary and frightening times indeed. At the end of five days, with Sherman getting closer and the dangers of the return trip mounting, the little family reunion ended. Rosa took Danda back to Columbus with her, and Cecilia and Wallace prepared to move to his plantation six miles away.

THE DAY AFTER Danda and Rosa left for Columbus, Peter drove up to the door of Sylvan Home in the largest barouche that Wallace owned. He stored Cecilia's boxes in the rear while Eleanor came down the steps with another armful of packages. When they were safely tucked in, Peter snapped the reins and the carriage rolled toward Wallace's Lawtonville plantation. Cecilia writes that she knew this day would surely come, but she dreaded it. Anna had called Wallace aside to tell him that her little sister was not prepared to be mistress of his plantation—that he must provide her with much additional help. He replied that he was not marrying a housekeeper, that he had a fine group of well-trained servants, and that she could leave the running of the house largely to them. He did not expect her—indeed, he would not permit her to do menial labor. Wallace's "place," as she always called it, "had a fine rambling, but very large and comfortable old house on it; beautiful shade trees, as well as a large and pretty flower garden. The place contained about 3,000 acres of land, much of it highly improved and very fertile." His house was surrounded by one of the finest collections of outbuildings that Cecilia had ever seen—a gin house, mule barns, a chicken house, a smokehouse, dairy buildings, pens for hogs, sheep, and cattle, and all enclosed by a wooden fence. Everything was freshly whitewashed. Whatever deficiencies she found in him, and there were some very disturbing ones, she could not fault him as manager.

The immaculate zinnia beds, the trimmed shrubbery, the neatly arching trees—quite aside from the large plantings of crops and the orderly slave quarters—all told her that her new husband was indeed master of the plantation.

But could she be mistress of the plantation? Cecilia recorded her anxiety:

> My extreme childishness at the time of my marriage showed itself in many ways. The night of my arrival Powell was there and other guests and when dinner was announced of course I was expected to take my seat at the head of the table opposite my husband. With this new position all the fearful responsibilities of the life I had entered upon seemed to loom up before me suddenly. I was completely overcome and somewhat hysterical.
>
> It was some minutes before I could be persuaded to take my place, for some unseen power seemed to be warning me against it; and whispering of all the cares that would come with the position. I suppose my husband was somewhat disgusted, but he tried to laugh it off.

Wallace fully intended her to play the traditional role of plantation mistress during his absence while serving on patrol under Colonel Peeples. He would frequently be gone for periods of a week. On the day he left for his first tour of duty, Maum Celie, his old nurse and housekeeper, came to Cecilia with a basket of keys, saying that her master wanted Cecilia to have them.

> I soon found that as much was expected of me as if I were a woman of thirty and of vast experience. The same duties that had devolved upon my mother as mistress of the plantation, as well as the house, now fell to my lot. What did I know of sick negroes and infants? Or even of providing clothing for the slaves which involved at that time having them spun and woven on the place.

Her lot was common in the South. An English visitor of the period wrote that although the master of the plantation appeared to rule like a tyrant, "he had little to do with administration. The legislative and executive powers of the home belonged to the mistress . . . she kept track of the finances and controlled the fate of a large retinue of slaves." As Anne Firor Scott writes in *The Southern Lady: From Pedestal to Politics, 1830–1930,* "Slavery influenced the lives and thoughts of southern women in many ways, not least in the kinds of work it created. Supervising slaves was difficult, demanding, frustrating, and above all never-ending."

Providing clothing and food for the slaves was nothing as compared to the problem of control and punishment. "I was only a child and tender hearted and the agony of my new position will be remembered until I die." Although Wallace had said repeatedly that Cecilia was not to do menial work—"I did not marry you to find a housekeeper"—he apparently had no misgivings in assigning her management responsibilities: "The most painful part of my duties, however, was the expectation that I should manage and control the slaves with whom I came into contact. I was only a child and a tenderhearted one who had known my father's slaves but as playmates and humble companions; and the agony of my new position will be remembered until I die." One can easily imagine the house servants bringing their problems to the new mistress. A loom breaks down and what does she wish done about it? Word comes from the slave quarters that a woman is having trouble with childbirth. In such a crisis sister Anna, whom Cecilia describes as "an excellent housekeeper," would come and give the necessary orders to quiet her distraught sister. A short time later Anna moved into Cecilia's house to find safety. The enemy was alarmingly close, and the most frightful rumors came from slaves and from Confederate soldiers of Wheeler's Brigade who were now roaming freely about the area.

The women who were left to manage Wallace's plantation were soon to have their first brush with fighting men. General Joe Wheeler's brigade of cavalry "raiders," whose mission was to harass the flanks of Sherman's far-flung army, were now appearing in the Lawtonville area. Like Sherman's troops, they lived off the land and were loosely disciplined. They expected any southern home to give them shelter and food and, if these were not forthcoming voluntarily, to take them.

During the three months that I remained on this plantation we fed hundreds of soldiers from Wheeler's Brigade especially in November and December—men from Texas, Kentucky, Tennessee, and other border states. And nearly all were dressed in blue uniforms captured from U.S. soldiers. One very large room about twenty-five feet long and built at an angle from the piazza was given up to the soldiers.

All were given an abundance of food—pork, bread, hominy and rice, also molasses. Coffee or tea we did not have. Their horses were fed, their clothing washed (we kept several women busy at this) and, what seemed to delight them most, their knapsacks filled with ground-nuts, which they called "grubers." As a rule, Wheeler's men were considered terrors, but they behaved beautifully to us. One day they saved our gin house when it caught fire. Had we refused to feed them, they would probably have helped themselves; soldiers in those days were compelled to do this or starve.

By carefully interrogating the successive groups of soldiers, the women obtained assorted pictures of at least one flank of Sherman's sprawling army and learned that it was not far away. They longed for verification, but all transportation and communication services had broken down. If one dispatched a trusted slave with a message he would probably not return, captured or lured to freedom. The stories were maddeningly conflicting, but there was a persistently recurring theme: the enemy was now closing in on Screven County, Georgia—which meant Blockade Place.

WHILE ON A SCOUTING PARTY, Wallace had visited Blockade Place after "Sherman's passing," as Cecilia put it. Destruction was so complete that Wallace was not sure he was on the right road—gaunt chimneys, charred trees, broken fences were all that was left of the homes he had seen on his first trip. Bodies of dead horses putrefied in the sun, and here and there a slave looked for food and firewood. The avenue of trees leading up to Blockade Place was destroyed, as were all the outbuildings. The big house itself was, to his amazement, untouched. Wallace sat on the porch that afternoon with Robert and heard the old man tell his story.

A small company of Yankees had come almost at nightfall and, liking the pleasant cleared space around the house, decided to camp there for the night. They even pitched their tents in the flower garden. Next morning they woke up hungry and went wild. First they looted the smokehouse of hams and bacon, which they brought to their campfires. What they could not eat they threw into their wagons. Then to the chicken coops. They tied the chickens' legs together in bundles and threw them into another wagon. Then to the cotton house and mule stables and cow barn. They burned everything. They spared the house because their tents were so close; they didn't fire the slave cabins for the same reason. "I suppose they didn't think the black people were their enemies," Robert said bitterly. "They destroyed the carriage house and my grist mill down by the river. They drove off thirty horses and mules, all the cows, sheep, goats and hogs— about two hundred head altogether. They took all the poultry, smoked bacon, and wagon loads of corn and potatoes. They ate for a couple of days and what they could not eat or carry off they dumped on the ground; they mixed thirty barrels of syrup and fifteen barrels of brown sugar with sand.

"Then they came into the house and took all my clothes and my wife's jewelry she had brought from New York. I had a wedding ring that belonged to my first wife's grandmother—she was a Singleton—hidden in the desk. But they found it. I begged them not to take a locket that had Cecilia's and Danda's pictures but they pocketed it. Then a corporal put a pistol to my head and demanded to know where I had hidden the gold coin. I had no hidden coins and he finally backed away."

Robert then proposed that Wallace and Cecilia move to Blockade Place at once. If Sherman moved into South Carolina—and he surely would— Lawtonville would be squarely in his path. Here they might be safe, Robert argued, for Sherman would not be likely to pay a return visit to the destroyed property at Blockade Place.

WALLACE WAS NOW FORCED to develop yet another evacuation plan. His father-in-law was right in supposing that Blockade Place was now safer than Lawtonville—as subsequent events attested. The air was thick with talk of Sherman's determination to march his troops through South

Carolina and northward to join Grant. Nothing could stop him now from capturing Savannah; even if General William Hardee put up a fight, his forces would be no match for the Sherman hordes. General Hardee might even find himself trapped between Sherman to the west and the forces on the coast—the federal fleet and the army at Hilton Head. However the struggle turned out at Savannah, Sherman would eventually head north and nothing would stop him. Wallace determined not to be in his path.

His plan was to take the women and a few servants immediately to Blockade Place and settle them quickly so that they could survive until he made the big move with his stock and the rest of the slaves. The house was still standing, one of the few blessings in all this carnage. There were several days of revolting work immediately ahead of him—he must bury the putrefying corpses of the mules and horses. From this distance we can only wonder that anyone had the heart to tackle the overwhelming problems facing him. Cecilia wrote several times of the oppressive stillness of a destroyed plantation—no human voices, no sounds from animals, no stirring of the wind in the trees because there were no trees, and no bird calls. The only movement she could see was the curls of blue smoke drifting up from the rubbish.

A matter that is probably not fully appreciated in modern times is the problem of maintaining sufficient "animal power" on a farm. At each of the destroyed plantations, the cows, hogs and chickens were gone—taken for food by the soldiers. But more serious still, the marauders killed or took away all the mules and horses. One can have land, slaves, and cotton seeds, but without mules the seeds don't get planted and man and animals go hungry. Furthermore, mules and horses were the transportation system of the time. Wallace seems to have had uncommon skill in preserving or acquiring such basic things as wagons and mules. Equally pressing was the matter of time. It would be quite possible for Sherman's troops to reach Lawtonville even before Wallace could return from Blockade Place and destroy his house, barns, wagons, and livestock. Cecilia wrote that they packed furiously, and soon the womenfolk, along with a bag of cotton seeds placed carefully under the front seat, were loaded into the barouche hitched to Bell and Beulah. A two-mule wagon full of hams, bacon, and hand tools was to follow. If the little convoy left early in the morning, a day's journey would bring them to Blockade Place, provided they weren't held up at the Savannah River.

Cecilia mentions several times her admiration for her Wallace's managerial ability; until now she had never seen her husband working under pressure. He gave orders like a commanding general. He knew how to set small groups to work on a task and apparently had a gift for being able to spot leaders. If his own vigor and enthusiasm did not energize a lethargic slave, a few well-placed cuts with the whip did. Cecilia was disturbed that Anna could not make the trip with them, because she had not yet returned from Sylvan Home where she had gone to gather up some personal treasures. Perhaps brother Robert had come on furlough and delayed her. Wallace would certainly take her back with him on his second trip.

The road from Lawtonville to the Savannah River was familiar territory and the two vehicles jogged along without incident. Peter drove the barouche loaded to the brim with three women, hat boxes, and valises. Wallace sometimes rode in the front seat with Peter and sometimes walked ahead as a scout. This enterprise was coming off as Wallace had planned it. The mules labored behind, hauling the wagon loaded with grain for the animals, two bags of cotton seeds, corn and peas both for food and seed, and Cecilia's trunk. Wallace did not load his wagons with the family silver and crystal, much as he would have loved to save them. He was carrying plow handles, ax handles, hoe and rake handles — the fire would surely have burned up these precious things.

And now the Savannah River, with a crowd milling along the bank at the ferry site overlooking the swollen stream. A company of Confederate troops had been allowed to break ranks and wander about the riverbank. When the Lawtons drove up, a dozen wagons and carriages were waiting for some means of crossing the stream. What were the chances of a passage over the river? None, Wallace was told curtly. The river was bank-full and too dangerous for flat-bottomed boats. Tied up at a little pier farther downstream was a paddle-wheel steamer emitting a wisp of blue smoke.

There was no sign of cargo on deck, and no one in sight except a gray-uniformed man in the pilot house. Wallace inquired about the moored paddle-wheeler from farmers loitering on the bank. The pilot, they said, was taking no passengers until the river went down.

Something about the boat, Wallace told Cecilia later, "didn't look right." It had either been conscripted by the military and was awaiting assignment, or it was owned by a trader on business — very private business. Wallace had never relied on other people's solutions to his problems, and he was not about to do so now. He sauntered along the riverbank and walked out on the boards of an improvised wharf. Cecilia, her face covered by a veil, sat erect and still in her buggy, as any lady should, and watched her husband operate.

Would the pilot be able to take him and his wife across the river? Absolutely not.

Wallace then turned to a man in Confederate uniform. Cecilia could not hear their conversation, but in a few minutes Wallace returned and told Peter to start moving.

Peter jumped to the ground to take the bridle of one bay, and Wallace took the other. Together they guided the team over the swaying gangplank and onto the steamer. Then the mule wagon. Cecilia drew her veil about her face and looked neither to the right nor to the left. Wallace had done it again. What had he said to the pilot? How much had he offered? No use in asking outright, because he probably wouldn't tell her.

Cecilia's memoir has an interesting postscript to this episode:

> Soon after, the owner of this steamer (Captain Dillon) headed her down with cotton which he had hidden in the river swamp, and slipped through the lines down river to Savannah. There he surrendered himself and his boat to the Yankee general in charge who allowed him to retain possession of the cotton. This he sold for a sum sufficient to yield him a comfortable future. Cotton was then selling for about seventy-five cents a pound. I have often wondered if he continued to prosper after this treacherous act.

FOUR

Black Men in Blue Coats

T HE CHARRED BOARDS, the gaunt chimneys, and the wandering
blacks along the route should have alerted Cecilia to the destruction
she would find at Blockade Place. Neither was she prepared for the stench
of decomposing mules and horses in the ditches. Wallace explained to her
that "they just rode the horses until they dropped and then got another."
As for burying the dead animals, there were no slaves now who had to
obey an order to bury rotting flesh. They drove past half-burned outbuildings, scattered bricks, flattened fences. The row of slave cabins was intact.

Although she dreaded meeting her stepmother, Cecilia was propelled
forward, she wrote, by the thought that she would be home for Christmas.
She would not let Ellen stop her.

Only Papa met them at the door. His wife couldn't come down; she was
"indisposed."

Later in the day, when Ellen Lawton came into the room where Wallace
and Cecilia were sitting, her first words were, "Oh, I hadn't realized you
were still here. I thought you would be staying at the hotel in Sylvania."

Wallace could have told her that he was about to buy the Sylvania
Hotel—which he did in the next few days—for Cecilia said that Wallace
had a "large amount of Confederate money." He no doubt wanted to invest
it in real property before his money became worthless. We do not know
how Wallace obtained the rather considerable amount of money that he
always seemed to have. He may have had a separate income during the
years he worked with his father. Winborn's will had provided no cash for
him. Cecilia said that the hotel, which he later bought, was registered in
her name, a wedding gift from Wallace; when it was later sold she never

received a cent, a matter that puzzled her but to which she seemed re-signed. We will probably have to settle for Cecilia's estimate of Wallace's business ability—that he was prudent, even frugal at times, and a good manager. Wallace's stay with his father-in-law was brief, because he had to return to gather up his livestock and slaves and move them to Blockade Place before Sherman's men reached Lawtonville.

The miracle was accomplished, and late in January Wallace's corps of workers was slowly bringing order out of the carnage about them. Field-workers under the overseer's direction were trying to get the land ready for sweet potatoes; Peter's wife, Emma, was down in the slave quarters taking care of children—Ellen Lawton wouldn't allow her in the big house; Peter was searching the ashes of the gin house for usable iron; and other men were improvising fences from scraps of boards and rails to make an enclosure. The mules and horses were on tethers, as were a half-dozen cows. Wallace had to divide his time three ways: patrol duty (he was still under Confederate orders), Blockade Place, and Judge Hobby's home, where Cecilia now lived. Ellen had ultimately succeeded in making life at the big house so unpleasant that Wallace and Cecilia had moved to Judge Hobby's home less than a week after their arrival. Mrs. Hobby, by nature a hospi-table woman, took in needy planters left stranded by Sherman's march as a patriotic duty and only reluctantly accepted the money Wallace offered her for room and board. As for their abandoned plantation back at Lawton-ville, a modern historian writes, "All other villages in General Slocum's path through the swamp country—Purysburg, Robertsville, Lawtonville, McPhersonville—were virtually obliterated." The [New York] *Herald's* man reported: "Whenever a view could be had from high ground, black columns of smoke were seen rising here and there within a circuit of twenty or thirty miles."

Cecilia's father had guessed correctly: the enemy, having passed through the area once, did not return. Wallace, however, picked up dis-turbing news of Sherman's invasion of South Carolina from a group of stragglers from Confederate general Wheeler's army. A loose, undisci-plined bunch, "Wheeler's Raiders" lived off the land in the manner of Sherman's men. They spread out to the sides and rear of Sherman's army to harass bummers and warn local citizens, but were almost as unwelcome as northern troops. They did not burn, but were accused of walking off with every bit of food they could find. Their report of the "invasion of South Carolina" was frightening, for Sherman had begun his systematic and supererogatory destruction. Modern historians attribute to him a statement that he "feared" his men would go out of control when they reached "the guilty state of South Carolina." Sister Anna and her children managed to reach Blockade Place before the destruction began, just as her husband, Robert, was suddenly transferred to North Carolina to join an army that would try to stop Sherman's northern progress.

When would Wallace return to Lawtonville? Southern generals had thought that the flooded swamps of the Salkehatchie River west of Beaufort would stop Sherman's progress considerably, or at least slow him long enough to give them time for regrouping. They were wrong. Wading in water up to their armpits, with their personal valuables stored in their hats, the vanguard of Sherman's army made the crossing and pressed on. Confederate general William Hardee was incredulous when he was told that the federal columns had crossed the flooded Salkehatchie, wagons, guns, and all. "I wouldn't have believed it if I had not seen it happen," he is reported to have said. Regarding this feat, the Confederate general Joseph E. Johnston wrote after the war, "I had made up my mind that there had been no such army since the days of Julius Caesar." Colonel Peeples, Wallace's patrol commander, finally determined that the main body of Sherman's army was well on its way to Charleston or Columbia— probably both—and advised Wallace to return home.

In mid-January Wallace set out on horseback for Lawtonville. He found a ferryman to take him across the Savannah River, and then entered into the worst scene of desolation and destruction that he had ever seen. He passed two women near a half-completed lean-to of old boards and burlap in which a chair and a table were the only pieces of furniture. They were tugging at a board pinned down by a fallen tree trunk when he rode up. They did not ask him to stop; he nodded and drove on. The next two women he met did not ask for help either. One had a shovel and the other a hoe; they were trying to dig a grave for a bloated, decomposing cow lying directly in front of the shed they were using for a house. Surely he could help these poor women if he only had a length of rope. They told him there wasn't a piece of rope left in the county. The women turned away and kept on digging.

SHERMAN'S ARMY HAD DONE its job well; the worst rumors that had come to Wallace were true. His commodious plantation house, which had stood at the end of a row of trees, was now only seven blackened chimneys and a pile of ashes. The gin house, the mule barns, the whitewashed fences, the poultry house, and the carriage house were charred boards and ashes. Not one of his sixteen outbuildings remained. Cecilia mentions several times that the invading army even destroyed the trees. "All the trees were gone." Did a planted avenue of trees send a message of lordliness and elegance that had to be brought down? "A row of twelve to sixteen cabins on the Gillisonville Road had not been touched. These were well built and comfortable for negroes. All of the barns, carriage houses, gin houses (with engines), store rooms, smokehouse, kitchen house, servants' quarters for house servants were gone — of the most commodious and substantial build and were therefore an immense loss."

While the magnitude of the task before him was staggering — and infuriating — we see Wallace plotting his attack. There was only one option open to him now, and there was not a moment to waste — he had to bring his fields back into production as fast as possible. The rich coastal fields made seeds grow faster than any land in the world, and they had to start producing food and cotton at once. Some kind of roof over their heads for shelter, and then to the land with all the forces at his command.

While riding to Judge Hobby's home where Cecilia was staying, he apparently discovered the farmer who sold him the tobacco that Cecilia was to describe as such a lucrative investment. Wallace, with a quick eye for a good business proposition, bought the man out. Cecilia reports that he invested several thousands of Confederate dollars and was later able to sell the tobacco at a handsome profit, "for every farmer must have his chaw of tobacco and all the coins in the area found their way to Wallace's pocket."

While Wallace was on patrol, Cecilia had an experience to which she devotes many pages of her memoir. Two ladies who had been refugeeing in Augusta stopped at Mrs. Hobby's house on their way back to their home in Savannah. Mrs. Hartridge was the wife of Confederate colonel Hartridge, and the other was a Mrs. Mollenhauer, "an intelligent and shrewd old lady who was reputed to be quite wealthy." General Sherman, after capturing Savannah, had issued an order allowing country people to bring in food and sell it unmolested. "It was under this order that the enterprising ladies resolved to attempt to enter the city disguised as country 'crackers'." Cecilia participated in their planning with such enthusiasm that the ladies asked her to join them in this venture.

They started from Judge Hobby's house, about sixty miles from Savannah, early one morning. Judge Hobby insisted upon driving them as far as Whitesville in his buggy, though Cecilia had a buggy and a pair of horses of her own. Judge Hobby had loaned them a cart to carry their "produce," which consisted mostly of a little bacon that Wallace had saved from Sherman's army and a few vegetables. It is interesting to note that Wallace saved enough bacon from the raiders to let Cecilia share it, and that she had "a double buggy and a handsome pair of horses." We also know that he maneuvered his mules and flock of sheep out of Sherman's way—all this at a time when most people lost everything. Cecilia's appraisal of him—"he was a good manager"—seems an understatement.

Judge Hobby offered them a "particularly faithful slave" to be the driver of their cart of produce. "However," Cecilia wrote, "he ran away that night to the Yankees, stealing the money he had been given to buy corn and fodder for the mule, leaving the poor animal half starved." The women spent the first night with friends in Whitesville. "In the morning we were startled to learn of the disappearance of the negro slave; we feared he would inform the guards of our assumed character and that we should be refused admittance to Savannah. But after some consultation we resolved to proceed and take the risk."

Cecilia then writes in great detail of the scenes of devastation through which they passed. "Scores and scores of blackened chimneys stood like silent accusing sentinels pointing heavenward and guarding the ashes of once happy homes."

They saw not a living animal on the entire trip, but hundreds, even thousands of carcasses were seen rotting at the roadsides and in the adjacent fields. "Vast numbers of cattle had been produced in this section which Sherman's men drove to the slaughter pens in Savannah to feed the troops and the hordes of negroes that accompanied them. All the animals that escaped en-route or were left behind were shot down."

One of the scenes that shocked her most was a huge pile of dead horses that entirely filled a country churchyard beside a neat little church. The animals, piled three or four deep, had been driven until they dropped, to be replaced by fresh horses as the army moved over the countryside. "We could scarcely endure to breathe the air and learned that the few inhabitants who were still living near the church had been obliged to fly from the pestilential odors."

Often they saw the dead and putrefying bodies of men near the road, sometimes in the wheel track. "Most were negro camp followers who had perished miserably from small pox or other diseases soon after gaining their new-found freedom. And everywhere the loathsome buzzard circled slowly above or perched gloatingly on his unresisting prey."

The ladies were now approaching Savannah and began to practice the "cracker" brogue. They had also changed dresses that morning "to become the characters we were assuming—that is, country people coming to town to trade the product of our farms for fine clothes." The major who met them at the outer line was suspicious and refused to let them pass. After much discussion he agreed that one lady should pass, leaving the other two as hostages. Mrs. Hartridge then drove into town, leaving old Mrs. Mollenhauer and Cecilia at the outpost. It was a Sunday afternoon and Cecilia later learned that the people coming home from church were shocked "as they saw this handsome country woman seated on her cart, who looked so much like their friend, Col. Hartridge's wife."

Mrs. Hartridge succeeded in obtaining a pass from the guard for the two hostages and sent it out by a friend. Cecilia says that she was much relieved when the pass arrived, because Mrs. Mollenhauer was having a heated argument with the major on the subject of slavery and the black race, and had made him furious. "Moreover," Cecilia adds, "he showed a disposition to gaze too long and too impertinently upon me, and made some remark about my rosy cheeks, though I scarcely spoke to him."

WALLACE MUST AGAIN DEVELOP a plan. He would go back to Lawtonville and begin all over. Somewhere among the smaller farmers near Lawtonville he would find a place to board his wife; the big planters had been the targets of the bummers, who had left the smaller farms untouched. Then he would take his slaves and mules from Blockade Place and start planting again. This was late January and there wasn't a day to waste.

"Wallace had been smart enough to save his horses, mules, cows, sheep, and meat when he left Lawtonville," Cecilia wrote. "The animals were all driven over to Screven County until the Yankees had passed over our section of South Carolina going northward; then he brought them back to his plantation near Lawtonville. He had a quantity of pork meat, bacon, lard, etc., having just killed all of his hogs." This simple statement barely suggests the complexity of his task, and again makes us admire Wallace's foresight and managerial ability. Who drove or carried that collection of animals several miles across rough country to the Savannah River, almost within sound of enemy guns, herded them onto boats and rafts, marched them to Blockade Place, and then repeated the maneuver a few weeks later? In spite of his fierce temper, Wallace seems to have kept the loyalty of most of his slaves, for Cecilia writes that they were lonesome for James Island and wanted to return. And Peter, of course, lived by the hope of eventually returning to the plantation of his childhood.

This moving back and forth—Cecilia wondered if it would ever end. The procession of carts and wagons, the screeching axles, the mules and horses on tethers, the slaves brandishing sticks behind a herd of cows, goats, and sheep. A harness was always breaking, a wheel coming off, or a cow straying into the woods, never to return. And axle grease! Wasn't there any left in the Confederacy? Wallace would gladly part with hard coin to stop that infernal squealing of dry axles.

Mr. and Mrs. Stokes lived only three miles from Wallace's Lawtonville place. They weren't really planters, Cecilia points out, but neither were they "crackers." They had a comfortable house and perhaps a half-dozen slaves. Yes, they would be glad to board Cecilia until Wallace could get his place in order.

With Cecilia safe, he could concentrate on his livestock, his slaves, and his crops. The slaves took their places in the old familiar cabins and seemed more content than they had been in days. Eleanor had to live with Peter and Emma—a marked change for Eleanor, who had been used to the servants' quarters of the big house and to the white man's food. Wallace cut the food rations for the field hands to the barest minimum. Normally three pecks of cornmeal and a slab of salt pork would do one person for a week, along with what sweet potatoes, turnips, and the like they could raise for themselves. Their gardens had suffered since refugeeing began and their diet had grown monotonous; Wallace had to cut the pork ration again, and the slaves were complaining. When slaves were complaining, they ran away and they stole. Scrounging up food for his workers consumed an inordinate amount of Wallace's time and money. But the slaves were his and had to be looked after. He couldn't dismiss a dozen of them and say, "Come back when times are better."

The Stokeses were generous and friendly people, but their house was too small for their large family and two guests. Wallace was steadily making plans to find a dwelling for Cecilia and himself on his own plantation. The only buildings left were the slave cabins on the Old Gillisonville Road, and here Wallace and Peter selected one with two rooms and a good roof. Somewhere Peter found enough boards to make a floor. For furniture they had nothing until Peter, searching among the ruins, was able to piece together two chairs. Mrs. Stokes gave them some kitchen utensils, a leftover table, and a straw tick, and with these Cecilia set up housekeeping on Wallace Lawton's three-thousand-acre plantation in Beaufort District. Since there was nothing salvageable that could be called a cook stove,

Peter quietly began to collect old bricks and assemble them in the shape of an outdoor fireplace. He found enough iron scraps to improvise a crane to hold a pot over the flames, "Just like the one I fix for Emma."

Cecilia records many of the details of her first days in the cabin by the Old Gillisonville Road, her first experience as "mistress of her own house," slave cabin though it was. From the stately Blockade Place with its staff of trained servants to this shabby row of slave cabins was surely part of what Cecilia was thinking when she wrote, "No one will ever know what I endured." It was a distance few girls had been asked to travel. When Cecilia awoke that first morning, Wallace had already risen and gone. No doubt he would be back soon and hungry. Breakfast? There were none of the morning sounds and odors that she was used to. There were no servants rattling pots and pans, and no cook muttering and humming to herself as she worked. Cecilia dressed hurriedly and went outside to make a fire. Only a cold, dewy silence. Peter had stacked some kindling in his improvised fireplace, and Wallace had left matches. Cecilia had never in her life boiled a pot of grits, but she knew it required a lot of water to a handful of meal. Why not cook the pork with the grits, since there was no other vessel to put over the fire? Peter, of course, did not eat with them, but he no doubt kept a watchful eye on his white master and mistress as they cooked their first meal. I find the picture a bit moving. A little salt? How much? Peter told my father that Miss Cecilia did not know a thing about cooking, "dat first time." In any event, the food was inedible. Cecilia writes about one of her failed meals, "We sat down and laughed at each other; and Wallace declared that I should never, *never* cook another meal." He assured her that he didn't marry her to have a cook; he would go over to Mrs. Stokes and ask her to help him find one.

By late afternoon Wallace had not returned and Cecilia began kindling a new fire. It would have to be grits again, with a few sweet potatoes that Peter produced from somewhere in his wanderings for her to roast in the coals. Wallace would be starved. At least this meal would be edible. While she was poking the fire and stirring the pot, Mrs. Stokes suddenly appeared in her farm wagon bringing a fully cooked hot supper. She had seen Wallace that morning when he was out looking for a cook, and had given him a few leads. Then, apparently taking pity on them, she had decided to bring them a hot meal of her own. Cecilia tried to thank her, but Mrs. Stokes had already mounted her wagon. The mules broke into a trot. Mrs. Stokes, bouncing on the high wagon seat and clutching her sunbonnet, turned and waved. Cecilia waved and waved until the wagon disappeared around a bend in the lane. "Kind Mrs. Stokes!" Cecilia wrote. "She continued doing this for three days—at the end of which time Wallace had procured a cook by riding the country over. He also succeeded in hiring a few black men to work his crops, but by far the larger area had to be abandoned, though up and growing well. He saved only a few acres."

It was while Peter helped Cecilia set up housekeeping that she casually referred to Emma as Peter's wife. He corrected her. He and Emma had never had a Christian marriage. Cecilia apparently made up her mind in an instant—they would give Peter a Christian marriage like one that she remembered as a child.

Peter and Emma were married on Sunday afternoon in late March—the 27th, to be exact. A Methodist minister, nameless to us, who had once served churches in three destroyed towns nearby and whose congregations were largely dispersed, now rode to plantations to conduct services by invitation. As a youth he had felt called to bring the gospel to the slaves; he was welcome at the Lawton plantation. Back on James Island, Winborn had always said that the slaves worked harder and stole less after a preacher had held services. Just be careful of the kind of preacher you let talk to them, was his warning—so many harbored secret abolitionist feelings.

Like the wedding that Cecilia remembered, this service would be held out of doors. Emma had swept the earth clean and cut some wild azaleas to fill a big pot by the door. The minister would stand in the doorway and face the little group in the yard, thus forming an intimate circle. The preacher read the service from the Methodist Episcopal church with considerable dignity and made a prayer and benediction that was long and personal enough to elicit some hearty "Amens" from the black guests. No one needed to tell the spectators that after the kissing and handshaking were over it was time to leave. The slaves returned to their work. Everyone returned to the old order, everyone to his assigned place for Monday morning, Tuesday morning, Wednesday morning . . .

TWO WEEKS AFTER Peter's wedding day, on Sunday, April 9, in a farmhouse in central Virginia, the southern dream and the southern cause collapsed. Despite broken telegraph lines and disrupted railroads, word of the Confederate defeat spread like a grass fire across the hinterlands of the South. Was the southern white man's century-old nightmare about to be realized—would the freed slaves rise up and kill their masters? For a slave, the prospect of running away was not wholly attractive. Run away to where? Many of those who had hung about the edge of Sherman's army had become detached and were wandering hungrily in the woods. Wallace's slaves were as unhappy with the frequent moves as he was, and openly said they longed to be back on James Island. The more thoughtful ones had made their choice. Peter, with his insight and intelligence, no doubt convinced some with his statement, "I'm staying with the Lawtons. I don't want to work nowhere else, and there *ain't* nowhere else to work." But even Peter's expressions of loyalty did not convince all the slaves, particularly those who did heavy labor in the fields.

Wallace decided to tell them—straight out, as he put it—how they might work for him and eventually go back to James Island. "People are already trying to drop ideas in their heads and 'make a deal' with them. I think the person who gets to them first has a big advantage and I intend to be first." Cecilia was apprehensive, but did not oppose him.

The next day he told Miles to gather all the slaves together under a tree by the whitewashed cabin. Wallace and Cecilia, standing in their doorway, watched the group—mostly field hands—come straggling in. The slower they walked, the less time to work in the field.

They are so quiet—too quiet, Cecilia thought as she watched them gather "under the wide-spreading branches of a large mulberry tree near the cabin we occupied." She was fearful for Wallace at a time like this—if only he would not get angry. This could be the situation in which Wallace was at his worst. He did so enjoy barking at his slaves; "the spirit of command," as Cecilia called it, was so deeply ingrained in him that he was completely unaware of it. Gallantry to white ladies and tyranny with the blacks came like flipping the pages of a book.

Cecilia gives us an almost verbatim report of his speech. "He stood upon a cart and addressed them — told them that the war was over; that the president of the United States had emancipated them; that, while he regretted it, he should submit to it as best he could; that they were now as free as he was." His listeners were now giving him close attention as he continued. "He no longer had power to punish or correct them in any way; that he wished to be on friendly terms with them and should endeavor to do so; and that such as wished to remain with him until the end of the year, and work for him, should draw a third share of the crop. Then we can all have money in our pockets when we go back to James Island."

An argument that his overseer used with them was that they must all stay together to stay alive. "'You have seen people out there in the woods with no place to go. What would you do if you were sick? You need me and the plantation, and I need you to help raise the crops. You keep on living in your houses, and I will give you as much food as I can find — but you will work as free men. We will draw a contract that each of us will sign — you promise to work and I promise to pay.'

"They received his speech in sullen silence," Cecilia writes, "and a few with such dark glances, that (from my cabin door), I trembled for my husband's safety. But they dispersed in silence to consider his proposition of working for him under contract.

"The negroes were all most anxious to return to their native home on the sea-island; but saw the force of their master's reasoning — that it would be better to go in December with money in hand, than at that time penniless.

"In a few days all had signed the contract and were working under it. Some of the more narrow-minded of the slave owners in the county spoke (at a safe distance) of mobbing Wallace because he told his negroes of their freedom! How foolish! They really *knew* it before, and a few days later *all* knew it."

How Grand A Flame

The field hands were slowest to respond. Was it because they had never worked for any goal beyond ending the day's labor and escaping into sleep, a regimen to be repeated endlessly until death brought release—no goals or choices, with rewards always at the whim of the master? We may well suppose that nothing in their experience had prepared them to choose a goal that was six months distant. Wallace's offer must have been too insubstantial to be taken seriously. It seems remarkable that Wallace was able to gain their allegiance as easily as he did.

PEACE MAY HAVE COME to the seats of government, but it did not come to the plantations at Lawtonville. "Troublemakers," as Cecilia called them, roamed the fields and woods seeking either to stir up discontent among former slaves or to recruit them for patrol duty. Patrol duty on a horse was a most attractive alternative to hoeing in the hot sun. Wallace would order the intruders out of his yard, only to find them reappearing at the edge of a distant field calling to his workers. Cecilia heard them say, "What you all work for? You is free. Uncle Sam take care of you. Come wid us." More and more black men were appearing on horseback in blue uniforms and carrying rifles. Their duty, they said, was "peetrolling" and "justice."

Confederate law was gone, and, much as Wallace and Cecilia hated Yankees, they longed for the imposition of military law by Union forces. There was no one to appeal to for protection from the stealing that increased daily. South Carolina law had collapsed and no system of justice had taken its place. Wallace's freed slaves would work under the contract until fall, but were not some of the fruits of their labor due now—today? A fat cow that came to the barn every night to be milked suddenly disappears. A hog is missing from the pen. How do a man and his wife protect livestock, tools, food from a hundred pilfering hands?

One morning Wallace's frustration turned to fury and he beat Peter. My father heard Peter tell of the time Wallace lost his temper, and it was surely the episode that Cecilia mentions in her record, although my father was unaware of the existence of Cecilia's memoir. By combining the two accounts, we get a fairly true picture of what happened.

Peter reported one morning that ten hens were missing. Wallace turned on him. "I told you to watch that pen every minute."

"How can I watch dem all de time when you send me down to de potato field?" His response was too spirited. "I can't be at two places at de same time."

Then Wallace swore at him, disappeared in a shed, and then came lunging at Peter with a length of harness leather. He brought it down on Peter's back, the end curling around his body. "You've had this coming to you for a long time, damn you. Your mouth is too big." He struck him again. "You're still working for me on my plantation. I've been wanting to give you ten cuts since you wouldn't tell me who took that hog."

"I tell you, I don' know who took dat hog."

Wallace told him he lied.

As Peter later recounted the story, "I told him to stop and I mean now. We were both yelling and making a lot of noise and then Miss Cecilia heard us and come running. 'Wallace, come here quick,' she say, 'I need you.' Mr. Wallace back off and followed her to the house. I don't know what she say to him, but I can guess. Miss Cecilia like me and always acted like she trust me. She come down the path cryin' and looking pretty upset."

A number of passages in the diary suggest what Cecilia might have told her angry husband. The countryside was swarming with bands of freed slaves, some in blue uniforms, who were looking for adventure, food, and former masters who had been cruel to their slaves. She would hardly need to remind him that two men on an adjoining farm had been murdered by a freed slave. Where were the magistrates and officers of the law to whom they might appeal? There was no law! And worse, suppose Peter *told* those men in blue coats that Wallace had beaten him?

Cecilia no doubt used a strong emotional appeal, for she knew that Wallace cared for Peter in a personal way. He had been their right-hand man through these months, staying by when it had been so easy to desert.

Peter was Wallace's last tie with the James Island plantation that they both loved, and to which they both longed to return. There was an openness and friendship between them so much of the time. Why must it stop? Wouldn't Wallace please say he was sorry? Peter told my father that Cecilia was a "fine lady," and I think he gave her credit for their ultimate reconciliation.

The turbulent friendship of Peter and Wallace! They needed each other in the way a man needs two hands. But there was an ancient and obdurate block in the stream of a smooth-flowing friendliness that each man secretly desired — a wrong as old as time lay buried in the stream waiting to wreck all decent human relations, a wrong that neither could completely renounce or expunge. One man was born free and the other was born a slave. Wallace stumbled on this block to the end of his life. We see Cecilia, in the revealing pages of her memoir, far excelling her husband in an honest perception of the social malignancy in which they were both enmeshed.

THE HEALING OCCURRED. Wallace was an intense, unrelenting man when he sought any objective he genuinely desired — whether in pursuit of love or a shrewd business deal. Did he seek forgiveness so earnestly, so compellingly that Peter — or any man — could not resist him? This time Wallace wanted a reconciliation, and he would not leave Peter until he had achieved it.

Cecilia learned at supper that night everything was "all right" between Wallace and Peter.

"ON A BRIGHT SUNNY DAY a few weeks after we had moved back to our ruined plantation, I was twisting some homespun thread on a spinning wheel (which I took a patriotic pride in managing), and Wallace was sitting in the door of the cabin reading, when I saw a squad of negro, U.S. troops with bayonets presented charging at double-quick right upon Wallace. The clinking of their arms as they halted suddenly by the steps made him start to his feet. But with wonderful control, he showed no terror, and *sternly* demanded their business.

"After a moment's hesitation one of the negroes in the front rank called back, 'We come to tell you all that the slaves are free. You got no right to work 'em anymore.'

"Wallace replied, 'I have told them they are free and they have agreed to work under contract for pay.' He said this with remarkable self control.

"Another man now stepped up and shouted, 'Have you taken the oath of allegiance to the United States?'

" 'No, I have not.'

" 'Then you got to go wid us to our Captain.'

" 'You must let me get my buggy because my wife will go with me.' Whereupon, Wallace went back into the house, strapped a pistol around his waist and headed for the horse lot.

" 'Why you got dat pistol?'

" 'It's for my personal protection,' Wallace replied.

"As he walked away to the horse lot, someone else in the troop shouted, 'Dat man mus' give up dat pistol!' Another one said, 'I don' trust him.'

"I said to him, 'Why do you mind one man with a pistol when there are fifty of you armed to the teeth? Brave men you are!'

"My remark infuriated them. 'Shut yo' . . . sassy mout. We as brave as you is,' as a dozen glittering rifles were pointed straight at me. The one who had spoken first came toward me menacingly with his bayonet pointed at my throat. 'Take dat back. Take dat back now!'

"I shall thank my kind Creator to my dying day that my courage rose to the occasion. At that moment I was my father's child. All feelings of fear vanished, and indignation and scorn controlled me. I stood erect before those brutal black men with flashing eyes. 'I will not take it back! You are inferior to white men. White men might be enemies but they wouldn't bully a defenseless woman. I'm not afraid of *you*.'

"One of them who looked superior to his companions now stepped up from the rear and said, 'She is right, boys! It is not brave to bully a woman,' and the others fell back muttering. I was thankful that my husband had not heard their language and seen the two threatening me, for I knew he was hotheaded; indeed, we were at the mercy of these troops, who could have murdered us with impunity. Several such murders by ex-slaves had taken place in our section."

When Cecilia went to her bedroom to get her hat, two men followed her and poked about the house. One pocketed Wallace's cut-glass scent bottle with a morocco case and a sterling silver cup. When she came to the door again some of the men continued their effort to intimidate her.

" 'You see dat man dere?' one exclaimed, pointing to a black soldier with a most *brutal* countenance, 'Well, he kill his master an his master son and den run away an come to us! He cut open both dem head with axe. His master was sleepin in his bed, and his son been sittin in front de fire!' The murderer was *swelling with pride* as his deeds were recounted! Another brute in blue uniform was pointed out who had come softly up behind his master in the field and split his head open with a hoe; and one or two others were almost equally famous.

"Some of them, seeking to tantalize me said, 'We are going to take all your colored people off. Now you look mighty tender; you can't work! What you gwine to do?' I replied with dignity, 'I am *very* strong, and can do any kind of hard work.'

"When Wallace drove to the door, I locked up our cabin and got into the buggy with him. One of the black soldiers in high good humor, jumped up behind the buggy just as negro slave footmen (or 'tigers') used to do!"

On the journey to the headquarters in Robertsville they met the white captain in charge, who, on hearing their story, released Wallace at once upon his promise to take the Oath of Allegiance as soon as possible. Cecilia explains that "the command was stationed at Robertsville about 15 or 20 miles from us. They were the nearest U.S. troops at the time, and had visited our neighborhood to arrest a white farmer on the adjoining place for flogging an old negro woman. Well, he deserved it. But Wallace had beat a young negro man for impertinence! The troops knew nothing of this, and had no right to invade our premises. But might made right in those days!"

While Cecilia and Wallace were at army headquarters, other black soldiers in blue uniforms were riding among his former slaves, spreading the word of freedom. All hands had been working near the cabin on cotton and corn crops that were growing well. The former slaves were more faithful to the terms of the contract than Wallace had dared to hope—faithful, that is, until the black soldiers in blue uniforms ran among them shouting, "What you workin' fur? Ain't you know you is free? Uncle Sam got nuff meat en coffee, and sugar to feed you all! An' he got gold fur you to walk on all de way to Beaufort!" Peter told the Lawtons later how it all happened. Almost as one the field hands dropped their hoes and started after the men on horseback; a few women ran back to the cabins to pick up their children. Within ten minutes they were all streaming down the Old Gillisonville Road.

Wallace and Cecilia, riding home in the buggy a half hour later, relieved that one crisis had passed, rounded a bend in the road to see a throng approaching. Men, women, and children, heads up, laughing, carefree. Their people! The very workers they had left in the field a few hours ago. This was not an angry mob, but a happy, almost playful crowd, grinning, expectant. Only Daddy Johnson was upset, weeping so hard he could barely speak. No, Marse Wallace, he did not want to leave, but his new wife said she was going and he had to come too. Many bowed and said, "God bless you, God bless you" and kept on walking, to where they did not know. Peter told my father, "I'm ashamed to say that Emma and me went along, too."

Wallace and Cecilia reached their silent plantation in late afternoon, unhitched the horses, tethered them, and then wandered about the vacant cabins. The bars of the sheep pen were down and the flock of twenty sheep was gone—the little flock that he had twice taken across the Savannah River. They stood looking at the empty pen sadly, too tired for anger. Such a stillness. A plantation for each of them had always been a community—always human voices, dogs barking, chickens cackling, often the sound of someone singing, but now this silence. The only sound they heard was of horses cropping grass in the night pasture. Cecilia writes that they were "too shocked and weary to speak."

When Cecilia and Wallace returned to their little two-room cabin that was almost devoid of furniture, sundown was approaching. But there was no time to rest, because the horses had to be fed — this time with no one to help. Cecilia writes that her husband went to the barn, which was only another cabin, and she followed him. Here they found some corn "in the shock" and together they shucked it until dark.

In the early twilight, they went inside and Cecilia lighted a candle. Then she set on the table a supper of cold grits, cornbread, and clabber. They ate in silence. They were so helpless — so utterly helpless. Bands of freed slaves, under cover of night, were at that very moment on the prowl through the fields and woods. Would they not return at any moment to even up old scores? Such men could not resist the appeal of a warm night to go adventuring. They would have heard now that Wallace had tobacco and money. Every extra coin for miles around had found its way into his pocket. Moreover, he was a planter with many slaves and a hard bargainer. At any moment she might hear the tramp of horses. To whom could they appeal? No one. Their bodies would be found in the morning — one more old score settled, never to be reported. It could be weeks before their family would know what happened to them — if they ever did. Why should an occupying army spend time on the disappearance of two former slaveholders? Everyone would lie. When a falling twig or a scurrying animal broke the stillness, Cecilia jumped. "I recalled the blood-curdling stories . . . about those brutal-looking black men; and the fact that Wallace that day had beat Peter Brown, one of his former slaves. I knew that he could return with others who had real or imaginary wrongs and murder Wallace and me and that no punishment would follow. Besides, we had a little gold money which probably was the only coin within miles of us and also some silver plate saved from the Yankee raiders. The negroes knew of this and robbery would be an additional motive. Should I live to be a hundred years old, I can never forget the unspeakable terror of that night.

"Wallace had retired to his bed and insisted upon my doing so. But I lay down for only a few moments. I rose, dressed and implored Wallace to go to one of the neighbors. He at last consented. We took the coins, Wallace armed himself with his pistol and an axe, and we made our way through the woods to the nearest neighbors, a family of well-to-do farmers named Ayers."

On the way they stumbled upon a deserted campsite a half mile from their cabin where a log was still smoldering. Men might at that very moment be lurking in the woods and watching them. "At last," she writes, "we routed out the Ayers, who had long retired, told them of the raid on our plantation, and of my own terror. They kindly and willingly took us in for the night."

Next morning, Cecilia and Wallace rose early and returned to their cabin, expecting to find it in ashes and their only cow gone. Nothing had been molested. Wallace gathered kindling for a fire and left Cecilia to struggle with the problem of breakfast. "I attempted to cook some breakfast . . . but I failed utterly. Neither Wallace nor I could eat the food I prepared. It was only hominy and fried bacon! There was no stove—only an open fire, and I burnt my hands and face over it. Wallace tried to milk the cows (they had come up themselves during the night). He came in disgusted with only a small cup of milk! instead of the two large bucket fulls."

When Cecilia and Wallace were standing at the door of their cabin one midafternoon, trying to decide what to do next, they saw a man on horseback far down the lane. He was slowly riding toward them. Oh God, what next? Then the man on horseback began to wave. The horse broke into a trot. It was Powell! He dismounted, and Cecilia and Wallace rushed up to embrace him.

He told them that Colonel Peeples had disbanded the patrol and that he was now discharged. He had stopped at Blockade Place and offered to help, but was treated so inhospitably that he stayed only two days. Ellen was as resentful as ever at having any of her husband's relatives in the house. Wallace assigned Powell to lodgings in one of the abandoned slave quarters.

Just before dusk, Peter and Emma, subdued and repentant, slipped into their old cabin. Cecilia went down alone to welcome them. That lapse of good judgment when he and Emma followed the blue coats always troubled Peter, and he told my father of the episode in considerable detail. I have Cecilia's diary in front of me now as I listen with new insight to Peter telling my father of their two days in the woods, and of his encounter with the black patrol. That night Peter may have performed his greatest service for his former master. "They told us how fine everything would be," Peter said, "and I gave in. Maybe I thought I might make a little money. I don't know why I left. Those men never kept any promises. All of a sudden they just ride away and left us in the woods. So we jus' keep walkin' and walkin' and lookin' and lookin'. Then I say dis is enough for me. I goin' back. Marse Wallace and Miss Cecilia they was real glad to see me. I told Marse Wallace that those men on horses was out lookin' for him. They said he was a very dangerous man and they was goin' to get him. Then they ask me if he beat his slaves. I told him no, Mr. Wallace wouldn't hurt a fly. We have good food an' a good house. He a very kind man. Den they leave me alone an' go off somewhere else."

I wish my father could have known of Cecilia's account of that frightful night, for it would have given him another precious glimpse into the character of Peter Brown to add to his store of memories of this remarkable man.

A young French artist, Augustus Paul Trouche, painted the Hundred Pines at the Lawton plantation early in the nineteenth century — *courtesy of the Gibbes Art Gallery, Charleston*

Left: Winborn Lawton II — *courtesy of Thomas Lawton*   *Right:* Lawton family coat of arms — *courtesy of Creighton Frampton*

Slave cabins on James Island — *author's photo*

Left: Wallace Lawton as a young man — *courtesy of Thomas Lawton*   *Right:* Cecilia
Lawton, age twenty-two — *courtesy of Mrs. Robert Campbell*

There is general agreement among
those who remember him that this
is Peter Brown as an elderly
man — *courtesy of Charleston
Museum*

Union warships off Morris Island, near entrance to Charleston Harbor, 1863 — *courtesy of National Park Service; copied by Willis Keith*

Battery Glover, part of the Confederate defenses at Stiles Point on James Island, adjacent to the Lawton plantation. During the late 1960s or early 1970s this battery was destroyed for residential development — *courtesy of National Archives; copied by Willis Keith*

(desolation caused by Sherman's Army).

scarcely endure to breathe the air; and learned that the few inhabitants who were still living near these unfortunate localities,
had been obliged to fly from the pestilential odors.

One of these ruins was a country graveyard, and adjoining
a neat, little church! It seems too monstrous to believe, but
I am writing only of what I saw myself.

These inhuman Yankees had driven herd after herd of horses
& mules into the graveyard, shooting them by scores, until they
were piled one upon another, entirely filling the small in-
closure and covering the sacred graves of their dead fellow-
men!

In several places, we saw dead and putrefying bodies
of men near the road. Most of these were negroes, camp followers, who had perished miserably from small-pox, & other
disease, even after gaining their new-found freedom.

In one place, the body of a white man, in blue U.S. uniform,
lay close beside the road, almost in the wheel-track — and
everywhere the loathsome buzzard circled slowly above, or
perched gloating upon his unresisting prey.

But these recollections, even now, sicken me. The country was
one vast region of silence, desolation and death!

Before reaching Savannah, we practiced the "cracker" tongue,
and had endeavored also dress as became the characters we were
assuming — that is, country people coming to town to trade the products of our farms for fine clothes, &c.

But the U. State major, (German without doubt,) who met us
at the outer line, seemed suspicious, and refused to pass us in
At last he consented for one of the party to pass, leaving the

Page from Cecilia Lawton's diary — *courtesy of Mrs. Robert Campbell*

U.S. flag-raising ceremony at Fort Sumter, April 13, 1865 — *courtesy of National Park Service; copied by Willis Keith*

Grave marker for Wallace and Cecilia Lawton's children, Herbert and Cecilia Lawton, who died in 1876, at St. James Church on James Island — *courtesy of Willis Keith*

Jetties at high tide, Charleston Harbor. Peter Brown saved Wallace Lawton's life here when Wallace slipped off the rocks while fishing — *courtesy of David May*

Cuthbert (now Heyward) House on Lawton plantation, shortly after the war. Note the boarded-up windows flanking the chimney — *courtesy of Charleston Museum*

The "store" that Wallace Lawton operated at the Bluff on Lawton plantation,
as it was in the late 1910s or early
1920s — *author's photo*

Cuthbert House in the 1920s — *author's photo*

Left: St. John Alison Lawton — *author's photo*   *Right:* Ruth Jennings Lawton — *courtesy of Creighton Frampton*

The St. John Hotel, now the Mills House, at the time when Cecilia Lawton sold it — *courtesy of Library of Congress*

The bridge across the Ashley River, with tollhouse, looking west, about 1901. Travelers from Charleston to James Island either crossed the river by this bridge or went via boat — *courtesy of Franklin Sams Collection, the Charleston Museum*

View of pasture on Lawton plantation in the 1920s, looking east from Cuthbert House, showing part of Alison Lawton's Holstein-Freisian herd — *author's photo*

Sam Gardner, grandson of Peter Brown, in the 1930s — *courtesy of Mrs. Marjorie Gardner*

Approach to Lawton plantation, 1947. The store is still visible, but the wharf is gone — *author's photo*

St. James Episcopal Church, James Island. Built in 1898, it was moved in 1959 to make room for a new building and torn down several years later — *courtesy of St. James Church, copied by Willis Keith*

Lawton family burial plot at St. James Church — *courtesy of Willis Keith*

View of Murray Boulevard in Charleston during a storm, sometime in the 1960s. The ironwork on the seawall is what remains of the wharf for the Battery Dairy that Cecilia Lawton operated — *courtesy of Post-Courier Newspapers*

White Point Gardens and the High Battery at the tip of Charleston Harbor. Cecilia Lawton's Battery Dairy was located just beyond the Fort Sumter House at the center of the photograph, and the dairy's wharf was not far beyond the wharf shown here. The shore of James Island can be seen in the background, at top left — *courtesy of Post-Courier Newspapers*

FIVE

On Trial for Murder

WALLACE SOON TURNED one of the cabins on the Old Gillisonville Road into a store; he seemed to have had a knack for merchandising, for Cecilia reports that all of his stores made a profit. The cabins in the little settlement now housed Cecilia and Wallace; a store; Wallace's sister Juliet and her husband, Asa; a hired white couple, Mr. and Mrs. Lucas; Powell; Anna's son, Robbie Oswald, the storekeeper; and a little farther down the road Peter Brown and other freed slaves. Asa and Wallace worked in an informal partnership on adjoining farms, and by pooling their labor and resources were getting their fields into production. Wallace soon discovered that he had too much land and that Asa wanted to buy a tract. They proceeded with plans for the sale, although they foresaw legal difficulties, because the line between federal control and local government was not clear.

Old slaves continued drifting back to work as employees, and they now possessed certain rights that the occupying federal government stood ready to enforce. Neither Wallace nor Asa was comfortable under the new regime. It was awkward and infuriating to have a former slave take you to a northern officer—to have his real or fancied grievance settled in a court of law. United States troops had come to Lawtonville and "encamped in the Baptist church yard under a beautiful grove of sycamores" bringing military rule to the region under the impressive rubric:

Department of South Carolina,
Second Separate Brigade,
Headquarters Dist., Port Royal
Hilton Head, South Carolina

Cecilia writes that minor disputes were handled by the officer at Lawtonville, with major ones being taken to Port Royal. She would come to understand this division of responsibility with shocking clarity in the next few months. The arrival of federal forces was doubtless the only movement of United States troops into southern territory that the local people ever welcomed. Military law was infinitely preferable to no law at all, for the unit's arrival ended the nightly depredations of the wandering bands of ex-slaves and northern adventurers. Of this trying time Cecilia writes "Nothing points more strongly to the docility of the negro race than the comparatively few—for there were exceptions—who committed outrages upon former owners at this period. Excitable they are; but docility and homage to moral superiority excel in them.

"But do not suppose," she continues, "that docility was allied to honesty in them. The negro was no sooner free than he began to argue that all his master's possessions were the result of *his* labor, and therefore belonged to him. Not being courageous enough to take forcible possession, he resorted to lies and strategy. Every few days a fat cow would be lost to us. One was found with her neck broken; another badly gored and had to be killed. In each case they were butchered and eaten by the negroes. At length one of their number hinted at the truth to Wallace, but warned him not to use any harsh means to suppress their robberies or his life might answer for it." One can but wonder if the man who gave this helpful warning was Peter Brown.

Despite the support they gained from each other, both Lawton families on the Old Gillisonville Road experienced periods of deep discouragement; the indifferent earth did not yield its increase to gentle efforts, there was too much or too little rainfall, a new pest would appear, and so on. Besides dealing with the thieving workers who were demanding retribution, the Lawtons worked under crippling shortages—never enough tools, harness, ropes, and a hundred other small items needed to keep the work of the plantation going. They must also have labored under the gloomy realization that never, indeed, in their lifetimes would the restoration they dreamed of be completed.

Cecilia writes late in the summer of 1865:

Many of the soldiers returned home in a desperate frame of mind, and really thirsting for blood! I heard two formerly good and worthy men say that the thirst for blood was almost uncontrollable in them. They had seen so much blood shed for four years past, had suffered so much, and had come to ruined homes to see their families suffer more. Their country was gone and they were almost ready to believe that God had deserted them. They were men who had been driven to desperation by the loss of kinsmen, homes, property, and were about to lose the cause for which all these had been sacrificed.

Besides, the morals of the men were corrupted. As soldiers, marching through the country, they had been compelled to capture their food or to starve. The habit grew on them. If a pig darted across the path, a pistol would be leveled upon it before the owner realized what he was doing.

They had practically raised the "black flag" — a measure which was then being discussed in the Confederate States. I believe that humanitarian, Robert E. Lee, opposed it.

Was Cecilia in these reflections searching for some justification — or understanding — of the tragic events that would close the year? The following excerpt from her memoir, dated 1865, is a passage that no reader can take lightly:

I pass over the fall months of this year as being too painful to recall. Few girls of 17 have been called upon to endure all that I suffered. In looking back, the one consolation left me is that I acted throughout the entire ordeal in a perfectly natural manner, and every impulse of my young heart was thus pure and right. Therefore I have never suffered from the pangs of an accusing conscience in connection with that sorrowful time. Thank God, my kind guide and protector, for this much!

I sought light on this passage from the one surviving man who knew

Wallace, Mr. Willie McCleod, his grandnephew. I called upon him in his colonnaded James Island home shortly before his hundredth birthday.

"I should be honest with you. My cousin Wallace was a man I could not admire—and I don't to this day."

"I have heard that he was a difficult man," I said in an effort to draw him out. "Didn't his wife come from the Beaufort area?"

"Yes, she came from Lawtonville." He chuckled. "I have always heard it put this way: A Lawton was married to a Lawton in the town of Lawtonville by a preacher named Lawton."

"I understand that her father opposed the wedding," I said. (I had been reading Cecilia's journal.)

"I'm sure he did. I don't blame him. I wouldn't let a daughter of mine marry him."

"I guess they stuck it out to the end, didn't they?"

"Of course. What else in those days?"

"Do you remember him well?"

"I was about twenty when he died. Old enough to know what there was to be known. Cecilia had a hard life with him. He came to be a big gambler in his later years—supposed to be a card shark. He was in serious trouble right after the war."

"That would have been around 1865?"

"Yes, I'd say about then. The family didn't talk about it—in fact they still won't, what's left of them. I think I know what happened, but I guess I'll leave it there."

"Some people who seemed to be in the know said it was pretty serious—they hinted something about a court-martial."

"Well," Mr. McCleod said, "I see you've been doing a little investigating. Yes, there was a court-martial at Hilton Head." He shifted in his chair as if he wanted to change the subject. "You can see why the family doesn't talk about it much."

A court-martial at Hilton Head? I would try the National Archives in Washington. There I found a complete transcript of the trial—168 pages of court-martial testimony before a commission of six officers. Everything was there—the charges, the specifications, the cross-examination of witnesses, the lawyers for the defense, and the verdict. The mystery of that short entry in Cecilia's memoir was at last solved.

The document is so detailed that one can easily reconstruct hour by hour — often minute by minute — the events of those autumn days.

SEPTEMBER 28, 1865 — A WEDNESDAY. We may suppose that the sun rose as serenely indifferent to the struggling families as it had the day before, and the day before that, a splash of light on the floor, the fire out, the water pail empty, the search for kindling. Wallace, restless for the dawn, would be up and dressed the moment he awoke, rousing his workers, down at the mule shed to apply tallow where an ill-fitting collar had worn the hide raw, wishing that the night had been shorter, that the day could be longer. There were animals to be fed, a cotton crop—such as it was—to be picked, corn to be shucked.

September 28 was the day when Asa and Wallace would close the deal on the land. Wallace would sell a tract to Asa for $6,000, half of this sum going to cancel a debt that Wallace owed Asa. The men had discussed the sale for several weeks, and both were comfortable with the arrangements. After the hands were at work, possibly around ten o'clock, Asa and Juliet would come over to sign the papers. Asa's brother, Judson, who lived six miles away, would come to serve as witness. By midmorning Mrs. Lucas was preparing dinner in the cook house to the rear, her husband and Monday Daley, an ex-slave, were loading corn near the barn, and Ellen Daley was also up at the kitchen. Surely, for the rest of her life, that scene would flash into Cecilia's consciousness. A sunny autumn day, everyone at work, the gloom lifting a bit, prospects brighter than they had been for years. Were there forces in the heavens, as some people said, emanations and influences from the stars that determined the affairs of men? Could anything explain how those men, Wallace and his brother-in-law, Asa—facing each other across a table—could blaze into such hostility?

The deeds for the transaction lay on the table between the two men. Judson, Powell, and Joshua Lucas were standing by to witness the signing. Cecilia stood near the bedroom door. Both men signed the papers and the promissory notes.

"And now for the Internal Revenue stamps. What will they cost?" Asa asked. "Does anybody know?"

"I don't know and I don't care," Wallace said.

"You mean . . . ?"

"I mean it's your job to pay for them. I'm not paying."

"The fair thing is to split the cost."

"Not with me, you don't." Wallace's moods changed quickly. "I'll tell you what. Make out new papers with the price at three thousand—that's the cash involved—and then the stamps won't cost so much. Everyone does it."

"That's defrauding the government. That's illegal," Asa said. "I don't like the sound of that. I don't like it a bit."

"Can't help how it sounds. I'm not paying for those stamps—any of 'em."

The watchers in the room were silent. Who would make the next move? Just then Robbie Oswald's voice outside: "Asa, I need you at the store for a minute."

Asa rose without speaking and left the house. The tension in the room eased momentarily. Wallace took the papers from the table, folded them carefully, and tucked them in his jacket pocket. A few moments later Asa, back from his mission to the store, returned to the table. "Have you made up your mind to pay for those stamps?"

"Hell, no. I'm not paying a cent for them."

"Then give me the titles."

"You can't have them," Wallace said, backing away.

"I demand you to give them to me!"

Asa lunged at him, brought his hands together around Wallace's neck and pushed him against the wall. Asa was forty pounds heavier than Wallace and taller; his grip caused Wallace to make gurgling sounds. Judson shouted, "Control yourself, Asa!" and seeing that Wallace was choking, rushed forward and locked his arms around Asa to pull them apart.

"Leave me alone, Jud. Let me finish him off!" Asa shouted, but Judson held him.

Wallace, choking and gasping, fell into a chair. "You can't do this to me in my own house!" He spat and swallowed. "We'll settle this honorably. And I tell you, Asa, you'll die for this!"

At this point the testimony is contradictory. Not all the witnesses agreed that they heard Wallace say, "You'll die for this."

"Stop that kind of talk!" Judson shouted, still holding his brother. "This can be settled in a court of law."

Both men, white-faced and breathing heavily, were apparently trying to decide upon the next move. Cecilia did not hesitate. She ran into the bedroom, grabbed her husband's pistol, and dashed around the table to where Powell was standing.

"Here, Powell, take this quick," she said, handing the weapon to him, "and get out of here."

Powell took the pistol and headed for the barn — as one cabin was called.

Judson, still holding Asa's arm, had cooled his brother sufficiently to lead him out of the house, up the path to the store and barn, with Powell a few yards behind them.

Cecilia rushed over to Wallace, trying to keep him from following the other men. "Don't go out there, Wallace. Don't follow them! Let them go!"

Wallace pushed her arms off his shoulders and ran out of the door, yelling to Powell, "Give me that gun. It's my property. Give it to me now or I'll kill you! Give it to me now!"

Powell stopped, wavering, looking in both directions. Wallace was beside him. "Give me that pistol!" Powell obeyed and Wallace started up the path toward the two men with the gun in his hand. Testimony varied on the exact wording of the exchange.

As Wallace moved closer to them Powell shouted, "Look out, Asa! Brother has a pistol."

Wallace was within ten feet of Asa and Judson when Asa suddenly whirled, raised his arms, and lunged at Wallace, relying on his weight to overpower his slightly built brother-in-law.

Was he attacking Wallace or attempting to defend himself by disarming him? The commission asked many questions at this point. Wallace stepped to the left; Asa changed his direction. Cecilia, standing by the corner of the house, screamed, "Don't shoot, don't shoot!" but before Asa made contact, Wallace fired. Asa plunged onward, driving Wallace to the ground. Unstopped by the bullet that the doctors later said cut through his lungs and liver, Asa sat on Wallace's chest and delivered fist blows to Wallace's face. By this time the weeping and screaming Cecilia, Mrs. Lucas, and Ellen Daley were down beside the pair, clawing at Asa's clothing in an effort to pull him off. He slowly got to his feet, clutching his abdomen.

"My God, I'm shot through," he moaned. Blood was oozing between his fingers and over his belt buckle.

Wallace rose to his feet and started for his cabin, blood coming from his nose and a cut lip. Cecilia did not follow him, but stayed with Judson and the other women. Judson called to Mr. Lucas, "Take his other arm and help me. We've got to get him to his bed."

Together they walked and half dragged Asa to his house. Juliet came running to meet them as Asa staggered through the doorway; Cecilia wavered between the impulse to help her and to find her husband, who was somewhere behind her. She decided to find Wallace.

She hurried to their cabin. "Wallace! Wallace!" She was screaming and running at the same time. "Where are you?" He was not in either room of the cabin; she raced to the kitchen, stopped—no, he wouldn't be eating. He wouldn't try to hide, would he? Then she ran to the edge of the yard, were she found Wallace saddling his horse. A cut over his eye was oozing blood that trickled down his face, his lip was bleeding, his nose actually looked off-center, his shirt was smeared with blood.

"You must stay here and let me bandage those cuts. You mustn't run away!"

"I'm not running away. I'm going to turn myself in."

"Where?"

"In Lawtonville. I'm not going to have some posse come out here and arrest me."

We do not know any more of the conversation that transpired between them. She did not convince him to remain, and perhaps on second thought she did not want him to. She had been married to this man for exactly a year and two weeks; she would write later that the first years of her marriage were the most dismal in her life. At age seventeen, she was seeing her husband turn himself over to the authorities for murder; he would do it with dignity.

IN ASA AND JULIET'S cabin two hours later, Dr. Baker was working over the wounded man. Cecilia started to enter the bedroom but then withdrew and returned to her own cabin, feeling distinctly unwanted by the group at the bedside. She cleaned a splotch of blood off one of the chairs and then decided to return to Asa's cabin. She hurried down the path to Asa's house and halfway there she met Mrs. Lucas, her cook, coming toward her.

"What does the doctor say? Will he live?"

"Oh, it's awful. He vomits all the time—then he will drift off for a minute. When he isn't fainting he can talk to you. The bullet is somewhere inside of him—maybe in his liver which is why he vomits so much. It pours a lot of bile into the stomach, the doctor said."

"Does he say there's any hope?"

"I think the doctor expects him to die. The doctor said he had paper, and asked Asa if he wanted to make any kind of statement—a deposition."

"Did he make one?"

"No. He said he had nothing to say against Wallace. I stood right there and heard—I was keeping wet cloths on him—'I don't want any revenge,' he said—'what we did was in passion—the heat of passion'—that's the way he put it—'and tell Wallace I forgive him for what he did to me.' It's those fainting spells that bothered me most," Mrs. Lucas went on. "When he drifts off you are sure he's gone—and then he opens his eyes and says something to you."

While they were talking, a man on horseback rode up to them and said, "Is this the Asa Lawton home? The place where a man has been shot?"

"It is," Cecilia said, "and may I ask who you are?"

"I am an army surgeon stationed at Lawtonville. I am Dr. Fox."

"You should go right on in," Mrs. Lucas said. "There's one doctor there already." Dr. Fox tied his horse and hurried into the house.

Mrs. Lucas and Cecilia apparently overcame their reluctance to enter the house, for in a few minutes they were among the group peering at the injured man as the doctors worked over him. They remained only a few minutes; they were distinctly in the way. All eyes and attention were focused on the bed. They found two little stools near the doorway, where they sat and waited silently. After what seemed an hour Dr. Fox emerged and went to his horse. Cecilia sprang to her feet and ran up to him. "I am Mrs. Wallace Lawton, Doctor, and I'd like to know . . . if he will recover?"

"To be honest, Mrs. Lawton, I do not think he will live out the day. I came with paper to receive a deposition. The military specifically requested that I do this, but he refused to make any final statement except that he had forgiven his assailant and did not want revenge."

Just as he turned away Cecilia spoke to him again. "Dr. Fox, can you please tell me where my husband is now?"

"When I left, he was under guard at the headquarters. I understand—although I cannot make any official statement because the matter is not in my hands—that he will be transferred to the prison at Hilton Head."

A few minutes before one o'clock in the afternoon Asa failed to recover from one of his fainting spells. Dr. Baker came into the yard to say that he was gone.

THE NEXT MORNING Cecilia prepared to go to Lawtonville with Powell. On that black day there was no one in her family to turn to for support; her mother was dead and her father's comfort could never get past his second wife. Ellen had always indicated that she despised Wallace, and Cecilia was convinced that "my step-mother turned my father against Wallace and me." Ellen would surely say that Wallace's crime did not surprise her, and she would force her husband to agree. Only the quiet, thoughtful Powell was left to help Cecilia through the days ahead. As the buggy carried them to Lawtonville, did Cecilia wonder if she had married the wrong brother?

How Grand A Flame

They did not find Wallace at Lawtonville. It was not the policy of that headquarters to retain prisoners accused of serious crimes. Mr. Lawton had been transferred to the headquarters of the Port Royal Separate Brigade at Hilton Head, the captain said. He offered to give them the name of the officer in charge of prisoners. Slowly home again, then, to await a second journey the next morning. There would probably be visiting hours.

Yes, she must surely go to Hilton Head—nearly a day's travel—and Powell would not think of letting her drive that far alone. The trip would give her the perfect excuse for missing the funeral. She would not have to stand the stares of the relatives, people filled more with anger than grief. What could she say to them? They had lost a husband, brother, father. She was the outsider who had lost no one—no one except a husband who might die for causing this tragedy. She would not attend. Surely her right to visit her husband in this crisis would have to be accepted by even the most unloving members of the family.

THE HEADQUARTERS DISTRICT of the Port Royal Second Separate Brigade was housed in an impressive complex of buildings, federal troops having occupied Hilton Head since November 1861. Cecilia and Powell were finally admitted to the office of the prison warden. We may presume that the visit was brief, probably no more than half an hour, and that it was conducted under the supervision of a guard. One outcome of the visit was the decision to engage William Chisholm as Wallace's attorney. Another matter of great importance was not decided until a few days before the trial began: would Wallace be tried under military law by the occupying forces of the United States Army, or would he be tried under the laws of the state of South Carolina.

A DOCUMENT IN THE National Archives bears the following handwritten inscription:

> Headquarters District of Port Royal
> Second Separate Brigade, D. S. C.
> Hilton Head, S. C.,
> Oct. 25th, 1865

The Commission met pursuant to Special Order, No. 71, the following members present:

Brt. Brg. General T. Seymour

Brt. Lt. Col. O. W. Howe

Major R. H. Willoughby

Capt. M. E. Davis

Capt. C. Sylva

Ist Lt. J. Schmidel, Judge Advocate.

The Commission proceeded to the trial of W. Wallace Lawton, a civilian, who was called before the commission. The accused requested that W. Chisholm, Esq., be permitted to appear as his counsel, which was granted.

The accused was, thereupon, arraigned on the following charge and specification.

Charge—Murder

Specification—In this, that he, Wallace Lawton did, willfully and with malice aforethought, shoot with a pistol, Mr. Asa Lawton, and did inflict a mortal wound by a ball from said pistol, which caused the death of said Asa Lawton; all this at a plantation about seven miles from Lawtonville, S.C., on or near the old Gillisonville Road, on or about the 28th day of September, 1865.

BEFORE THE TRIAL BEGAN, William Chisholm, Wallace's attorney, raised the question of jurisdiction. Could a military commission legally try a citizen for offenses not military, since the civil courts were even then beginning the exercise of their function? The commission discussed the matter in private, but being unable to reach a conclusion referred the matter to a higher authority who ruled that the trial must continue. Apparently several attorneys were consulted or participated to some degree in the defense, for letters exist emphasizing the importance of a civil trial, "for if there is a conviction of murder we may have to rely upon appeal. We cannot afford to throw away that chance . . . Mr. Lawton's life is of too much consequence to neglect any reasonable means of saving it." Another communication expressed some concern on learning "that General Seymour is at the head of the Court. The General is a member of the Church and is not likely to look highly upon the taking of human life under any circumstances of private feud."

The first witness called was Judson Lawton, brother of the murdered man. His account of the struggle in the house minimizes the fierceness of Asa's attack on Wallace and attributes words to Wallace that other witnesses did not report. Asa's struggle with Wallace to recover the deeds was indeed violent, leaving Wallace with cuts and bruises that bled profusely. In the words of Monday Daley, a former slave now employed by Wallace, "Mr. Asa rushed at him and squashed him to the floor. He was about three times bigger than Mr. Wallace." There was surely much shouting in this fracas and both men may have made life-threatening statements. Neither Emma nor Mrs. Lucas "heard" Wallace shout, "You'll die for this!" as Judson testified he had done. Wallace, stinging from defeat at the hands of the heavier and stronger Asa, was obviously bent on revenge, as evidenced by his demand that Powell give him his own weapon, the one that Cecilia had tried to remove from the scene. By now she had known what to expect when her husband was angry.

Attorney Chisholm would have problems with one part of Powell's testimony:

Ques. by Judge Advocate—Did Wallace Lawton ask you for his pistol, after Mrs. Lawton gave it to you?

Ans.—He did; he came to the top of the steps and asked whose pistol it was. I said, his; he then said, give it to me.

Ques. by J.A.—Did you give it to him then?

Ans.—I said no pistol should be used.

Ques. by J.A.—Did Wallace reply to your refusal and if so what were the exact words used by him?

Ans.—I did not hear any reply.

Ques. by J.A.—Did he say anything at all to you for not giving up the pistol before the shot was fired?

Ans.—As I took the pistol from Mrs. Wallace Lawton, he said, "If you don't give me the pistol, I'll kill you."

Ques. by J.A. — When you handed the pistol to Wallace was he excited?

Ans. — He seemed very much excited.

Ques. by J.A. — What led you to exclaim, "Look out, cousin Asa, he's coming?"

Ans. — I wanted to warn him to get out of the way in case anything should occur.

Ques. by J.A. — Was there anything in Wallace's actions or words that led you to make this exclamation, and that led you to believe that he would shoot Asa; and what was this in his actions and words?

Ans. — Nothing in his words, but his actions led me to believe that he was again going after Asa as he walked down the path.

Ques. by J.A. — Was his walking down the path his only action that led you to believe that he was going after Asa?

Ans. — Yes, sir.

One witness reported hearing Wallace shout while he was down the first time, "I am being insulted in my own house. Get off of me and we will settle this matter honorably." The last word, honorably, had only one meaning to an antebellum southern gentleman. He was talking about a duel.

The record contains pages of questions about the movements of Asa and his brother as they returned to Asa's house with Wallace in pursuit of them, armed with a loaded pistol. How fast was he walking? One witness said "running." Did Asa turn when Powell shouted, "Brother has a pistol!" and did Wallace actually say, "Stop or I'll shoot"? Was his weapon raised? Was it cocked? When and in what direction did he veer when Asa turned? Did Asa turn on Wallace to attack him, or was he attempting to ward off an attack—which is to say, in self-defense?

We do not know whether Cecilia was present at the trial or not; the record makes no mention of spectators or of "clearing the courtroom." Men knowledgeable in such matters tell me that she was probably excluded.

How Grand A Flame

AFTER NINE DAYS OF cross-examination, Attorney Chisholm concluded his defense by reading a lengthy statement citing precedents and laws. He worded it in the first person, as if Wallace were speaking. I have made an abridgment of the address.

Mr. President and Gentlemen of the Commission—For several days you have laboriously engaged in the consideration and investigation of a cause which to you has been doubtless an onerous and a disagreeable duty. To me, however, this trial has been far different. Upon the issue joined are periled not only the happiness of my family, my honor, and my personal liberty, but life itself and perhaps the loss of a human Soul . . .

In the state of South Carolina the grades of homicide are punishable as follows: Murder with death; Manslaughter with fine or imprisonment at the discretion of the Court; Excusable Homicide in which the slayer is not considered altogether without blame and there is no punishment; Justifiable Homicide where the slayer is altogether free from fault and there is no punishment . . .

All the witnesses, with but one exception, not only agree but corroborate each other in narrating the circumstances of this most unfortunate affair. The witness, Mr. Judson Lawton, has told a story and painted a picture which would scarcely be recognized by the other bystanders . . . Either his prejudices, or a desire to revenge upon me the death of his brother, must have obliqued his vision and biased his understanding. From beginning to end, he has been unjust in giving his testimony. All moods, actions, however favorable to me, have faded from his memory; he recollects none of them . . . During the assault in the house, he did not see Asa charge me, he only saw him put his arms around me; he did not pull Asa off from me, but says that Asa let me go. He heard what no other witness heard Powell say: "Look out, brother is going to shoot you." He saw what no other witness saw—he saw me "running toward" Asa with the pistol . . .

If then the witness Judson Lawton has misstated the evidence and the facts, no matter from what motive, I invoke in my behalf, the maxim of law *falsus in uno, falsus in omnibus* . . .

Asa Lawton, be it remembered, had provoked the whole difficulty, he had beaten me in my own house because I would not yield him my rights, whilst choking me he had objected to being separated in order that he might take my life, he had notified me that unless I yielded my rights he would kill me or I would have to kill him, leaving my house and proceeding to his barn an unfortunate expression of my brother caused him to turn and rush me; he was vastly my superior in physical strength, he was rushing upon me violently with his right hand raised, when he rushed me I retreated to the left, when near me I warned him to stop, but he heeded me not, and when he was in the act of springing upon me I fired . . .

There is a case in the 31st Georgia Reports which decides that a man is not compelled to retreat before he can defend himself— "that when an attack is so sudden, fierce and violent, as that a retreat would not diminish but increase the danger, you may instantly kill your adversary without retreating at all."

If you have any reasonable doubts that the homicide was not murder, you must acquit me of that charge; and if you entertain any reasonable doubts as to whether it was or was not excusable homicide in self defense, you must acquit of manslaughter and, giving me the benefit of your doubts, find Excusable Homicide in self defense, to which in the United States, as already quoted, there is no punishment or criminality attached. This principle is no arbitrary rule of the courts. If you will analyze it for yourselves, you will perceive that it is founded upon reason, philosophy, and the precepts of the Christian religion.

In conclusion, Gentlemen, allow me to thank you for the kindness and courtesy you have extended respectively to my counsel and myself. Having presented to you my views of the law and the testimony, my person is now subject to your decision for weal or for woe. I trust that you will do unto me as you would have others do unto you, under similar circumstances. I beg that you will be merciful. Nothing is so becoming to power as mercy. With the prayer that the God above us will enlighten your understanding and guide you to a judgment which shall be consistent with truth, justice, and mercy, I have the honor to be

Respectfully, your obedient servant,
W. W. Lawton

THE COMMISSION THEN retired to consider the evidence; twenty-four hours later they submitted the following report to the Adjutant General:

Hilton Head, South Carolina
Nov. 4th, 1865, 10 A.M.

The Commission met pursuant to adjournment. Present, all the members and the Judge Advocate.

The Commission having been cleared for deliberation and having considered the evidence adduced, find the accused, W. Wallace Lawton, as follows:

Of the specification, Guilty, except with "malice aforethought."

Of the charge, Not guilty, but guilty of "Excusable Homicide" and do therefore acquit him, the said W. Wallace Lawton.

T. Seymour,
Brt. Brig General

WALLACE WAS RETURNED to prison to remain until the proceedings had been reviewed by an officer in the Judge Advocate Department. Four days after the verdict was announced — which seems a surprisingly short period of time — the reviewing officer made his report:

Headquarters-District of Port Royal
Second Separate Brigade
Hilton Head, South Carolina
General Orders — No. 88
November 8, 1865

. . . The proceedings in the case of W. Wallace Lawton, a civilian, are hereby approved, but after a careful and considerate perusal of the Evidence the reviewing Officer is compelled to disapprove the finding. In his opinion the Prisoner has been proved guilty of manslaughter. Wallace Lawton will be released from confinement.

By order of Col. J. Durell Greene

The trial had been carried out properly, and so the decision of the court stood, although in Greene's opinion the proper verdict should have been manslaughter, not excusable homicide. In any case, Wallace was now free to resume his life as a planter.

SIX

Return to the Bluff

WE SHOULD LIKE TO KNOW more of the days immediately following Wallace's release from prison, but the record is silent. He and Cecilia must have sensed a bitter rejoicing when they drove into the Lawton settlement on the Old Gillisonville Road. It is hard to imagine anyone from Asa's household rushing out to greet them. An exultant but subdued Wallace gave orders to his workers that evening. Without a doubt, Wallace had had a narrow escape; the finding of the reviewing officer that he should have been found guilty of manslaughter, an offense that would have carried the sentence of imprisonment, must have left Wallace a chastened man. Surely the picture of Wallace hurrying after his brother-in-law with a loaded pistol in his hand, a weapon that he had angrily demanded from Powell, is not easy to interpret as other than indicating the intent to inflict bodily harm or worse. The authorities may have freed him mainly because of the chaotic condition of the whole legal system at the time. I never heard my father say anything about Wallace's trial; his silence makes me think that Peter did not speak of it. The whole disgraceful episode may have been off-limits to conversation, and as the years passed slipped slowly into welcome oblivion.

In her diary, Cecilia writes in the paragraph already quoted that she will pass over the months of "that fall" in silence as too unpleasant to record, but she then leaves six inches of room, as if saving it for possible future comments. These she never made. At the bottom of the page she begins to talk of something else, as if to say, No, enough of that—get on with the business of living. We read: "During a short visit to Savannah I purchased new clothing for myself and for the coming babe and considered myself very fortunate to have fine things. Money was so scarce that most of our people still wore the faded garments that survived the war."

In early December brother Aleck visited Cecilia and Wallace, having just spent a few days at Blockade Place. He brought the bad news that Papa was failing fast. Aleck told a pathetic story of seeing his father in the field of corn following unsteadily behind a one-mule cultivator. Aleck thought the old man would never make it to the end of the row, and came to his aid by leading him to a shade tree and finishing the task himself.

Sister Rosa and the doctor stopped on their way to Savannah with their son, Douglas, who had just gotten out of a northern prison. Cecilia writes touchingly of him: "The poor young fellow, only 29 years old, had been starved, deprived of water and change of clothing, and closely confined in a damp, underground cell at Fortress Munroe and came home a physical wreck. He never recovered his health and died early in life."

IMMEDIATELY AFTER CHRISTMAS—the family did not attempt a party—Wallace announced another plan. He would sell out in Lawton-ville and return to his home on James Island, the land he loved best. There was little in Beaufort District to hold him now. His relationship with Juliet and her family was shattered. There were problems with others, too; not everyone saw eye to eye with a judgment that cleared a man who had killed his brother-in-law in a family squabble. Self-defense? Excusable homicide? Well, call it that if you want to. When the court has spoken, people must, of course, try to forget and move ahead with their lives, but more than a few in that rural community must have lifted their eyebrows and shrugged their shoulders at the mention of Wallace Lawton's name. The murdered man's father was a preacher-planter; the family had lived in the Beaufort area for two generations. Wallace, from the Charleston area, was the intruder. Certainly it was best for him go back to his family place on James Island and make a new start.

But first Wallace made an exploratory trip to Charleston. Peter told my father that he went with Wallace because a man should not travel alone in the backcountry. Both men were eager to start, for this trip would be "going home," with all that expression implies, provided at least some of the rumors were false. Wallace had learned that Sherman's main force had crossed the Ashley River west of Charleston and that the city had been spared. But what damage the far-flung bummers and scavengers had done to his property was a worrisome thought. Peter did not tell how they got across the several rivers on their route, but using the "short-cut" roads they knew well, they arrived at the far side of the plantation in late afternoon.

Peter's few words to my father about their anger and sorrow and a sentence from Cecilia's diary are all we have, and perhaps all we need, to fill out the picture for ourselves of the grief and rage they must have experienced. Cecilia wrote: "Wallace's large and handsome mansion on the 'Bennetts' part of the plantation, just opposite South Battery, had been swept away by the war."

The big house was a pile of ashes, charred boards, and a collection of chimneys. The outbuildings, all of them, had been destroyed. And again there was that strange openness to the sky because all the trees were gone. The boles of giant pines lay crisscrossed where they had fallen, except where someone had sawed off the best parts and carried them away. This silence. Did even the birds so dislike the smell of rain-soaked ashes and blackened boards that they would no longer light in the bushes? Wallace and Peter dismounted and walked to their old workplaces—where once the carriage house, the gin house, the stables, and the barns had stood.

This was the second time he had walked among ruined buildings of his own. Did Wallace think of the Book of Job? Houses and cattle and servants gone. Not his family, however, or the land. Cecilia wrote twice in her journal of how the faithful land had produced bountifully and sustained them. This fertile, obedient earth had never failed them yet, and it would not again. The land was their only hope.

Wallace and Peter walked to the front steps of the big house and down the brick path to the marsh. The wharf remained, but the boats were gone. We do not need to be told of the memories—and dreams—that must have overwhelmed them as they stood there. In the old days this was where you made a choice—the club in the city, a game of cards, good drinks, and love, if the signs were favorable. Or, to withdraw from it all, take a seat on the piazza, and, from the shelter of pines and with a sound roof over your head, scan the harbor and the city skyline. Like his father and grandfather, Wallace could choose the city's pleasures or else let the Ashley River become a moat between him and an unruly world.

Peter and Wallace left, gazing across the water at the city, and took the field road, now overgrown with weeds, to James Island Creek. On a little rise of ground, "the Bluff," they found the small frame house that Wallace was hoping had escaped destruction. Wallace saw at once that this two-room house, with a little patching up, could be made suitable for Cecilia.

Down at the edge of the creek a man with a fishing line was perched on a half-submerged piling of the bridge that used to go to Frampton's Point. Peter recognized him and asked him to look after their horses while they crossed the river to the city. Somewhere along the creek they found a rowboat.

Wallace's chief business in Charleston was to talk to his banker. Finances in the city were in a chaotic state. There was business also with the Freedmen's Bureau and the reclaiming of his land, much of which had been dispersed among the ex-slaves. One wonders how a man so beset with problems of safety, food, finance, housing, labor, land ownership—all requiring immediate solutions—kept his sanity. Perhaps most disquieting of all was the knowledge of who it was that had destroyed his home and outbuildings. Cecilia writes: "Our own soldiers, those belonging to the 'country cracker' class, who hated all wealthy planters, had wrought this destruction. Some of the places on James Island were destroyed by the Yankees also, so that from friend and enemies that doomed island suffered the worst."

As for the Lawton plantation: "Almost the only building left on his three James Island places was a small, two-roomed cottage at the Bluff." It was neatly lined with boards, had a porch in front and was *tolerably* comfortable for those hard times. "In sight of the Bluff," Cecilia tells us, "was Cuthbert's House, on one of Wallace's places, but it was badly out of repair and 500 negroes had died in it of smallpox during the summer and fall of '65. Therefore we shunned it."

Meantime, back in the Lawtonville area Cecilia was awaiting the birth of her first child. Shortly after Christmas she had moved in with Anna at Sylvan Home. "They were about as destitute of furniture as we were, but their comfortable dwelling had not been burnt.

"Here my first baby, 'Bertie,' was born Jan. 23, 1866—and I came near losing my life by the most brutal mismanagement. I had only an ignorant negro midwife to attend me. The nearest doctor charged $25.00—and to save this sum my health was wrecked. Up to this time I had enjoyed perfect health all my life. Dear Sister Anna was as kind and attentive to me as she could be. Wallace was with me when my baby arrived, but soon returned to Charleston."

A WEEK AFTER Bertie was born, Wallace was back on James Island struggling with obstinate officers and suspicious ex-slaves. The problem of regaining his land was compounded by an order that Sherman had issued a few months earlier. When Sherman was in Savannah his troops were besieged by thousands of blacks who had left their homes and followed his army in search of food and freedom. Besides commanding his occupation forces, Sherman was also confronted with the problem of finding food for this vast throng or of dispersing them in some way. He appealed to Secretary of War Stanton for help and the two men, after conferring with a group of fifteen black ministers, were persuaded to follow the counsel of one of them: "The best way we can take care of ourselves is to have land, and turn and till it by labor . . . and we can soon maintain ourselves and have something to spare. We want to be placed on land until we are able to buy it and make it our own." Sherman then issued an order that set aside the coasts and riverbanks thirty miles inland from Jacksonville to Charleston for freed slaves. Each family could take up to forty acres until Congress "shall regulate the title." Wallace found that his plantation had been cut up and given away to freedmen, some of whom had been his former slaves.

His first impulse, no doubt, was to "drive the bastards off by force," but fortunately he chose diplomacy. Cecilia writes: "Wallace experienced much difficulty in gaining possession of his James Island property; he finally had to pay several hundred dollars—a big sum then—to buy off the negroes who had land claims from the U.S. government. Each had a claim of forty acres, and the total made more land than Wallace owned. The general in charge told Wallace he had given his lands to more loyal citizens." Wallace was caught in the middle of a bureaucratic conflict, but, characteristically, he got what he went after—land. He might have reclaimed his land for nothing had he waited, because the administration in Washington changed its position, leaning more to consideration of the planters' rights, and issued an order that "the former owners of the land in the Sea Islands on the coast of South Carolina will be permitted to return and occupy their lands."

When her baby was five weeks old, about March 1, Cecilia went to Charleston to join her husband. Powell Lawton and Robbie Oswald drove Cecilia, her nurse, and the baby to Blacksville, where she took the South Carolina Railroad. The nurse, Maum Bess, "a superior servant," returned to Lawtonville because Wallace had a new nurse engaged in Charleston. This was Cecilia's first visit to Charleston, where she knew no one in the city save her husband. She spent the first two days in the boardinghouse alone because high winds kept Wallace from crossing the river. Thereafter, he came nightly when he could, but there is no doubt that she spent a wretched two weeks before they finally moved to James Island.

"I was in poor health for the first time in my life, and I had a young infant to take care of—so that my two weeks' stay there were not pleasant. We boarded on Limehouse Street, near the water. One lovely spring day in the middle of March, Wallace took me over to James Island to live. Under happier conditions I would have enjoyed the row across the river; but, as it was, I wept bitterly and silently the whole way, and heeded none of the beauties of nature. With my babe pressed to my bosom, and a veil over my face, I approached my new home. Unhappy omen!"

While our sympathy goes out to this frightened young girl-mother, I cannot help wondering how Wallace felt as he sat there pulling heavily on the oars, watching the tears stream down his wife's face; I conclude that he wasn't exactly having a lark that morning, either. His weeping and heartbroken wife wasn't the only person who faced despair and a black future. He had been working to regain his land, direct the laborers—such as he could find—and had likely been trying that morning to ready the old two-room house for Cecilia and the new baby. He too had been reared in luxury and was just as painfully aware as Cecilia of the distance they had fallen down the economic scale. We can only wish that he had possessed Cecilia's gift for written expression.

Cecilia continues: "My poor little baby was ill when we reached James Island and immediately became much worse. I had no experience and did not know what to do. In my ignorance of medicine, I gave him a teaspoonful of laudanum. He went to sleep immediately and came very close to death. We sent for the doctor as soon as I told Wallace of the baby's long sleep, but he did not arrive until the next morning. He, Dr. Robert Lebby, Jr., said the child's life was saved by a miracle, as he could not understand it.

"Wallace with his usual thrift soon started a small store at 'the Bluff' and sent for Robbie Oswald to clerk for him. He also made a little money nearly every day by taking passengers to and from the city in a *long* canoe boat called *Stark Naked* because of its trim appearance. He had recovered this boat from some negroes who had stolen it from his James Island place during his 'refugeeing' absence."

He and other planters on the island had trouble obtaining field labor, because the blacks objected to working for their former owners. Field-workers ranked at the bottom of the slave hierarchy and rarely find a place in the touching folklore of the devoted slave. Maids, cooks, nurses, yardmen, and carriage drivers often stood by their masters when adversity struck, but the cruelly driven field hands did not chant about the virtues of "ole Massa," or often come to his defense. Wallace was discovering what the managers at the Port Royal Experiment had discovered five years earlier when they had tried to induce former slaves to return to their plantations and work for pay. The field hands would hoe and plow and plant beans, sweet potatoes, and corn, but they would not pick cotton. It was in the cotton fields, working from daybreak to dark with sore and cracked fingertips, that they had suffered most, and they would have no more of it.

Wallace hit upon a plan of renting his land to a man whom the blacks would accept. Luckily, he found such a man in the vicinity, a Mr. Habenitch, a German immigrant who had never owned slaves; he would pay $1,000 rent for fields on Wallace's plantation—a large sum, but then Sea Island cotton sold for a dollar a pound. We do not know the exact financial arrangements Wallace made with the man, except that some months later Cecilia tells us that he had not paid the rent.

Getting started in the little house by James Island Creek was painfully difficult. The Lawtons did manage to buy some new furniture in Charleston and made the house tolerably comfortable, but "my life was hard," to use Cecilia's words. To make matters worse, little Robert Themistocles—Bertie for short—was often sick, and Wallace was developing boils. Like her husband, Cecilia could find no reliable or competent servants; she had no conveniences for housekeeping and no knowledge of the art of cooking. "Most of my nights seem to have been spent in nursing Wallace or the baby, and much of my days in weeping. Let no one accuse me of weakness —for none knows all the discouragement and sufferings I underwent."

Wallace and Powell, working in their informal partnership, surely had worries and discouragements that Cecilia does not record. Because of the nature of their work, the men did not suffer from loneliness and confinement as Cecilia did, but they were never free from the unremitting strain of providing food for their family while at the same time getting the plantation to turn a profit. "I never saw a white woman from month to month for very few had returned from their refugee homes at that time," Cecilia wrote. "I heard that some ladies had returned to Secessionville—six miles off— but they had no means of visiting me. No one could then afford pleasure horses or vehicles. William Hinson and Elias Rivers, who were planting on the island, were almost the only visitors we had."

This rigorous life almost broke Cecilia's health. Dr. Lebby, who was her attending physician, called Wallace aside and told him that he must take Cecilia away from James Island or the life would kill her. Fortunately, a family in the city, the Joseph Dills, were glad to have Cecilia board with them; Wallace was the godson of Mrs. Dill's father. Both Cecilia and Wallace moved to the city and boarded with the Dills for about two months, although he returned daily to James Island, weather permitting.

Wallace now sold the store at the Bluff to the German, and since he was free of management problems on James Island, decided to resume planting on his land back near Lawtonville. Why own two farms if you don't use them? Sister Anna and her husband, Robert, would be glad to have them stay at Sylvan Home. An outbreak of dengue fever in Charleston was an added reason for the move. Once settled in Lawtonville, Wallace began extensive planting on his former plantation. Brother Aleck now joined Wallace and Powell in the farming partnership, Aleck having left Blockade Place because of unjust treatment by his stepmother. The spiteful stepmother was still in command at Blockade Place. Sister Georgia (Danda) at last found a husband and was married at Blockade Place; the stepmother refused to let her husband's children attend the wedding.

During 1867 events seemed to have moved swiftly. The cotton crop yielded abundantly, Cecilia tells us, but "the depredations by the negroes was beyond belief. They seemed to spend their entire nights picking our cotton and selling it to unscrupulous neighbors—including our former friends, the Ayers." Then on July 8, 1867, little Bertie died after eight days of a sickness called cholera infantum. "He was buried in the old cemetery of my forefathers at Lawtonville—and there is his grave stone."

Wallace's business problems never let up. He could not collect the rent from the German, who now owed him $300, and so decided to sell his Lawtonville land and go back to James Island, get rid of Mr. Habenitch, and operate the plantation himself. Cecilia fell to counting the houses she had lived in since the war began; she reached a total of nine. Although she did not know it, she was far from through.

Wallace believed that he might now be able to secure workers for his land on James Island, since some of his own former slaves were drifting back. Peter Brown had apparently stayed on James Island to work with the German, for he did not mention, so far as I know, the sojourn in Lawtonville.

The trip back to James Island in 1868 would follow approximately the same route Wallace had taken nearly five years before, using his own mules and wagons, but this time without the procession of slaves and cattle. Wallace begged Cecilia to remain with her sister until he could get properly settled—excellent advice—but Cecilia insisted on going with him. The country through which they passed was "desolate and somewhat lawless." The effects of Sherman's march were still on the land, not only in the destroyed property but in the disillusioned and hostile people. To Cecilia the poor farmers along the way seemed "half civilized and altogether selfish and uncharitable. They refused us even the shelter of their roofs and no amount of money or persuasion could make them relent. They seemed a species of Ishmaelites, whose hands were against every man."

Their refusal to give housing to Wallace's party underscores again the gap between the "cracker farmers" and the planters. A great many farmers called the Civil War "the planters' war." Here, obviously, is a well-to-do man who comes to the door with a six-mule-team wagon, a three-mule wagon, and two buggies, all loaded with expensive-looking furniture and supplies. He thinks his money can get him anything! Let this rich scoundrel who can come out of the war with all those goods take care of himself!

"So we were compelled to camp out, and without a tent. A mattress was put under the largest wagon, protected on the sides as well as possible under the circumstances, and here Wallace and I slept. Brother Robert and Powell slept in the wagon which had a canvas cover. We slept one night in an outbuilding, and one night I had a room with the Warings, the family who had adopted Wallace's mother during her orphaned girlhood.

"We bought some food along the way and the gentlemen drew coffee when we wished it, but most of our food was cold.

"On the afternoon of the fourth day we reached St. Andrews Parish on the Ashley River opposite Charleston. There Powell and Robert remained with the horses while Wallace took me into the city. We crossed the Ashley River in a rowboat used by the Charleston and Savannah Railroad to transport its passengers, for no bridge had been built to replace the one destroyed during the war.

How Grand A Flame

"We had heard that horse cars were running in Charleston, but we walked all the way to Broad Street before we saw one. I boarded on Broad Street for about two weeks, Wallace being with me occasionally. While in the city I was confirmed at St. Philip's Church by Bishop Davis.

"As soon as Wallace arrived in Charleston he heard that upland cotton—the kind we raised at Lawtonville—had suddenly jumped in price. Nearly the entire crop was still held by Anderson and Sons, cotton brokers of Savannah. He telegraphed them immediately to hold it, and received answer that it had been sold before the rise and at the *lowest* price. (I had asked W. before we left to please write Anderson *not to* sell, but he refused.) We lost several thousand dollars."

At the end of two weeks Cecilia was back on James Island in a barnlike structure at the Bennetts' end of the plantation, near the site of Wallace's old home, "with the city in full view across the river." They whitewashed the walls of the three large rooms, set up a stove, and lived in this "barn" for a while. Then Wallace had an idea. He would move her to Beck's Point on the other side of the plantation, near the third bend of James Island Creek. This move, Cecilia wrote, was a perfect example of Wallace's impulsiveness and lack of consideration for others once he made up his mind to do something. He rushed in one morning and informed her that this house was to be pulled down immediately and that she must move— today—now! A gang of men was at the door ready to fall to work. She had not expected the move to occur for several weeks.

"But Wallace made the men tumble the furniture and all our belongings pell mell into a filthy little negro cabin nearby, and then he went off leaving them to demolish that larger house, and poor me, appalled and confused, to set up some of the furniture and mend the chairs as best I could. He never did have any idea of arranging comfortably before hand for a move and I suffered many hardships in consequence. We occupied this cabin for about two weeks.

"I had a *hard* and revolting experience while in this miserable little cabin."

The remodeled "barn," now moved to Beck's Point, turned out to be a neat little house with three good-sized rooms, a piazza running along one side, a kitchen, and a storeroom. It was plain, but vastly better than any house they had lived in since Sherman had burnt them out.

WHEN I LIVED ON James Island in the nineteen-twenties, Beck's Point was not part of the Lawton plantation. It had the last wharf on James Island Creek at which freight boats could tie up at low water; beyond that point the creek wandered off in little tributaries and got lost in the marsh on its way to the Stono River. Tom Welch, Sr., who had married the granddaughter of sister Anna, did some planting on Beck's Point, and he also operated three freight boats with which he conducted a thriving business hauling produce from the surrounding islands to the city. A freight boat—or launch, as Alison Lawton called it—entering James Island Creek from the harbor would pass first the two Lawton wharves, then a public wharf, and following a bend to the right it would come to Beck's Point. I did not know until I read Cecilia's story that the Beck's Point acres ever belonged to the Lawtons. Wallace's reason for moving there was to escape the summer diseases—a bad decision, it turned out, for both he and Cecilia came down with malaria the first summer.

In the year 1868 the Lawton fortunes seemed to have turned a corner. Powell was now working regularly with Wallace and was living with his brother and Cecilia in the new house. For the first time since her marriage, Cecilia was able to do serious housekeeping; she was determined to do her own cooking in order to save money for improvements, but Wallace objected because he thought she would save very little, and besides, he did not want her doing "menial labor." Although Cecilia does not mention it, Wallace may have had a clear memory of her cooking skill. Fortunately, Maum Celie, a former servant of whom Cecilia was very fond, returned at about this time and Wallace hired her to cook and wash.

"At Beck's Point," Cecilia wrote, "I had a busy and useful life until prostrated by illness in the late summer. I began at once setting out fruit trees, trimming up those already around us and planning future improvements. I attended entirely to the milk, setting, skimming, and even churning butter myself. I also began to raise chickens and took great delight in them.

"We were real farmers that year and our cows, pigs, and chickens were important elements in our lives. I did *all* my own sewing and even made underwear for Wallace and Powell."

We know many details of this eventful year because Cecilia resumed the practice of keeping her diary. Through it, we see the Lawtons' slow but steady effort to regain the life they had once known. The struggle to return to an orderly, dignified, and productive life without the help of a corps of slaves was a difficult one. Wallace was forced to become a laborer as well as a manager, and Cecilia began to do work that was distressingly like that of the "crackers." I get the impression that Cecilia did not find these new activities particularly disturbing — she seems actually to have enjoyed them. Her major concern was that Wallace would be upset and would not approve. Of the two, Wallace was the more rigid, the least willing to compromise as he met new forces and demands. As a young male growing up in the slave culture, he had enjoyed far more status than had his wife. He could give orders to satisfy his slightest whim without having his authority gainsaid. For women like Cecilia, who never possessed as much authority as men, there was a shorter distance to fall.

CECILIA DEVOTED SEVERAL pages of her diary to the delightful details of that memorable Easter of 1868 — the first since the war to be celebrated in a setting of friends and beauty and overflowing goodwill.

Easter fell on the twelfth of April — the middle of the flowering season. Spring had come to the Sea Island just as it had come for countless centuries before the white man's invasion. It was a morning whose beauty all but obscured the scars left by the war. The jasmine blossoms poured their lemon-sweet fragrance over the hedgerows, Cherokee roses were flinging their white streamers over old earthworks, and young green plants in long, straight rows were appearing in the fields. The dark soil of the islands was responding at last to the hand of cultivation. The black people were seeking their little churches tucked in obscure crossroads, and the

Lawtons were setting out to spend the day in Charleston.

Wallace, Powell, and Cecilia—with a basket of orange blossoms that she would carry to church—stood on the shore by the Lawton's tiny wharf ready to embark on the *Stark Naked*. When Peter had tied the craft securely he would bid them to board. An obliging tide had slipped under the weathered planks, and the wavelets that swirled around the unsteady pilings made warm, cheerful sounds as they came rippling through the new marsh grass at their feet. This Easter morning brought a boundless invitation to life. From the air warm against the cheek, the water whispering under the wharf, the dipping sea birds, the sunshine on blue water to the red-roofed houses and steeples across the bay, it was a morning to be remembered. Wallace would return to the plantation at nightfall and Cecilia would spend a week with the Dills.

As Peter paddled them toward the city, Cecilia and Wallace could look forward to a day when things would be done right—a bit of the old life they had known before the war. For a day, at least, under Mrs. Dill's skillful hand things would be done with dignity and a touch of elegance. There were some Easters in the past few years that were best forgotten. They were returning to the city without little Bertie. He had left them last July in one of those wasting-away diseases of babyhood that no doctor knew how to stop. For a moment, did her first trip across the Ashley come out of the past—a gentle day in spring like this one, Wallace at the oars, Cecilia hugging little Bertie? This Easter day would end quite differently from that lonely one by James Island Creek.

The old skyline came closer and closer. Touch land at the foot of Legare Street, join the Dills for a carriage ride to St. Philip's, and then Easter service in the church where Cecilia had been confirmed three months before. There would be church bells ringing, friends to touch, everyone wearing flowers, singing in the choir, and a sermon by the Reverend Dr. Miles. Then back to the Dill home for a leisurely dinner. Afterwards, the men would drift out onto the piazza to talk business; Mr. Dill would pass around his imported cigars; their fruity-sweet aroma would drift through the windows where the ladies were holding session. Then slowly, slowly, back to the world they must live in on Monday—the world of cotton markets and caterpillars, of workers who came late and stole you blind, of shortages in the barns and pantries, of unjust taxes.

It is refreshing to read of the Lawtons' growing social life in 1868. Mrs. Joseph Dill was a surrogate mother to Cecilia, her adviser and confidante. Cecilia often crossed the river by rowboat or ferry to spend a day with Mrs. Dill, with whom she might recoup her strength for the next week. She frequently brought "butter which I made with my own hands" or shrimps and crabs from the creek. Mrs. Dill often returned Cecilia's calls, and once when she dropped in to spend the day she found Cecilia in a pleasant social whirl. Mrs. Dill ran into Mrs. Hinson and her sister, Fanny, who had come for the day, and a few hours later Mr. Washie Clark and Vergi, his wife, appeared, along with his sister, Lily, and Miss Annie Baynard. "The ladies rushed up to me and kissed me and were delighted with our house." In the afternoon Mr. Dill and Mr. Hinson called and they all stayed until sundown—so late that the Dills missed the ferry and Wallace had to take them home. This may have been one of the many trips that Peter told my father about when he spoke about being escort and oarsman for many trips to Charleston. Cecilia had a delightful day, but "begrudged the time taken from my sewing."

"I would so much like to improve the tone of my home," she wrote one day, "and thought to do it by reading. When in Charleston on a shopping trip I subscribed to *The Land We Love*, a southern magazine, with money Wallace had given me to buy stockings; I decided to darn the old ones." She liked to write letters "but Wallace was always forgetting to mail them." An entry for April 19: "Wallace forgot to mail my letter." On April 25 she wrote: "Wallace attempted to paint his boat himself, but got *full* of paint, clothes, *face* and hands. He went to town in the afternoon and took a nice plate of my butter that I had just made to Mrs. Dill. But he forgot to mail my letter." Another entry, April 27: "Got my letter mailed at last. Wallace often lost my letters in crossing the river—those coming to me and those to be mailed. My correspondence was carried on with great difficulty."

As I read her pages for the year 1868, I sense that most of the references to unpleasantness or distress of mind—aside from the attacks of malaria—

have to do with Wallace. How selfish and inconsiderate was he in his deal-ings with Cecilia? There is no word of physical violence; if violence did occur, I think she would have been too proud to mention it. Cecilia reports her troubles with a touch of self-pity and conscious poignancy. How difficult was *she* to live with? We must read her account of the times when Wallace hurt her, or fell short, with the full realization that Wallace did not keep a diary and did not record *his* daily frustrations and disappoint-ments. He was probably less introspective than Cecilia. I started to add that he was a person "less finely tuned" than Cecilia, but I might mean only that he was less articulate. Because he does not leave us pages of words, it is hardly fair to conclude that Wallace was utterly indifferent to the feelings of others.

The question ever before us in reading Cecilia's writing is how to use personal documents in understanding a life. There have been many inves-tigations of this topic by students of personality, and surely Cecilia's memoir is a suitable candidate for study. The notion that people write or create just to get something "off their chests" is largely discredited by studies of human behavior. People create in the visual arts to be seen, musicians compose music to be heard, writers write to be read.

We peruse personal documents in the belief that, being private and per-sonal, they will plumb to truths that we assume lie buried beneath the words. Who were Cecilia's imagined readers? If we knew, our search for the truth would be easier. She clearly did not write for Wallace; if she had, she would have deleted many pages. Sometimes the future reader appears to be herself; she wanted to leave something that would jog her memory. Regarding her early proposals of marriage we read: "In December, 1862 I visited relatives in Lawtonville and while there had my first proposal of marriage—I was fifteen on December 11th—." Between the lines she wrote "D.P." A few months later a similar entry: "I made the mistake of engaging myself to a very faithful and persistent lover who had known me since my 8th or 9th year . . . I knew him to be noble and honorable and most devoted to me; and in an impulse of gratitude and self-reproach for my former coldness, brought on by his deep feelings which he could not hide, I accepted him. Then I set myself to the task of persuading myself that I returned his affection, and for a few weeks succeeded. Then came the discovery that I had made a mistake and could never love him save as a dear friend—G.C.D." There is still another offer of marriage with initials: "While in Augusta I had my fourth offer of marriage—H.C."

At times she sees herself as a girl in a picture frame—pretty, popular, and intelligent—but, alas, all that was brief and long ago. Then again, she stands back from herself and looks with outright pity at a girl who is having more trouble than she deserves. As matter of fact, she *did* have more trouble than she deserved. Does this hint of paranoia in her diary come from unwholesome self-pity, or from an honest appraisal of the painful experiences that she underwent? I think that both she and Wallace should, in all fairness, be permitted a degree of self-pity. According to Cecilia, Wallace was hard to live with, and her contemporaries seem to have agreed with her. But how hard was Cecilia to live with? Was she a fusser and a complainer? We do not know.

We do have a considerable record of Wallace's harsh, inconsiderate, selfish behavior. He would provide for all her "creature needs," as she admitted, but seemed to bypass her feelings and wishes in the daily round of life. If, in the grand strategy of running the plantation and providing a suitable home, it was suddenly necessary to move, then do so at once! "He never did have any idea of arranging comfortably before we had a move, and I suffered many hardships because of this. I had wanted a few days to prepare, but he said to do nothing until he came to move us back to Bennetts. Of course, I obeyed him. But judge my confusion when he rushed into my room early before either baby or I was quite dressed, and telling me that boats were waiting and that men were coming in to move the furniture and bedding. I begged him to give me a short time but he flew into a rage. Then he called the men and everything was dragged out and flung pell-mell into the boats or flats. Even Catherine was sorry for me."

An earlier entry: "Mom Bess is still with me and I have a fair cook (though a notorious thief she was). Cash is scarce and the food procurable is not of the best and there is no variety. Hominy, bread and salt meat. These days went very hard with me, but other things in my life were even harder to bear."

In August: "It's pouring rain. I am very unhappy in my home. I *do* try so hard to do my duty and yet I cannot get on smoothly. Had a serious talk with Wallace about his conduct."

A few months later: "The hardest part of our financial troubles seemed past, and we had money for the necessaries. My future sufferings were of the heart and from bad health and a lack of fore thought or care on Wallace's part to provide comforts for me."

Sunday, September 24, 1868: "In bed at home, as I am still sick. This is the fourth anniversary of my wedding. Four long dreary years."

Reading all this in the light of the circumstances surrounding her wartime marriage, her stated regrets, the murder of Asa—which though unmentioned must have overshadowed all else—we get the picture of a very burdened young woman trying heroically to maintain a marriage.

Peter told my father that he had never seen "such a ruckus" on the plantation like the time Wallace discovered a caterpillar in the cotton field. Cecilia notes the event, too, with the following entry for July 6, 1868: "Wallace went fishing this morning. This afternoon he discovered a caterpillar and couldn't help showing it to Willie Hinson when we drove over that way."

July 17: "We went to town and he showed his caterpillar to Frazer, Dill and Pelzer and a crowd of others. Willie Hinson borrowed it last evening and carried it to Clarks and those down that side. Said he never saw men so crestfallen. Nearly all in the city and country exclaimed, I am a ruined man! Such a furor over one little worm. Mr. Dill sent it to Europe."

Twenty years earlier caterpillars had appeared and destroyed nearly the whole cotton crop on James Island. For unknown reasons the little larva did not reappear until 1868, but the memory of its destructiveness was vivid. Its ways were capricious, for all the cotton plants in one field would be stripped of leaves while those in an adjoining field would escape. Mr. Seabrook had lost nearly his entire crop in that outbreak, while the Lawtons' cotton escaped serious damage.

Even though anxiety over the caterpillar was intense, it did not stop social life. In August Wallace and Cecilia were invited to watch the sailboat races from Mr. Hinson's summer place at Fort Johnson. There is no spot on James Island that offers a more impressive view of the city and harbor than Fort Johnson. It was the quarantine station for incoming ships when I was a child, with a physician and a small hospital to retain those with contagious diseases who would be removed from a ship before it docked in Charleston. For us James Islanders, it was a delightful excursion site— especially for picnic suppers. A brisk breeze kept the air free of mosquitoes, and while our elders laid out the meal we children followed a dozen mysterious trails among the bushes and up and down the old earthworks that still remained. We did not know then that we were playing over unexploded shells that were concealed in the sand and vines. A tragedy occurred, long after I had left South Carolina, when a James Island youth, playing as we had, was killed by an exploding shell that had lain dormant for over seventy years.

At Mr. Hinson's party the guests enjoyed the unique setting much as we would years later. They gazed over the harbor, walked on the beach, and partook of refreshments. An added attraction for the ladies was a tour of the area—six at a time—in Washie Clark's ambulance. There must have been war surplus sales in those days, for, says Cecilia, "Washie Clark obtained the ambulance, a cheap substitute for a carriage, as a bargain after the war." The abominable caterpillar was not forgotten, however, for "the gentlemen all agreed that each one who said the word caterpillar should take a drink each time. This was to keep off the blues. Elias Rivers was very tight and carrying on ridiculously." The party lasted until sundown, when all left at the same time.

The next day, Sunday, saw all three Lawtons at church. Mr. Law, a Presbyterian, preached. "Everyone was as blue as indigo about the caterpillars." On the following Tuesday, Cecilia entertained three guests for the day and had a delightful time. "I served chicken-pie and fish and then a little custard pudding. Simple occurrences all these—but in my old age they will help me to recall the days long past and my favorite friends of that time."

Wednesday, August 12: "Wallace and I went over to the fields at Bennetts this afternoon to look for caterpillars, but could not find *one*. If they have not eaten us out by the 15th I am to go up country for my health."

When I read Cecilia's repeated descriptions of malaria, chills, and fevers, I wonder that they had energy enough to make a living, let alone enjoy a social life. The trip "up country" turned out to be a trip to Atlanta, where sister Rosa and her doctor husband lived. Cecilia was sick half of the time and took quinine steadily as prescribed by her brother-in-law, Dr. Douglas. Back on James Island, Dr. Robert Lebby, Jr., was her physician. He had practiced during the war, and no doubt had as much skill as anyone in those days in setting broken bones, lancing, and amputating. He applied poultices and administered the standby remedies of the day—quinine, calomel, and purgatives; on one occasion he treated Cecilia's inflamed throat by swabbing it with turpentine. Viewed from our vantage point at the close of the twentieth century, their efforts were too often futile or damaging.

Historians tell us that a few people were, even then, beginning to suspect what Immanuel Kant had noted years earlier, that people who did not go to doctors lived longer. A doctor then often felt that he must establish his professional worth by doing something. But already the belief was growing that the body might heal itself better if left alone, or aided by mild medicines, rather than by dramatic and heroic treatments. We do not know how Dr. Lebby practiced medicine, other than from Cecilia's comments, but families leaned on him heavily, respected him highly, and always called upon him with utmost faith. Too often he seems, however, to have arrived at the bedside in time to watch the patient die.

Cecilia had regained her health by November, for she and Wallace attended a large dance at Mr. Hinson's summer home. "I wore my hair crimped and hanging down my back and about my shoulders, as was then fashionable. It fell below my knees and was *wonderfully thick* and luxuriant. It was a dark brown, almost black, and very glossy. Wallace thought it was beautiful and approved my wearing it down, but Powell said a married woman should not wear her hair down."

Wallace appeared to have been unpredictable at social occasions. One evening he was expected to remain for dinner at the Dills in Charleston, but for some unexplained reason he suddenly refused to stay and went back to James Island, although he did allow Cecilia to remain. She was naturally very embarrassed. When they were summering at Secessionville to avoid malaria, the Seabrooks gave a large party to which the Lawtons were invited. Part of the entertainment was to be an elaborate charade in which Cecilia, because of her long dark hair, was to play the part of Pocahontas. Cecilia was dressed and prepared to walk to the party, but wait — Wallace was not dressed yet. He continued dressing ever more slowly — obviously not intending to be there in time for Cecilia to perform her role. He stalled until they arrived an hour late; the charade was over, and Cecilia was heartbroken. At other times, he was permissive. They attended a number of parties where there was dancing. Cecilia loved to dance; Wallace did not, and sat out while Cecilia danced with Powell. Powell was a "lovely dancer, and often accompanied us to parties." We are inclined at this point to speculate on motives and desires, but we should refrain for lack of evidence.

BECK'S POINT WAS a much better place in which to endure the pains of Reconstruction than was the city of Charleston. Wartime fires and the shelling of 1865 had left whole sections of the city in ruins, with almost all basic services suspended. Cecilia found serious deficiencies in her little house, but she did not have to deal with racial riots, filthy streets bordered by ditches that were little more than "lines of cesspools," polluted water supplies, epidemics of malaria and yellow fever, to say nothing of ruined churches and stores. The Dills, being well-to-do and living in a favored part of town, doubtless enjoyed many conveniences that Cecilia did not have, but it appears that they were glad to spend many days on the Lawton plantation. Masefield's lines about old London may well have been written about the crowded Charleston peninsula: "Wretchedly fare the many there, and merrily fare the few."

We are now in the middle of Reconstruction days, but I do not think that Peter and my father spoke of that term as it is now used. From the extensive literature of that troubled period, we see that its manifestations varied greatly from state to state and even from town to town. "In every part of the South beyond the immediate reach of federal troops," writes

Page Smith, "the lives of blacks who engaged in political activity, who tried to own property or start a business, or who in any way drew the unfavorable attention of whites were in constant danger." It was much easier to kill a black man after emancipation, now that he was not worth any money.

No South Carolinian can consider the two decades following the Civil War without thinking of Wade Hampton. His picture, along with those of Beauregard, Lee, and Johnston hung over the blackboard of my James Island grammar school. Born in Charleston, he fell heir to vast holdings of plantations and slaves in several states, a legacy that he increased by shrewd management until at the outbreak of the Civil War he was reputed to be the richest planter in the South and one of the richest men in America. A man of remarkable vigor both physically and intellectually, he epitomized the best qualities of the rich planter. He was a skilled horseman, master of all weapons, and an avid hunter. One of his favorite pastimes, writes Manly Wade Wellman in his biography of Wade Hampton, was to hunt black bears on his estates with a pack of hounds. Mounted, he would follow the hounds until they had cornered the animal in a thicket or forced it back against a tree, where it would lash out with its front paws, boxer fashion, at the ring of hounds just out of reach. "Then Wade Hampton would swing out of his saddle. With one hand he would draw from its sheath a long, keen, heavy knife, almost a sword in size and design. Commanding the dogs to get out of the way he would charge the bear. It was over in a moment—a darting swing of the huge talon-armed claw, a quick dodge by Hampton to avoid it, a deadly counter stroke with the steel . . . this he did fully eighty times."

The love of violence, which we have noted before as characterizing many southern slave owners, seems not to have spilled over into Wade Hampton's social life. He never fought a duel and was reported to be gentle with his slaves; indeed, he spoke and wrote often of the ultimate freedom of the blacks. While governor of South Carolina he vetoed a bill that would have set up chain gangs for blacks under sentence in county jails. He had opposed secession, but like Robert E. Lee cast his allegiance with his own state and served for four years in the Confederate army as a commander of cavalry. After Appomattox he urged the southerners to support the lenient policies of President Johnson and "render full obedience to the government, always reserving to themselves the rights of free speech and free opinion." While Hampton opposed the manner in which the amendment abolishing slavery was passed, he said, "But the deed has been done and I, for one, do honestly declare that I never wish to see it revoked. Nor do I believe that the people of the South would now remand the negro to slavery, if they had the power to do so unquestioned."

But vindictive elements in Washington would have nothing to do with leniency and objected particularly to allowing the seceded states to set up their own conventions and constitutions unsupervised; their objections were given validity by the Black Codes that white southern governments sought to enact immediately after the war ended and that attempted to perpetuate the virtual fact if not the name of slavery. Typical of these was one of South Carolina's many restrictions: "No black man shall pursue the practice, art, or business of an artisan, mechanic, or shopkeeper or any other trade or employment besides that of husbandry, or that of servant under contract for labor, until he shall have obtained a license from the district court, which license shall be good for one year only." A black shopkeeper had to pay $100 a year for such a license. Punishment was the theme of the day, and this could best be achieved by allowing freed slaves full control of government in this period of history known as "Congressional Reconstruction." Nearly ten years passed before the white people regained full control of the legislatures, but when they did so they began passing a series of laws designed to return the blacks to a servitude distinguished by all the disadvantages of slavery and none of its advantages.

Over against this we hear Wade Hampton demanding constitutionally protected rights for all men, black or white, saying that to deny basic rights to one man or group was ultimately to deny them to all. While governor of South Carolina, he said of the blacks, "We intend to try to elevate them, to educate them, and show them the responsibilities as well as the blessings of liberty. We want them as citizens of America and of South

Carolina to be worthy of the great boon of citizenship and of this great republic." Although his concern for the black race now appears a bit pater-nalistic, few influential Confederates—let alone war heroes—voiced such sentiments at the close of hostilities. He demanded, moreover, that the same literacy test for voting be applied equally to both races, and to all voters in the North. So intense was the opposition to this sort of talk that his enemies were reduced to spreading a story about him that, if true, was worse than the crime of treason: he had dined at the same table with black men. The accusation was true, for at a dinner given by a professor at Claflin College in Orangeburg, a state supreme justice and a professor were guests. Both men were black. The story goes that Hampton was the per-fect gentleman in his demeanor throughout the evening.

WE DO NOT KNOW HOW this stormy period affected the daily round of life for blacks and whites on the Lawton plantation. Since the freed slaves' main employment was husbandry, there was probably less conflict with the Black Codes than in upstate areas. A rifle club known as Haskell's Mounted Riflemen was formed at about this time and met for regular drills. Its purpose, of course, was to demonstrate white supremacy, al-though there is no record of armed conflict. The group's self-imposed mis-sion was, as an old resident told me, "to preserve order by having a mili-tary presence on the island"; whether this mission included appearing in force on Election Day, I do not know. Clashes were so severe in many areas of the South that President Grant would later order all armed groups of citizens, meaning of course the rifle clubs, to surrender their weapons to United States marshals. Most did not comply but went underground, call-ing themselves by such innocuous names as baseball clubs and musical clubs—"we play with eight-pound flutes." The absence of rioting and armed conflict on James Island may be attributed in part to the absence of a numerous poorer class of white people. In some areas, writes Page Smith, "the entire apparatus of civilized life had been destroyed. In many parts, the white rural underworld swarmed out of the swamps and hills to loot the planters whom they envied, and kill the Negroes whom they hated. They probably did as much damage as did Union armies . . . [If] the

landed base of southern wealth was still there, and in regions where invading armies had not penetrated, Negroes continued to work for their former
masters, and life went on as before the war." Several historians have noted
that in areas of well-established plantations, particularly along the Atlantic coast, many freed men continued to work as hired employees of their
former masters. Cecilia does not mention any violence on the plantation,
although I am certain that the blacks were entirely subject to white rule.
It is perhaps not too much to hope that the influence of the great moderate,
Wade Hampton, might have softened the racial tensions on James Island.

The prevailing attitude on James Island was expressed, I think, in Alison Lawton's response to a letter from my father inquiring about the blacks
on the plantation. He wrote: "The Negroes are not our intimates and they
have been taught to look up to white people. This requires strict honesty
on the part of the white people; a Negro would trust a white man rather
than one of his own race. As fine and honest and as refined people have
grown up on these Sea Islands as you will find anywhere in the country.
The Negroes are respectful of white people. On the whole sea coast of
South Carolina there has never been known an attempted case of rape; and
there have never been any lynchings or that kind of carrying on as there
have been in some parts of the South."

The plantation was largely unaffected by the riots of 1876, although in
Charleston Hampton's supporters were brandishing weapons and attempting to keep from the polls any blacks who might vote for the recon-
structionists. The violence in the city was so severe that scores of rifle clubs
from the surrounding area were pressed into service to patrol the streets for
several months. Surely the mounted riflemen of James Island would have
volunteered for this duty.

The Haskell's Mounted Riflemen of the Charleston area continued to
drill long after the stress of Reconstruction had subsided. They slowly
turned into sporting teams and display units that appeared at public cere-
monies. A headline in the *News and Courier* in 1883 reads: "A Close
Cavalry Contest—Inspection of Jenkins Mounted Battalion. The Tilt—
the Dinner and the Dance."

Major John Jenkins's battalion consisted of companies from the city,

James Island, Johns Island, Wadmalaw, and Edisto. The James Island company was hosting the event on the McCleod plantation on Wappoo Creek. Most of the guests came by water. A tugboat, the *William C. Nichols*, conveyed the team from Charleston to the landing on Wappoo Creek. The steamer, *St. Helena,* brought the riders with their mounts from the more distant islands. The newspaper account calls the McCleod plantation one of the most attractive in the low country, "picturesque and charming with its avenues of grand old live oaks which afforded a grateful shelter to the hundreds of ladies who were present.

"The tilt," the account continues, "was one of the most spirited and closely contested ever held in the State. Each company was represented by four members, who were allowed three runs. The James Island company won the challenge cup with a score of 205 points."

In the afternoon the company sat down to "a bountiful dinner of succulent James Island mutton, fresh butter, poultry and other choice viands. In the evening the belles and beaux passed several hours in dancing. Everything passed off pleasantly and the guests were pleased with the hospitality of the James Islanders."

WALLACE, WHOM CECILIA several times calls "prudent" and "thrifty," was not content to be a one-crop planter, although cotton was his chief source of income. While at Beck's Point he started the business of raising hogs, having at one time two hundred animals. He was forced to close down this prospering business "because of the number of hogs stolen from him by the negroes." The chief vice of the newly freed was theft. When I lived on the Lawton plantation about the only "problem with the help" that I heard my elders talk about was stealing. There was no breaking in or violence, but a few of the workers would simply walk away with the necessities of life—hammers, wrenches, saws, ropes, hoes, a piece of harness—none of which could be purchased on the low wages paid at the time. Instead, they were "borrowed" overnight. In retrospect, I marvel that the workers on the James Island plantations accepted their impoverished lot with such grace.

Wallace's store on James Island Creek was becoming a money-maker. Located on the shore end of his wharf, it was able to capture customers both coming from and going to Charleston. It was the last loading point on the way to the city and a natural meeting place for blacks and whites even up to the time I lived there. On a Saturday night dozens of black people, coming by foot or by cart, gathered on its porch or lounged under the big oak trees to enjoy a soft drink, visit, flirt, and possibly wait for the return of a late boat.

Another enterprise sprang up at this strategic location on James Island Creek: the James Island Milling Company. Immediately after the war, the planters on James Island had no place to gin and store their cotton, all gin houses having been destroyed during the federal occupation of the island. Three men—Wallace, William Hinson, and Joseph Dill—pooled their resources and formed the James Island Milling Company. Wallace's contribution was the land and the wharf. The company began auspiciously and gave employment to all the white men of the Lawton clan, but it lost money. Cecilia tells us that "at length Wallace was persuaded to buy out the firm, and assume the debts, thinking he had the good will of Mr. Hinson and Mr. Dill. But a few months after the sale, Mr. Hinson appeared with his wagons to appropriate the gins and machinery. Wallace had no legal papers to restrain him." We do not know, of course, Mr. Hinson's thinking in this matter. I do know that he was a man of many friends on the island, and that Wallace was considered a hard man.

This episode may have been the reason for Alison Lawton's statement to my father that his father, Wallace, and Mr. Hinson feuded for years. Peter told my father that for many years Wallace would not let any workers from Mr. Hinson's place cross his land. One day Wallace took down his shotgun, announcing that he wasn't going to hunt partridges. This moment must have had special terrors for Cecilia and may have been the incident she describes in veiled language: "I had a revolting experience today that I cannot forget," and a sentence later, "I had a long talk with Wallace this afternoon about his conduct." Wallace with his gun in his hand planning to even up an old score was frighteningly like a day she remembered all too clearly. According to Peter, she did not restrain him when he decided that "none of the Hinson niggers would cross his land again." For Mr. Hinson's workers, the shortest route to Charleston was by boat from a wharf on James Island Creek; they would pass through the boundary hedgerow onto a field road that led directly across the center of the Lawton plantation to the store and wharf. When I was child this was almost a public road, except for a series of gates that we unlocked for our neighbors. Shutting off this route to Mr. Hinson's help meant a three-mile trip via Three Trees and Camp Road. Peter said that Wallace stationed himself "not too far" from where the field road came through the hedge and fired bird shot at any trespassers. Peter never reported that any blacks had been shot; if anyone did go to his cabin and pick out bird shot, we didn't hear about it.

Life went on busily: "Finished making two and a half gallons of blackberry wine.

"Made myself a new sunbonnet while I was in bed recuperating from malaria.

"The black hen brought out nine chicks today.

"Mrs. Dill was over and I served calve's head soup and sea crabs roasted in the half shell."

(Cecilia wrote the words "sea crabs" three times in her journal; there is no mistaking the word "sea" in her clear handwriting. It was not "she." Since there is hardly a misspelled word in the whole document, and the punctuation is done meticulously, I conclude that Cecilia served "sea crabs" in soup or in the half shell. Is the current expression "she crabs," now used so relentlessly in Charleston restaurants, a corruption of the words "sea crab?" Local chefs will shout that down, I'm sure. Another possibility: Cecilia was writing in very "proper" Victorian times when, for example, a lady had a limb, not a leg. My great-grandmother in helping herself to chicken could select a "drumstick" without a scruple, but never a "thigh"; she would have, please, "the second joint." Cecilia may not have been able to offer at the table anything so blatantly sexual as "she crabs." I leave the matter to further research.)

Later in 1868: "Wallace brought me a sewing machine today—a Wil-

How Grand A Flame

cox and Gibbes—price $75.00. I bought a lot of dainty fabrics and went to work with 'making up a small wardrobe.'" A baby was on the way. "I had been invited by my kind friend, Mrs. Dill, to stay with them during my sickness—and Mrs. Dill now urged Wallace to bring me over at once. There was no physician on James Island at that time. I was sick and confined to my room all Saturday with a doctor and nurse in attendance. It was a heavenly day and I looked out and saw a crowd of happy children hurrying past to attend May Day parties and picnics.

"Sunday, May 2nd, 1869, my second child, Alison, was born at about 10:30 A.M. while church bells were singing joyously, and the sun shone mellow and brightly. I was living at #15 Legare Street—now #19. I gave the naming of the child to Mrs. Dill—who was the godmother—and she begged me to allow him to have the middle name of her daughter, Gena. Thus he was called Alison, and Mr. Dill put Joseph before the Alison. (Joseph was later changed to St. John for my mother's ancestors.)"

WHEN THE CATERPILLAR was eliminated a few years later by an arsenic spray, cotton production on James Island jumped from 165 pounds per acre to 205 pounds in two years, and climbed steadily until 1879, when it reached 415 pounds per acre. Cecilia says of those years that they were able to afford the necessities of life and, indeed, were better off than most of their neighbors. The home at Beck's Point proved to be no protection against malaria, however, and as the farming operation grew, it was found to be too far from the center of activity. Wallace therefore built a new house back in the Bennetts' area, near where the big house had stood, a one-story bungalow-type house with a kitchen. This was the house they were moving to when Wallace unceremoniously dumped the household goods into the waiting boats.

Cecilia finally got the furniture repaired that had been broken in moving and her house in order, "and on a lovely spring-like day in late January I strolled out on the river bank enjoying the glorious weather and the lovely view. But my heart was heavy within me. Wallace was very repentant and trying to make amends for his rudeness in the sudden move. The next day he went to town and bought a carriage for baby and also a new mule for $250. 00." She planted a dozen orange trees and other shrubs and continually reveled in the view from the new house. "There could not be a lovelier situation. The whole city lay spread out in full view and I was within hearing of the city's bells."

Her home across the bay was mercifully excluded from the widespread misery in Charleston. The pain of Reconstruction on James Island was, as I have noted, probably less severe than it was in other sections of the South. The plantations were larger and could offer employment, such as it was, to many freed slaves. Those who were unhappy could easily slip away and lose themselves in the city. As a youth, I was told—whether true or not I cannot say—that the Africans who came to "our islands" were characterized by a more reasonable, gentler, and more tractable disposition than many, and that these qualities accounted for the more harmonious relations enjoyed by the blacks and whites on the islands near Charleston. The patronizing note in this observation is distressing, even if it might contain a bit of truth. As Cecilia gazed at the handsome houses on the Battery, she was probably not aware that many of their owners were destitute, reduced to taking in boarders and waiting in line for handouts or rice. Many houses on East Bay degenerated into bars and bordellos, according to one historian, and were some of the "wickedest and filthiest" in Charleston.

We should hardly expect Cecilia to mention that South Carolina was readmitted to the United States in 1868, but she does tell of a newly opened theater, the Academy of Music, in December 1869. Charleston seems to have had a continuing love affair with theaters, for distinguished performers began coming well before the city had put itself in order. Cecilia tells of seeing one famous actress: "Friday, April 1st, 1870. Sis (Georgia who was visiting me at the time) and I went to town upon an invitation of Mrs. Dill and Mr. Dill escorted us to the theater. We saw Laura Keene act and enjoyed it immensely." She does not tell us whether she knew that Laura Keene was the famous actress who had attracted Abraham and Mary Todd Lincoln to the theater on the night of April 14, 1865.

Some months after the Lawtons were settled in their new house by the harbor, they received an invitation to attend a large picnic at the McCleod plantation on Wappoo Creek. All the principal planters on the island were invited, along with a boatload from Charleston—relatives, bankers, and cotton factors. The planters needed to keep on good terms with the businessmen of the city. Mr. Dill said the guest list was "a very mixed one." A sizable party from the Lawtons attended; besides Wallace, Cecilia, and little Alison and his nurse, there was sister Georgia, who was visiting, and her baby and nurse. They traveled by boat—or boats, Cecilia does not say —and Peter may or may not have been the oarsman. Small engines were in use then, but we do not know whether or not Wallace possessed one.

Cecilia's contribution to the picnic was a high mold of butter in the shape of a pineapple, "made with my own hands." This Mrs. McCleod placed in the center of the table "where it was much admired." The early guests wandered across the broad lawn to the water, to wait at the wharf for the Charlestonians who were to come in a "rice schooner."

If we may judge by references to parties and dances, Cecilia and Wallace were sought after as guests. At this picnic she was not only the maker of the wonderful butter sculpture, but was now a published poet. A few months earlier the *Charleston Mercury* had printed a poem, "The Ocean's Lament," by an author named "Cecilia." To have published the full name of a married lady would have violated the social protocol of the time. Cecilia states that, regrettably, she has lost her copy and cannot include it in the memoir. I found it on the front page of the *Mercury* for Thursday, September 4, 1868.

The Ocean's Lament
Written on a deserted Sea-Island Plantation
By Cecilia

Sitting by the ocean's side
Where the restless billows ride
Where the ever-flowing waves
From the sea's bottomless caves
As they dash upon the beach
Sigh and moan as if they each

Had a mournful tale to tell
And sang the happy past a sad farewell.

THEN FOLLOWED SIX melancholy and wistful stanzas in the same tone
—lament for a ruined plantation home and bygone days of happiness that
are no more.

She describes the conclusion of the McCleod party: "At sundown it
began pouring in torrents and blowing hard. The rice schooner came for
the town folks but we were forced to stay all night. We left for home early
in the morning so as not to inconvenience Mrs. McCleod. When I got
home I found 21 of my beautiful Brahmin chickens drowned in one barrel—after all the trouble I've had with them. But tired as I was I went to
church." In parentheses, she writes: "I had a special reason." No subsequent entry in her diary explains the meaning of that sentence. It was a
comment added years later when she assembled her memoir. Her special
reason, whatever it was, must have stayed fresh in her memory for many
years. I do not think her "reason" for going to church on that rainy morning was to hear the gospel preached or to transact some bit of everyday
business. One does not write so mysteriously of mundane matters.
Neither do I believe that it was romantic speculation to think that her
"special reason" was a person. Who was the person, I ask myself, whom
she wanted so much to see but could not reveal by name?

LIFE IN THE LITTLE cottage with the beautiful view of the city was not
the happy experience that Cecilia and Wallace had envisioned. Cecilia's
malaria flared up again, and she began to suffer from a throat problem that
would plague her for many years. Between illnesses, she and little Alison
and his nurse spent weeks in Charleston at the Joseph Dill home. When
the strain of living on the plantation threatened her health, Cecilia would
rest and recover at the Dills. Cecilia writes that her return to James Island
after one such sojourn was particularly distressing because Catherine, Alison's nurse, refused to go with her. "I get so lonesome on James Island,"
she said. Cecilia arrived at the little house by the harbor, "thin, weak and

in very poor health, the doctor told me." Wallace and Powell, deeply involved in the cotton harvest, were unable to be with her for long periods, and "after three dreary, desolate days at Bennetts, I moved back to Dills. Baby Alison was so excited at being with the Dills he jumped up and ran—his first steps. His good nurse, Catherine, came back and I settled myself comfortably for the winter. Wallace came over every night unless it was too stormy." But in a few days, Wallace, as if he were placing a horse in another stable, "soon changed his mind and moved me back to Bennetts."

The new cottage with its five little rooms, too small for the Lawton family, now had to make room for sister Anna and her family, who had experienced land troubles at Lawtonville: "Wallace, baby and I occupied a room about ten feet by ten feet—most uncomfortable."

In 1870 Wallace made another one of his business decisions that was to have far-reaching effects. He agreed to provide milk for the Mills House, Charleston's leading hotel. Again he was capitalizing on the strategic location of his plantation. The big planters on Edisto Island, for all their fertile fields, could not even entertain the thought of transporting fresh milk to Charleston, but from the wharf on James Island Creek little freight boats could carry Wallace's milk to Charleston in half an hour. The Lawton plantation never ceased to produce milk until developers bought the land seventy-five years later. Milk gave Wallace a "cash flow," to use a modern expression, that the single-crop planters did not enjoy. Dairying and cotton came first; then with the demise of Sea Island cotton, the combination was dairying and truck crops; finally, dairying alone. Wallace did not have to contend with health and sanitation inspections or with pasteurization; he simply had to get the milk into cans, onto the boat, and to the back door of the Mills House. Ice to cool and preserve milk was cut from the frozen Hudson River and stored in big houses of sawdust on East Bay. Those dealers who peddled milk in the streets simply dropped a few chunks of frozen Hudson River water into their portable tanks and ladled the milk into jars that servants brought down to the curbside. I have no record that Wallace sold milk in this fashion.

Even as the plantation prospered, Cecilia's health problems grew worse. Dr. Lebby called her infection "catarrhal fever." She became well enough to spend two weeks in Savannah, where she still "felt miserable." Then she visited Blockade Place, "which father and his wife had vacated for a small house (Oak Hill at #5 on the Halcyondale Central R.R.), having sold the land." She was now pregnant and it was time to get back to Charleston. Here at the Dill home her "sickness," as she calls it, ended on July 2 when her third child, little Cecilia, was born.

"In September we moved to Secessionville on James Island fleeing from yellow fever which had broken out in Charleston a few days before. Wallace wanted me to remain and become 'acclimated,' but Dr. Horlbeck said I was almost sure to take the fever and if I did it would *kill* me. We left at once and boarded with sister Anna. During the fall none of us dared to go to town (except Wallace who said he was proof against Yellow Jack). The fever raged with considerable virulence until December. Eddie Clark went back to the city to go to school—but too early, because he contracted the fever and died of it. Wallace made a good crop that year and considerable money as the caterpillars gave us a respite that year and prices were good."

In the year 1870 Wallace was facing problems that were quite unrelated to cotton and milk production. News of his prosperity may have reached his half brothers and sisters and their children, for they now decided to take legal action on Winborn's will. Wilhelmina Lawton, a granddaughter of Winborn, instituted a suit on behalf of herself and all the legatees against Wallace, the executor of his father's estate. In the records of the Supreme Court of the State of South Carolina we read these words on page two of a ninety-three-page document:

And your oratrix and orator further shew unto your Honors, that they have repeatedly applied to the executor, Winborn Wallace Lawton, for the payment of the legacies due to them and for the one-ninth of the residuary estate bequeathed to them by their testator, and that he refused to pay them the said legacies and their portion of the residue, although more than six years has elapsed since the death of the testator.

In three more pages of tortured legal phrasing they present the details of a simple complaint: Wallace, "who took upon him self alone the burden of execution of the said will," had not paid up. It was also noted that the $65,000 he owed for the land and slaves—minus the $10,000 that his father had given him—constituted nearly the whole of the estate.

His reply was that he had made substantial payments according to the schedule agreed upon; indeed, he had paid sums well before their due dates—he was permitted to do this—into the estate account in the Bank of South Carolina. This he continued to do even after the Confederate army occupied James Island. One does not have to be a very astute businessman to understand why he was paying so generously ahead of schedule. He was doing so in inflated Confederate currency. He had acquired the hotel in Sylvania and the $5,000 of tobacco in the same way. At the close of the war the currency had ceased to be legal tender, and the Bank of South Carolina had gone into receivership. He would gladly show receipts for his payments to the bank.

No doubt this all appeared to the twenty-eight legatees as too neat and too crafty a maneuver, by a man who was reputed to be crafty. The suit drifted on for at least ten years, and we see its effect on a number of business transactions that Wallace was to make during those years, and later. The Judge assigned a referee to study the suit and recommend a settlement. The judge first concealed the value of the slaves—$45,000—for obvious reasons. His next rulings hurt: First, the debt of the executor to the estate was payable only in gold or silver or other legal tender. Second, the deposit by the executor in the Bank of the State of South Carolina of any funds other than gold or silver, or other legal tender, did not amount to payment, or protect the executor from liability. Using some funds found in the bank, the referee finally named a sum to be paid to each legatee if all would so agree, thus closing the matter. Two people did not agree and stated their intention to sue for more. The financial bind in which Wallace found himself may explain several hasty business transactions that Cecilia mentions—the sudden transferring of land to Brother Powell and the sale of the Sylvania Hotel in Screven County, a property that he had originally deeded to Cecilia. Wallace had this suit hanging over him until the turn of the century and it seems to have affected several subsequent business decisions. I have been unable to discover how the suit of the two displeased legatees was finally settled.

Cecilia's last move on the plantation was about to occur. The little bungalow was just too small. The presence of two children and their nurses, the influx of company, and Cecilia's continuing poor health made the Bennetts' cottage unacceptable. The one remaining house was the Cuthbert House on an elevation of ground not far from the Bluff. Seven years had elapsed since the five hundred Negroes were supposed to have died there of smallpox, and the Lawtons now felt it was safe to occupy. "It had once been a very nice house, built in the old Dutch style and with *beautiful* grounds around it. Even after the war a fine grove of cedar trees encircled it but the German cut it down and used them for fence posts the year we were refugeeing."

This house is now the Heyward House on Fort Sumter Drive, owned by a descendant of the builder. The original house remains—the four big rooms, the large chimneys at each end of the house, the four fireplaces, the dormer windows; the only changes are additions to the rear to provide rooms for modern living. Peter Brown told us that a road lined with Osage orange trees had once run out to the Ashley River. As I have said, the view of the city, unobstructed by trees, was unique. During the early plantation days the house stood on a little knoll in broad fields that produced cotton and corn. In my childhood, when dairying flourished, the house was surrounded by pasture on three sides. Cecilia seemed to enjoy the house, even though there was then no kitchen in the rear. Wallace insisted the cook use two of the newly invented oil stoves, which he had just purchased. Cecilia feared and hated them. "The cook nearly blew us up several times before I got them removed."

On a November afternoon in 1921, almost fifty years to the day after Cecilia set up housekeeping in the Cuthbert House, my parents, my brother and sister, and I moved into the same house. My mother also began cooking on a new two-burner oil stove that my father had bought. Like Cecilia, she feared and hated it.

How Grand A Flame

WALLACE HAD TOLD CECILIA soon after they were married that he wanted her to produce only boy babies. It is exactly the kind of remark one would expect from a man with his distorted notion of masculinity. We do not know what Cecilia said in reply. If one may judge from her comments in her diary, she doubtless listened to what her husband said, and forebore making the obvious reply: that what he wanted in such matters had nothing whatever to do with what he would get. If so, she would scarcely have been the first woman, whether planter's wife or not, to learn very quickly that the best way to handle a foolish husband is to nod and pay no further heed to what he said. Cecilia Lawton might admire Wallace's energy and his skill at managing a plantation, but it must have been clear to her, too, that when it came to intelligence and insight, she was considerably better endowed than he. In the years to come, once the duties of tending to small children could be put aside, she would prove herself to be a businesswoman of no small ability.

In point of fact, Cecilia complied tolerably well with her husband's demand; she produced three boys and one girl. She goes on to note in her diary that Wallace became "very fond of—even worshipped" his little Cecilia, a development that probably surprised him as much as it did his wife.

The fourth child, Herbert Singleton, was born February 23, 1874, bringing the family in the Cuthbert House to five members, with Alison, age five, the oldest child. He would have been old enough to play in the shallow tidal inlet behind his house where nearly fifty years later the Bresee children would spend most of their free time. Here a small arm of the Ashley River meandered into a depressed corner of the pasture, an area that at extremely high tide might become a tiny pond a foot deep. Except on those rare days, it was firm earth covered with short marsh grass through which the tiny stream looped and curled. Nearby were thickets of cassena bushes that offered mysterious trails and hiding places for birds — and little boys. When my brother and I played there, no one told us that the owner of the plantation surely must have waded in the little stream and searched for crabs and tiny shrimp when he was a boy. No child could possibly resist the lure of what we called "the tide."

Alison was seven years old when little Herbert, who was approaching his third birthday, suddenly fell ill. If Cecilia kept a diary of this sad period, she did not include it in her book of memoirs. We do not know the name of his sickness, but it was probably diphtheria, a disease that often spread through a family and took out several children in a few days. In the Lawton family plot at St. James Church are two sculpted lambs in white marble resting on a granite base, a monument that must tell us all we can know at this far time of little Herbert and his sister. Herbert died on December 2, 1876, and little Cecilia died five days later. On the granite base are words that read almost like a stifled sob:

> Cecilia — Herbert — Our Darlings
> Thy will be done

No diary has come down to us for the period 1870–80, and what we know of the Lawtons' daily life must be inferred from other sources. In the decades of the seventies and eighties the Lawton plantation was apparently making money. The economy had its fluctuations, and though the price of cotton never returned to the dollar per pound of 1865, the plantation prospered. In 1880 James Island cotton production averaged four hundred pounds to the acre—the black-seeded, long-staple cotton that commanded the highest prices in the world. Increasingly the James Islanders enjoyed the advantages of Charleston suburbanites. For Wallace there were more trips to the city to chat with friends at the Charleston Hotel and at other clubs that were now being revived. The James Island Agricultural Society, a branch of the state organization, routinely invited business and professional men of Charleston to their annual summer meeting—a practice that continued into the decade when I lived on James Island. I am told by several of Wallace's cousins "twice removed" that he became skilled at cards and was a successful gambler.

It may have been while spending a pleasant afternoon at the Charleston Hotel that he heard of Mrs. Charles Manigault's intention to sell Marshlands, her large plantation on the Cooper River. Marshlands, which had once been in the Heyward family, had been one of the largest rice plantations on the coast. Its most notable feature was a commanding three-story house mounted on brick columns eight feet high; with a broad piazza surrounding the first floor, it was one of the finest houses on the Cooper River. A large plantation up for sale sets every businessman to examining his resources and wondering. Land is the ultimate mark of rank and affluence and sends a clearer message than does a distinguished name—unless, of course, the name is backed by land.

In 1880, Wallace bought Marshlands. He did not live there, but rented or leased it in some fashion until it was sold twenty-five years later. The transaction, no doubt, created the pleasant, anticipated stir—"Mr. and Mrs. W. Wallace Lawton of Marshlands on the Cooper and James Island" made a most agreeable sound. They could visit their new property more easily now, because the streetcar lines were pushing farther up the Cooper each year. The records show that Wallace immediately transferred the title of the plantation to Cecilia—a move about which we can only speculate. One theory: gamblers in those days were known to transfer titles of real property to their wives so that a run of bad cards would not ruin them. Wallace could fit into this category. Another: Wallace had not yet resolved the problems of his father's will; if the two unhappy heirs sued for more money, this land, at least, would be safe from attack.

On James Island the major planters resumed the practice begun long before the war of spending their summers at Secessionville or Fort Johnson to avoid malaria. William Godber Hinson, Wallace's neighbor at Stiles Point, writes in his *Sketch of James Island* (1888) that "There were twenty-five houses at Fort Johnson before the war of Southern Liberty, all of which were destroyed by the Confederate engineers. Occupying soldiers (Confederates) on James Island destroyed thirty dwelling houses in sheer wantonness." His remark confirms Cecilia's observation in her diary about the destruction of the Lawton house. Hinson's *Sketch of James Island* reflects the gloomy, postbellum views of the large planters who were ruined by the war. He casts a last, unrepentant look at what has been called America's greatest wrong. "It is to be hoped that when the world recovers from its insanity on the subject of African slavery that an impartial posterity will adjudge it fairly and correctly and the old slave-holders will not be slandered and abused as it is the fashion nowadays to do." William Hinson served throughout the war in the Army of Virginia and came home to find that his fiancée had married someone else; he settled down to bachelorhood and became one of the largest landholders and most prosperous planters on James Island. He concludes his *Sketch* on a sad and wistful note: "The future looks uncertain. Trade and farming are depressed, politics degraded and the war of the races imminent. It is to be hoped that Providence will dispel these clouds, imaginary or otherwise, and that a permanent prosperity and perfect confidence will come to the Garden spot of the South, the Sea Islands of South Carolina."

THE EIGHTEEN-EIGHTIES find Wallace and Cecilia living in the Cuthbert House with their only remaining child, Alison, now in his teens and thinking about college. He probably got his grammar school education on James Island; later, I suspect, he attended a school in Charleston with tutors. Wallace must have held some idealized notion of how the eldest son of a planter should develop—energetic, able in firearms, full of masculine assertiveness but obedient to parental authority, courteous to women but quietly preparing to dominate them, always conscious of rank, and ready to carry on the family business. If Wallace accepted without question this picture of a planter's son, as I think he did, he was surely devoid of the genius to bring it to pass. Worse still, Wallace gives us no sign that he appreciated the unique combination of talents and disposition that a youth brings into the world, and of his precious right to pursue and develop those endowments. All he saw was an irritating boy who had gotten hold of this drawing craze. A boy should be hunting, sailing, fishing, interested in science or business—not sketching pictures.

There is no evidence that Alison loved guns or horses or sailing. He liked the visual arts, for he was to become an architect, and he liked mathematics. How could there have failed to be angry confrontations? I do not like to extract from the situation more than is there, but I doubt that Cecilia had an easy time of it. She could sympathize with a mother who once said to me, at a bitter moment in her own family relationships,

"Every man I ever knew had to have a son, and almost every mother I know has spent half of her life standing between them to keep the peace."

One of Cecilia's last entries in her journal tells of Livie Oswald's marriage. Livie was a daughter of sister Anna, and although she was Cecilia's niece, the two girls were nearly the same age. Livie's marriage to John Calhoun Clark took place in Cecilia's house "after which they went to his new home at Ocean View where he had a very nice and comfortable house for her—furnished and complete." Surely Cecilia was remembering the hectic beginning of her own married life. Her next sentence describes an ideal as fine as any girl could desire. "He is such a thrifty young man, steady and amiable, and a most devoted husband." Livie had all the luck.

SEVEN

Restoration

THE ASHLEY AND COOPER RIVERS, which make a peninsula of the city of Charleston and offer miles of waterfront for commerce and recreation, suffer one drawback—they disgorge tons of channel-clogging silt into Charleston Harbor. The shallow channel at "the bar" had hindered shipping since the city was founded; the larger vessels had to wait for high tide to enter and sometimes even then were grounded. The decision was made around 1880 to let nature—the movement of the tides—assist in keeping the channel open. Two great walls of rock would be built, each approximately a mile long, one extending from Sullivans Island and the other from Morris Island, designed to narrow the route for the outgoing tide so that the swiftly moving water would keep the channel clear of silt.

The U.S. Army Corps of Engineers required nearly seventeen years of dumping lighter loads of huge rocks to complete the two arms of "the Jetties." Besides keeping the channel open, the great rocks resting on the level floor of the ocean produced one of the finest fishing spots on the south Atlantic coast, and soon a fishing trip to the Jetties fulfilled every fisherman's dream. Although work was not completed until 1896, good fishing came some years earlier when in the first phase of construction great rafts of logs were sunk (by piling stones on top of them) to serve as a foundation for the larger rocks to follow. Sheepshead and bass soon collected in great numbers to enjoy the protection from enemies and to obtain their own food from the marine life that was fostered there.

The point in this bit of history is that Peter and Wallace went fishing one day at the Jetties—a day that neither of them would ever forget. Pleasure trips in the harbor were common then; Cecilia wrote in the summer of 1868 that "Powell and Wallace went sailing to Fort Sumter in the big boat. They got home at nine o'clock because they had to row 'agin the tied.' I told them it served them right for going sailing on Sunday." Peter did not tell my father the date of their adventure at the Jetties; it was probably in the eighteen-nineties.

On this journey Peter was the oarsman, but I am sure that Wallace took him on the trip because he was good company. After a row through quiet waters to the Sullivans Island end of the Jetties, they decided to leave the boat and fish off the newly deposited rocks. Peter was actually the hero of this fishing expedition, although he never presented himself as such and the details are not clear. I am told that now the rocks are extremely slippery from algae and other marine growth and that moving about them is dangerous; they were probably not so slippery when Wallace and Peter climbed out of their boat to perch on a little shelf ten feet above the water. Peter simply told my father that in casting his line Wallace lost his footing and slid down the rocks into deep water. Peter did not at the moment fear for Wallace's life, because he thought he could swim and make his way to a little ledge; Wallace slid out of sight and came up waving his arms and gasping and calling for help, only to start sinking again. Having no lines or floating objects to throw to him, Peter took off his shoes and jumped into the water. He said Wallace kept his control enough not "to grab me around the neck and pull me under." Wallace hung onto Peter's clothing as he swam the few yards to the boat where they clung for a moment and caught their breath.

My father said to Peter, "You saved his life, didn't you?" Peter replied that he didn't know about that, but "Mr. Wallace said I did. He told me on the way home that if it hadn't been for me he would be out in the Atlantic Ocean. I don't know if that is true. He asked me not to tell his wife about it and I tell him I wouldn't talk to no one. And I didn't." My father always felt that modesty kept Peter from telling the full details of the rescue. Soon after the near-drowning at the Jetties, Wallace must have sensed his indebtedness, for he told Peter and Emma to move into the now vacant cottage by the harbor that Cecilia and Wallace had once used, a house incomparably better than the cabins of the other workers. Many years later—when we were living on James Island—Alison said to my father the day after Peter died that he had always had a special place in his memory for Peter. "You know, Mr. Bresee, Peter Brown saved my father's life when they were fishing at the Jetties. He told me that Peter was to have that little house rent-free as long as he lived, and I have followed his directions."

WHEN IT WAS TIME to select a college for Alison, I think his father prevailed; Alison would go to a southern military college. Wallace no doubt thought that if anything could straighten his son out, a good military college might. The South Carolina Military College—now called The Citadel—was a clear possibility, and near home, but "everyone" went to The Citadel. I can hear Cecilia making this point. Virginia Military Institute had just the right combination of prestige and location, a little "northern" but located in a state rich in southern tradition. If he went there, Alison, let it be hoped, would not be tempted to study art! Cecilia must have seen the rich possibilities of such a school—a place to meet scholars and scientists, men not tied to the slow agricultural life of James Island.

At VMI Alison was soon drawn to architecture, a field perfectly tailored to his needs. It would allow him to create artistically, satisfy his interest in mathematics, and please his father by "studying something practical." His first two years seemed to have passed routinely—home for the Christmas holidays and summer vacation and back to school in the fall. How their relationship fared during the summers is left to our imagination. Peter Brown told my father that "Mr. Wallace was very hard on his son," a statement that tells us nothing specifically because Wallace was hard on everyone, if I may believe the remarks of distant relatives. (A lady who lived across the creek at Frampton's Point, a cousin of Wallace's, never spoke to him, always left the room when he entered, and is known to have said that he was "the devil incarnate.")

At the close of Alison's junior year Cecilia and Wallace waited for the letter from Virginia telling them when Alison's train would arrive in Charleston. The letter did not come. After some days or weeks — we do not know what transpired in that time — a letter came, I am told, from a business friend in New York City, probably a cotton broker, saying that Alison had been located. Another story has it that his parents hired a detective to find their son. Both accounts agree in that he was found shining shoes in the lobby of a New York City hotel! The stories agree also in telling us plainly that Alison was not filled with a longing to spend the summer on his parents' beautiful plantation by Charleston Harbor. Peter remembers being called to the house suddenly and told to take a telegram to the city and to wait for a reply; if none came by nightfall, he was to leave money for a messenger service. A reconciliation must have been effected ultimately, because Alison returned to Virginia in the fall.

Alison did well at VMI, graduating in 1891 with high honors and winning a prize for oratory. Sometime in those years he met and fell in love with his future wife, Ruth Jennings, of nearby Lynchburg. She was from an old Virginia family and had lost relatives in the Confederate War, thus earning double accreditation to the Lawtons of James Island.

Upon graduation, Alison did not return to practice his profession in Charleston, but took graduate courses at the Massachusetts Institute of Technology and then secured employment with a firm in Washington; later he was to work in New York City. It took the tumultuous events of the turn of the century to bring him back home. Both the city and his family could use his skills. Uppermost in everyone's mind was the Charleston and West Indian Exposition, an enterprise that its organizers thought would draw the attention of the world to Charleston as a trade center. An elaborate complex of buildings appeared in what is now the Hampton Park area, replete with sunken gardens, a zoo, auditorium, and pool. The exposition created great excitement in the city and drew some notable visitors, although it failed financially.

AS THE CENTURY DREW to a close, Charleston was to have another war scare, again fearing an attack by sea. The harbor defenses were woefully unprepared. If Wallace Lawton had come down to the waterfront of his plantation in the autumn of 1897 with his field glasses in hand and focused on the walls of Fort Moultrie, he would have seen a stir of movement on the old fortification. The Corps of Engineers was rebuilding rotten gun platforms on the channel side in an attempt to shore up old defenses, because new weapons, ordered years earlier, would surely not arrive in time to meet the pending emergency. The "Spanish situation" was getting serious. No city on the south Atlantic coast felt secure, so ill equipped and poorly manned were the harbor defenses. Fort Moultrie had had no regular garrison for thirty-one years until late October of 1897, when a battery of artillery arrived from St. Augustine. The fear in Charleston was that the powerful squadron of Admiral Pascual Cervera would cross the Atlantic undetected and bombard the cities and forts. On April 5 it was announced that the harbor would be mined; by the end of the month war would be declared.

An Associated Press dispatch of April 7 reported that a detachment of engineers was en route from New York "to lay cables and electrical apparatus for operating the controlled mines." The *News and Courier* assured its readers on April 16: "If the declaration of war is delayed a short time, Charleston will be impregnable. The famous 'disappearing rifles' from England have arrived and by working 200 men on round-the-clock shifts, they are finally installed. When these ingenious weapons are fired the recoil causes the twenty-eight-foot rifle barrel to sink automatically back into the protection of its concrete base. By the end of the month," so the papers reported, "four twelve-inch mortars would be clustered to loft their 700-pound projectiles simultaneously to crash down vertically on the thinly armored decks of warships. The ten-inch flat trajectory weapons will be able to hurl their 571-pound shells into ships eight miles out to sea." With the actual declaration of war on April 21, 1890, the fear mounted in Charleston that Cervera's fleet would bypass the U.S. Second Fleet based at Hampton Roads and shell East Coast cities.

The first bad scare came when Cervera's armored cruisers, destroyers, and torpedo boats were reported hovering off the bar. "Wild excitement gripped Charleston," according to one account, "and soldiers rushed to their Fort Moultrie battle stations. A naval fight was reportedly raging off the South Carolina coast. Anxious hours passed before investigations revealed this as a rumor." Then a week later came another message that set the city and the surrounding islands on edge. Someone had received a cable from the British War Office stating that British naval circles believed Cervera's ships would evade the American fleet and bombard the city. To calm the people, newspapers pointed out that the Sullivans Island batteries were in fine fighting condition and well garrisoned, and that all the defenses were "in the charge of the most skillful and experienced men." Neither attack came off, but Charlestonians again gathered at the end of the peninsula and scanned the harbor entrance.

The "splendid little war" ended August 12 and Charleston relaxed. It had raised all the old questions of harbor defense that had troubled the city and the surrounding islands ever since Charleston was first settled. It was all very well to have a fine harbor and a United States Naval Base now, but with them came new hazards as well as opportunities. The outbreak of World War II forty years later and the appearance of German submarines in Atlantic coastal waters brought the old fort to life again. A new fortification was also built on the north end of Folly Island, although I think neither of these installations actually fired on an enemy.

Fort Moultrie is a national park today. Concrete walks, signs to guide the visitors, and neat lawns surround the gun emplacements. The big varnished cannons are now curiosities and look a little pompous as they face bravely out to sea. Tourists come in throngs to see them, the men to pat them appreciatively, children to climb over them, and everyone to take their picture.

THE OPENING OF THE twentieth century must have brought special joys to Cecilia, one of which was that Alison was securely back in Charleston. We are not quite sure how her son spent all of the decade since graduation, but in 1901 he was home at last. The *News and Courier* for May 17 carried the following announcement:

Messers Rutledge Holmes and St. John Alison Lawton, two talented young Charleston architects, have formed a partnership for the practice of their profession. Mr. Holmes, whose excellent work is already known favorably from one end of Charleston to the other, has for a number of years been a successful architect here.

Mr. Lawton graduated with honor from the V.M.I. and then pursued the study of architecture at the Massachusetts Institute of Technology. He practiced for a time both in Washington and New York.

The friends of both of these gentlemen wish them every success.

James Island, as we might expect, could not hold permanently a woman of Cecilia's intellect and ambition—not with the city of Charleston so close. Thirty-five years had elapsed since she and Wallace had begun the task of restoring a lost way of life, and they had succeeded better than most. The main elements were in place: a plantation that was making money, a second home in the city, and a son in professional work.

The City Directory for 1900 has the following entries:

> Lawton, W. Wallace (Cecilia) planter, and propr. James
>   Island Dairy; residence 43 S. Bay.
> Lawton, St. J. A., Architect, planter, res. 43 S. Bay.

There were very practical reasons for moving to the city and the purchasing of the property on South Bay Street (now South Battery). The dairy badly needed a retail distribution center in the city, and the property at 43 South Bay, now suddenly announced for sale, met every specification. The lot extended east to King Street and down to low water on the Ashley, making possible the dairy's own private wharf and providing also abundant land for a bottling room, icehouse, stable, and wagons. And so the Battery Dairy came into being on the site of what is now the Fort Sumter House. The dairy's name suggested history and social class and fell easily from the tongue. Who thought of the little addendum—"Oldest Dairy, but Freshest Milk"—which appeared on all the wagons, we do not know. It sounds like Cecilia to me.

Alison had made a good marriage. Ruth Jennings was bright, dignified, poised, well educated, and, surprisingly, quite acceptable to both
Cecilia and Wallace. Like her mother-in-law, Ruth was entitled by her
noble family lines to membership in the DAR and the UDC. She was the
first white lady I saw when I came to James Island as a child of five. She
was seated on the porch of her home (now gone) and rose to greet my family as Alison presented us on the day of our arrival. Her voice impressed
me then, as it did every time I heard her speak — rich and expressive, like
the voice of an actress but with no trace of artificiality. As national president of the United Daughters of the Confederacy, she addressed our little
James Island School at celebrations of Lee's birthday; her earnest but warm
and polished manner of speaking I have never forgotten. Her pronuncia-
tion and intonation were like that of Franklin D. Roosevelt. We at the
Bresee house believed she could have addressed a joint session of Congress
with distinction.

On a trip to James Island in the nineteen-fifties, some twenty years after
the Bresees had returned to Pennsylvania, my wife and I stopped at the
Squirrel Inn in the town of Summerville, twenty-five miles above Charleston. It was lunchtime and the hostess seated us on the piazza where we
could gaze at the banks of azalea blossoms under the pine trees. From an
open window behind me I heard a lady in the dining room giving instructions to her waitress. I could not see her from where I sat, but without
turning my head, I said to my wife, "That lady speaking is Mrs. St. John
Alison Lawton." My wife, less bold than I am in such matters, said, "Are
you sure?" "Of course," I said. "I'm going to introduce myself." I did, and
we lunched together. The years had not changed her expressive voice. She
was saddened by the recent death of Alison and inquired about my parents. We were remembering life on the plantation when she said quietly,
"I'm sure those days on the island were not always easy for your father and
mother." In this remark, which I did not quite understand, she revealed
a quality that all of us admired in her.

ANOTHER EXCITING DEVELOPMENT glimmered on the horizon in the
early nineteen-hundreds — nothing substantial yet, but if rumors were

true, something intimately related to the Lawton fortunes. The Navy Department wanted a base on the south Atlantic coast—that much was certain. Would the admirals choose to enlarge the Parris Island Naval Station at Beaufort, or decide to move the whole enterprise to Charleston? Mayor Adger Smyth and Senator Tillman were doing their best to have it located on the east side of the Cooper River. The city would gladly contribute Chicora Park, but more land was needed, especially the Lawton plantation known as Marshlands. Cecilia was thought to be asking a good price, for if the navy got Chicora Park for nothing, they could afford to pay her price for land to complete the site. She found ways of getting out the word that Marshlands could be bought.

Cecilia had no trouble in letting Marshlands go. The plantation was always a rented property—she and Wallace never lived there—and the abandoned rice fields were not well suited to modern agriculture. The Department of the Navy cared for nothing but the precious acres fronting on the Cooper River and offered to buy it for $50,000. Wallace is not mentioned as being present at the formal signing, having retreated, probably, to his world of card-playing. Mayor Smyth was there to cede 178 acres of Chicora Park, which, with Cecilia's 258 acres, would create at Charleston, according to Captain Longnecker, "the greatest naval station of the South." Cecilia, with her ever-present sense of history must have thrilled at the thought of her land being put to an undertaking that could only bring wealth and recognition to the city.

THERE WAS ANOTHER MATTER for Cecilia's attention at the moment: Alison was applying for membership in the Camp Moultrie Chapter of the Sons of Confederate Veterans. Whether this was his idea or his mother's we do not know—more likely hers, for she filled out the application form. The war was already well behind, and some of the old anger in her generation was being replaced by philanthropy, anniversary celebrations, parades, and even reunions where survivors of both sides shook hands. Symbols and fraternal gatherings like the Moultrie Camp were slowly beginning to preserve the memory without some of the bitterness.

"To the Officers and Members of the Camp Moultrie Chapter: The undersigned respectfully applies for admission to your camp and presents the following record of services of his father, W. W. Lawton." The application must have caused her to pause often, for under "Battles" she could write only of minor skirmishes around Pocotaligo, and, to make matters worse, the Rutledge Mounted Riflemen were not members of the Confederate army when Wallace rode with them. She wrote: "Was in active service on James Island and on the mainland near Charleston and Port Royal during which time his valuable estate on James Island was undergoing destruction." There was nothing to say, really, under "Wounded," but she wrote: "Being prostrated by a desperate case of malarial-typhoid fever in 1862, he remained an invalid for two years but re-enlisted in 1864 under Captain F. H. Peeples, during which time he was frequently exposed to danger in the front and rear of Sherman's army." As if to suggest that his "fighting" had engaged the attention of the enemy, she wrote after "Remarks:" "The Union forces arrested him immediately at the end of the war for not swearing allegiance to the United States." She concluded with: "Sherman annihilated his valuable home and surroundings in Beaufort District." Another paragraph told of how he aided the Cause when he was ill by providing food and a horse for families of servicemen.

Finding supportive evidence for Wallace Lawton's military career was not easy; one of the men she listed as a reference wrote that he could not remember any service with Wallace, but begged to assure her that he did not want to predispose the committee, and urged her to continue the search for information elsewhere. I do not think that Cecilia's rich prose was sufficient to gain for her son membership in the Camp Moultrie Chapter of the Sons of Confederate Veterans.

As Wallace seems to have declined in vigor, restricting his social life more and more to the club and cards, Cecilia, his intellectual superior and ten years his junior, was there to fill the gap. The postwar struggle for survival had only served to sharpen her business acumen. She was now ready to turn her $50,000 to more profit, and, just as the lot on South Battery came up for sale at the propitious moment, so did the venerable hotel known as the Mills House at Meeting and Queen Streets. The West Indian

Exposition, it was assumed, would draw thousands to Charleston who would need lodging, and, moreover, Charleston needed a fine hotel where planters and professional people could find privacy and charm for work or relaxation. "The most distinguished hotel in the low country" was Cecilia's dream. She bought the hotel in 1901.

Everyone said that Cecilia named the hotel after her son, but that is not quite true. Her maternal grandmother was a St. John, a name that seems to have had a special fascination for Cecilia. Not many people liked it as a first name, and Alison did not so use it except in his signature. But for a hotel? A name with a hint of aristocracy and old-world elegance—the St. John Hotel of Charleston, of course. She immediately assigned Alison the task of drawing new designs for the lobby and dining room. He was also charged with designing two apartments on the second floor for the Lawtons.

The City directory for 1906 lists:

> Lawton, St. John (Ruth), Sec. & Treas., St. John Hotel—
> res. —same.
> Lawton, W. Wallace (Cecilia), Prest., St. John Hotel—res. —
> same.

FOR ALL ITS NEWLY acquired elegance, the St. John Hotel was not the place where Wallace Lawton wanted to spend the few remaining years of his life. He was listed as president only because he was the senior male; Cecilia and Alison provided the energy and direction that elevated the hotel to the top position in Charleston. As often as he could manage to do so, Wallace fled to James Island, telling his friends that he wanted to get out of that "hot hell." Their old home at 43 South Bay would have offered cooling breezes in the afternoon, but that house was rented to Captain and Mrs. Thomas Pinckney.

Cecilia and Alison had chosen the apartment in the St. John Hotel, and that is where Wallace was to live. But he had an escape. All he had to do was to walk over to his own wharf, on what is now Murray Boulevard, and cross the Ashley River on a milk boat from his plantation. He made this trip often. The operation of the plantation was now in the hands of two managers—one a field and crop man, the other in charge of the cattle. A cluster of cabins near the store housed the steady black workers, a few of whom might rise to leadership positions because they could read and write. The more fortunate men found their way to the dairy barns, where the pay was a little better. I do not know exactly what position Peter held during this period. He was not a field-worker, I am sure; I suspect his position was similar to what on most plantations was called a yard man. Often such a position amounted to that of a low-level manager, for he had his hand in everything and was at the beck and call of nearly every white person on the plantation. He could safely be entrusted to take messages, run errands off the plantation, and "check on things." Such a person was often the maintenance man for the twenty-five or thirty buildings on the place.

My father once asked Peter, "What was Alison's father like?" or words to that effect. It was then that he said that "Mr. Wallace was hard on his son," and went on to tell about Wallace's last years. "I knew him longer than anyone else—longer than his wife—and I have outlived him and Miss Cecilia." It was then that Peter said, "I stayed on with the Lawtons after freedom." I am sure my father asked "Why did you stay, Peter?" and the answer came not in formal statement, but in anecdotes, asides, and casual observations made during the four years of their acquaintance, some of which I have suggested earlier in this narrative. Perhaps his deepest reason surfaced in a remark he made to my father when they were standing on our back porch looking at the city, "Mr. Bresee, I love dis plantation." I think that Peter died only two or three years after this conversation, at about age eighty-five.

His old master demonstrated all the ambivalence of the slave owner— violent fluctuation between despotism and compassion. The habit of command that Cecilia talked about was still embedded in Wallace, and, although more disciplined since freedom, it flared uncontrollably at times. Peter seems to have looked behind the fierce exterior, choosing apparently to see the almost childlike kindness that might follow an outburst. As the years passed, the wall between them crumbled. I think Peter could now look at Wallace eye to eye without wavering, not across the old chasm. While Peter seemed to grow in insight and—to put it simply—wisdom, Wallace was stationary. For Peter his freedom had meant upward movement, a growing expanse of sky overhead; for Wallace, who saw himself wronged and defrauded, his loss of power meant a downward movement of which he now found daily reminders. He would continue downward unless by some reversal of his perceptual schema he could be delivered from the evil residue of his youth. Such a reversal did not come.

Characters in fiction are sometimes led through long periods of adversity in which they make discoveries that modify their personalities in some favorable direction—toward deeper wisdom, more compassion, or even acceptance. The errant son in the famous parable at last "came to himself." We have no evidence that Wallace did. Certainly he did not, as the bit of verse puts it, "grow lovely growing old."

One of Wallace's visits to the plantation stood out in Peter's memory. "I think it might have been his last trip over here—it was when he came to leave a present for little Sam." Sam was Peter Brown's grandson. Wallace had come over on the morning boat, wandered around the dairy buildings for a few minutes, and then asked one of the yard boys to find him a buggy. There was a time when he had surveyed the plantation on horseback, but in the later years he had chosen to use a buggy. Peter said that he and Emma were working in their garden when Wallace drove up to the little cottage at Bennetts. "That was the part of the plantation that he liked best," Peter said. "It probably seemed more like home to him than any other place." The morning at the hotel had not left him in a good mood. "He said he had never thought he would live in a box with people above and below him."

Peter and Wallace walked to the site of the big house, now only a faint outline of bricks in the tall grass. "The old part of the plantation meant a lot more to Mr. Wallace then it did to me," Peter said to my father, not a surprising remark when we remember that Peter was a slave when he lived at Bennetts. Emma had lived across that hedge and Peter had come to within a hair of losing her when Wallace refugeed to Lawtonville. "We walked around for a few minutes and then went down to the wharf when all of a sudden he pulled a fifty-dollar bill out of his pocket and said, 'I want you to give this to your new grandson when he gets older. Tell little Sam that it's from an old friend of his grandpa.' I'm saving that money until Sam is about ten years old. Mr. Wallace would do nice things like that and then be mad the next minute when he remembered how someone had done him wrong. One time I told him that he had to do some forgettin'. I tell him *I* have to, and everyone has to if they get along in dis world."

Years later when we were talking about Peter and the days at the Bluff, my father remarked when he was going over that scene, "I suppose we're asking the old man to forget a great deal. Having two plantations de-stroyed—houses and everything—once by soldiers and another time by vandals. Maybe a man can't ever forget that. I never saw the big house, of course, but I've stood there a few times looking at those bricks in the grass. I felt for him."

A few weeks before Wallace died, Peter called upon him in the St. John Hotel—a maneuver accomplished by advance notice and using the service entrance on Queen Street. Wallace had sent a note over on the morning boat asking him to come and to bring some pecans from the tree by the lit-tle cottage; he should use the note for entrance. Peter said he put on his best clothes, and Mr. Waters, the manager, told him they would hold the boat for him until he was ready to come back. Alison and Ruth had gone off for a meeting somewhere when Peter arrived at the hotel. He found Wallace sitting in a big chair with a lapboard in front of him and his feet on a stool. Peter handed Wallace a pecan, but told my father, "He couldn't crack it in his fist as he used to, so I broke the shell for him. He was playing solitaire when I came, but he stopped and we had a good talk. The drawer in his table had about fifty packs of cards. I don't remember what I said but I told him a lot of things that was on my mind, and when I stood up to leave, he said, 'Peter, you ought to have been a preacher.'"

A James Island cousin called on Wallace only a few days before he died and found him in a hostile mood. Again, he was sitting in a gentleman's chair, feet propped on a low stool, and fingering a deck of cards. The conversation apparently took a wrong turn, for one of the last remarks he is reported to have said was, "I'm mad as hell at everybody."

He died on November 30, 1906, in the St. John Hotel. It was probably no place he would have chosen for a deathbed. Peter learned of his death when Mr. Waters, the manager, called him down to the store to read a letter that came on the morning boat. The funeral was to be the next day at the St. James Church, and the older plantation workers were invited to attend if they cared to. "Be sure to get word to Peter Brown," a sentence in the letter read that Peter said "made me feel good." He and Emma borrowed a plantation cart for the trip to the church and sat in a pew reserved for blacks at the rear. It was Peter's and Emma's first experience with the Episcopal funeral "where they spent most of the time reading from a prayer book. Those people should have had a good sermon." Wallace was buried in the family plot in St. James Episcopal Church on James Island, next to the tall monument that he had ordered for his father.

Wallace Lawton did not make a will, a decision that suggests to me his usual obstinacy. His resentment at hotel living was profound, and he may have felt that his business-minded wife and son could "do as they damn please" with his property. After the funeral service, there was the usual gathering to discuss the distribution of personal items. Mr. Willie McCleod, a cousin whom I have mentioned earlier, told me that the matter of Wallace's portrait came up. Who would like to have it? No hands were raised. Again the question was asked, and again silence. It was clear that no one wanted Wallace's picture. Finally someone said, "Willie, you take it. You can find somewhere to put it in your big house."

WITH WALLACE'S DEATH, the center of gravity for Alison and Cecilia changed sharply. Even in his declining years Wallace had taken the responsibility of managing the plantation; now the task was theirs. Where did their interest and loyalty lie? With the plantation, of course. As exciting and absorbing as was the hotel venture, it was never a matter of the heart and could never even approach the pull of the family lands. The St. John Hotel may already have lost some of its seductive charms, and it may also have been losing money. Anyhow, what were the descendants of three generations of planters doing in the city, suddenly transplanted there and trying to run a classy hotel? For reasons either economic or emotional—I suspect the latter—Cecilia sold the hotel and made plans for Alison to return to James Island.

Peter was glad for the move, because he liked Alison. James Islanders liked him, too, and continued to wonder at the difference between father and son. He was absentminded, the planters all said, and maybe a little eccentric, but never mean or vindictive. He had a reputation for transparent honesty and for kindness. My father, who loathed profanity, once remarked, "I never heard Mr. Lawton swear." Before our arrival on James Island and during the period when they were corresponding, my father's mother died. In a letter that suggests his sensitive nature, Alison wrote in part: "I know it must be a great loss to you. We can have only one mother, and no one can take her place. It is bad enough to lose a true friend, as we have so few in this world. I know that a man of your caliber did your part for her while she lived, and therefore there should be no regrets at this temporary parting in the firm belief that, being a Christian, you know that it is so ordained by our divine maker for the best."

WHERE WOULD Ruth and Alison live? The Cuthbert House needed repairs, and was, of course, old. A recently married couple should have a new house. The plantation did not lack for attractive locations, as subsequent real estate developers have demonstrated. The site the Lawtons chose was the high ground by James Island Creek. I would probably have chosen "the Point," but that location was a bit too far from the dairy buildings and the gin house. The Lawtons built a plantation-type house, with a broad porch or piazza, two large rooms on either side of a central hallway, with an open staircase, a long sloping roof, and a second floor with dormer windows. Broad steps from the west end of the porch led to a shaded lawn that sloped down to the creek. The kitchen was behind the house, a small room reached by an enclosed corridor. This was the dwelling that I saw when we first came to James Island in 1921.

How Grand A Flame

One could travel to James Island by then via the new Ashley River toll bridge, completed in 1899, but it was a long eight or nine miles by sandy road from downtown Charleston; the Lawton milk boats were still the best way to get to the Bluff. Ruth could sit on her new piazza and watch them go chugging by as she gazed across a broad marsh to the Elias Rivers's plantation known as Centerville. We can only guess about her happiness in the new location. Sitting on her piazza the first afternoon of our arrival, she told us that she missed the rolling hills of her native Virginia. The record shows that she was active in social clubs, particularly the United Daughters of the Confederacy. Although a planter's wife living on one of the islands, she had ready access to all the advantages of city life. She told us of a delightful way in which she entertained friends. Early in April, a launch picked up guests at the Bluff, and then went to the Lawton wharf on the Battery where more guests were waiting. When all were on board, the boat took them up the Ashley River for a day at Magnolia Gardens. The guests strolled down the garden paths, enjoyed a picnic lunch on the boat, and then floated back to Charleston in late afternoon. It would be hard to imagine a more pleasant day.

The Lawton plantation continued to be unique on James Island in that it was both a cotton and dairy plantation. The "oldest dairy with the freshest milk" was prospering. Each year Cecilia added more customers to her lists, even though, for no other reason than snobbery, she would not allow her wagons to deliver above Calhoun Street. Cecilia controlled the Charleston operation, owning the land, the wagons, the bottling equipment, and hiring her own manager. Alison sold milk to his mother at a price dependent upon what she could obtain from the retail market. Cecilia kept an alert eye on Alison's business, and since the Battery Dairy determined what Alison would receive for his milk, people said that "the old lady runs the show."

My father, a few years later, was to discover to his regret that this was true. He had agreed with Alison that Cecilia should turn over the management of the Battery Dairy to her son, "but," Alison wrote, "she has steadily refused to release it to me. It is absolutely absurd her keeping same. She is 72 and has not been out of the house for over two months. We have the right, I should think, to offer her so much for a lease and if she will not lease it to us, we can sell our milk elsewhere. She cannot continue as she is, as she is getting more in debt and owes me $4,000.00 now. It would be great help to me if I could have *you* put it to her." I find it quite revealing that even before my father had been officially hired, Alison was seeking his help in dealing with Cecilia. Apparently both men lost their nerve, for Cecilia retained control.

Alison's planter friends often urged him to devote more of his land to cotton production, since the long-staple variety was commanding such high prices. He steadily refused, for reasons probably dictated by his mother, but the decision proved wise in the long-run. The reign of Sea Island cotton was to be brief.

PETER BROWN'S LIFE in the twenty years after Wallace's death were certainly the most peaceful he had ever known. I do not think that Peter ever feared that Wallace would dismiss him from the plantation, but he was continually faced with the task of adjusting to Wallace's unpredictable behavior. Wallace may not have attacked Peter personally in his later years, but he was harsh and punitive to those Peter loved. Alison was quite different. He never threw tantrums or made threats. Peter was also having the pleasure of rearing his first grandson, his daughter Sara's boy. She had married Tennie Gardener, a good and dependable employee of the plantation, but he found more lucrative work in Mount Pleasant, coming back to the island only on weekends. His son, Sam, spent more and more time with Peter and Emma, finally making his home with them. After a few years, his parents moved to Mount Pleasant. The Lawtons took an instant and enduring interest in little Sam. Peter's children were bright and so was his grandson. Sam was a boy of high energy who darted about his work with twice the speed of others, had an alert and expressive face, and deftly used all the social amenities. He was unusually tall and strong for his years, Peter told my father, and Sam felt so embarrassed in school with the smaller children that he sought every means to avoid attending and never received the schooling that he deserved. The people on the plantation called him Smilin' Sam, an expression that stayed with him for the rest of his life.

Peter Brown's loyalty to three generations of Lawtons made Cecilia especially determined to keep Sam on the plantation, and she succeeded. He continued working there long after we returned to Pennsylvania in 1930 and, indeed, until the plantation was sold in 1947. Bonum Wilson, a young Clemson graduate who worked for Alison after my father left, told me that Sam was the most able man with whom he had ever worked—able in the sense of awareness, thoroughness, and foresight. "He seemed to enjoy a complicated task. It was a pleasure to work with Sam," he said, "because he always knew what he was going to do next."

I WISH I COULD write more about the last days of Peter Brown. He quietly slipped out of my life in the mid-twenties, perhaps three years after the death of his old mistress, Cecilia. If my father were living, he could probably tell me the exact date. I remember only that he stopped bringing a string of fish to us on Fridays, and we did not see him walking across the pasture in late afternoons. Then one night at the supper table my father said simply, "Uncle Peter died today."

We may believe, I think, that he was not unattended in his death. I am sure that Alison would have monitored his last days. I do not remember his funeral; it probably occurred when I was in school. He was buried in the plantation cemetery, the one that my brother, Jamsie, and I had visited a few years earlier, which had now fallen to only occasional use. His wife was buried there, and how many of his ancestors we do not know. Those of us who knew Peter can be thankful that he was buried in the land that he loved. I have looked for a marker among the brush and tangled vines that now cover the burial ground, but have found none. At one time I was distressed to think that he and his family lie in unmarked graves; the thought no longer disturbs me. To lie in the earth under water oaks and sweet gum trees in the soil that received his enslaved ancestors may be right after all, not needing inscriptions carved in stone that, sadly, they could not read. Better the smilax vines and pine straw and finally the sheltering woods.

THE PLANTERS ON James Island had for many years gathered on the Fourth of July at their hall near the school for the annual meeting of the James Island Chapter of the South Carolina Agricultural Society. The state secretary, Dr. Harry Freeman, told me recently that South Carolina was one day short of having the oldest such society in the nation; the Pennsylvania Agricultural Society was founded one day earlier in Philadelphia. An old James Island resident remarked lightly that the South Carolina Agricultural Society was considered to be the Saint Cecilia Society of the planters. In going over some old records recently, I was happy to discover that my father was elected to membership in 1922. Traditionally the James Island meeting was the gastronomic and social event of the year—the time when planters "rode the crops" and then sat down to a sumptuous two o'clock dinner with their wives, children, and bankers from Charleston. The wives came to the Agricultural Hall in midmorning to "set up" for the meal and lay out their most elegant dishes of shrimp and crab casseroles, red rice, fried chicken, and multistoried cakes. After dinner the children would play under the trees, the young people leave for the beaches, the ladies gather on the wide porches to chat, and the men settle down in the hall for their annual meeting. Most of my Fourths of July on James Island were spent in this manner.

The meeting of the James Island Agricultural Society on July 4, 1917, was probably the dreariest one on record. For like a candle snuffed out, or a bubble when it bursts, the Sea Island cotton crop on James Island was gone. I shall try to recreate that day from information I gathered in talking to old residents who attended the meeting and from my own memories of similar occasions.

At this meeting the quality of food was undiminished, but there was no life in the party. Riding the crops—the annual fraternal appraising of the fields in midsummer—had been a dismal procession of men on horseback riding from one desiccated field to another. During this survey of the crops there was no actual competition among the planters, for an excellent crop at Seaside in no way threatened or diminished the one at Stono. For all the men, it was a day of learning more about seed selection, drainage, cultivation, the handling of labor. But this year there was no cotton—only endless rows of sick cotton plants with heads drooping, the "squares," as the fruiting sections were called, empty, their innards having been gnawed away by the grub of a little beetle one-fourth of an inch long.

The little pest had destroyed cotton in far-off Mexico before the turn of the century, a few years later in Texas, and then in the gulf states. As it crept eastward, adding annually a few counties or states to its domain, no sprays or dustings would stop it. No one was prepared for its sudden leap onto the Sea Islands in 1916, nor was anyone prepared for the fact that the valuable long-staple cotton was particularly vulnerable to this voracious beetle. Suddenly the boll weevil was here and the precious Sea Island cotton was gone.

After dinner the president of the society, Mr. Jenkins, rose to say that the State Department of Agriculture in Columbia had offered to send an expert to address the club, and of course he had invited the gentleman to come. He was happy now to present a bright young entomologist who would speak on "The Present Menace." Fuller King remarked under his breath to the man who sat next to him, "That topic doesn't help my digestion a bit."

The speaker, an earnest young man who had studied entomology at Clemson College, plunged at once into "background material," detailing the origins of the boll weevil in southern Mexico, its movement across the southern states, its mating and egg-laying habits, its hibernation. He told of how the females gnaw a little cavity in the fruit bud in which to deposit their eggs, the female being so respectful of property rights that she will not trespass on a boll where another female has preceded her. She will reluctantly, the speaker pointed out, lay a second egg only if all virgin territory has been exhausted. The planters fidgeted in their chairs, but tried to remain polite.

When the speaker paused momentarily to shuffle his notes, Alison rose and spoke, "May I ask a question, sir? We have been reading for months about these little pests and how they operate. My question is—can you tell us any preventive measures? Is there any way to rid ourselves of these little devils?"

He sat down to a patter of applause and the nodding of heads.

"Of course, I can get onto the subject of control."

"Yes, would you please?" a member remarked loudly.

The young scientist shuffled his papers again and said that the state was now conducting some research, but the results were not in yet. Some of the leads looked promising and he wished that he could bring them some really good news in this area, but he was afraid that at the moment he could not. The outlook was grim indeed.

Mr. Grimball rose and in a truculent voice said, "Then as the state department sees it, we can go broke." He did not wait for a reply but walked out on the porch.

The society president, apparently feeling that the speaker's audience would disperse unless he acted, rose and thanked him for this informative talk, adding that "all we can do is trust that the next year will bring some kind of relief."

The next year did not bring relief, nor the next ten. Certain less valuable varieties of cotton might be grown along the Carolina coast; Sea Island cotton was finished.

THE LAWTONS COULD be thankful indeed that they had decided to remain in the dairy business. The cotton farmers moved into truck crops, but the transition was difficult. Alison was already developing an interest in breeding registered Holstein cattle, for him a completely new field, but one that fascinated him. By the time my father arrived he was attending state meetings of cattle breeders, subscribing to the leading magazines on the subject, and able to discuss blood lines with my father. He had come to the conclusion that there were no local men who possessed the training he thought necessary to operate the kind of dairy plantation that he envisioned. He would advertise for a manager in one of the leading cattle-breeding magazines, the *Holstein-Friesian World*.

Placing the advertisement got postponed until the next year, although the need for such a person intensified. Alison, Ruth, and Cecilia were absorbed in preparations for an event that would be a kind of culmination of all their labors since the war: the South Carolina Agricultural Society had accepted their invitation to hold its annual summer meeting at the Lawton plantation on July 12. It must be a grand occasion, held out of doors under the live oaks, with a marquee for the dining area, a lavish meal, guests from all over the state, and the principal speaker from Cornell University. The entire plantation would be on display, the herd especially, and the new pasteurizing equipment.

An idea like this could send Cecilia into a transport of excitement; this would put the Lawton plantation "on the map." At last the hard work and good management were paying off and planters and dairymen from all over the state would see the results of their labor.

In a letter to my father a few months after this grand event, Alison wrote: "The oldest agricultural society in the United States held its 147th annual meeting on my place last Tuesday. I am enclosing a clipping from the Evening paper. I wish you could have been here."

The article read in part:

In the midst of the stately oaks surrounded by broad green acres in which a herd of pure bred Holstein cows were grazing, the 147th annual meeting of the South Carolina Agricultural Society was held yesterday on the James Island plantation of St. John Alison Lawton. A large number of members and invited guests were present. A prettier spot could not be found for such a meeting.

Under the shade of the great oaks and with the ocean breeze keeping everyone delightfully cool, the gathering was a success by the unanimous consent of the crowd. The bountiful dinner served in the open played no small part in the success of the occasion. With one great harmonious "aye" the diners declared it to be the best feast ever spread before the society in the many years of its existence.

Mr. Samuel Stoney, the president, introduced Professor Fripin of Cornell University, who spoke on the importance of lime, and Mr. James Henry Rice, who was seeking to develop agriculture along the Atlantic coast by encouraging farmers to settle there. Among his statements was one that had special meaning for Alison: "The greatest need for the coastal region is more educated farmers." He also heard Dr. Leon Banov, the young county health officer, outline health and sanitation needs of the area by saying, "It will do little good getting settlers for the coast unless we can keep them."

Alison's advertisement for a dairyman brought over seventy replies. He chose to answer first the one from my father. Ruth was now helping him with some business details, and his four page letter, which began in her handwriting and concluded in his, described in much detail his herd of cattle, the handsome location of the plantation, and its relationship with the Battery Dairy. This letter began a correspondence that lasted over a year, culminating in my father's decision to visit the plantation for two weeks in November 1920.

Alison Lawton met my father's train at four in the afternoon and drove him, in his quaint, boxlike car known as "the Anderson," directly to his home on James Island. They arrived in time to observe the end of the evening milking and make a cursory survey of the fields and buildings. Alison—always "Mr. Lawton" to the Bresees—invited my father to a light supper at eight-thirty that Flora, the cook, had remained on duty to serve. Ruth Lawton was attending a day-long meeting in Mount Pleasant and would return on the late ferry.

My father rose early next morning to watch the milking and look at the cattle more closely. Alison had apparently thought it wise to let his guest roam freely for an hour or two. He returned to the house at eight and found the Lawtons ready to serve breakfast. He was presented to Mrs. Lawton, who led them to the dining room and said that they were going to serve him a typical southern breakfast of grits, scrambled eggs, and bacon. He found the grits bland and uninteresting but ate them anyhow. He often spoke of how that breakfast in the setting of their pleasant dining room, with the windows open, contrasted with what his family in Pennsylvania was experiencing: bare trees, the fall flowers all frost-killed, the cows safely tucked in barns, and an all-night fire in the stove. Here, a mockingbird perched in a fig tree was singing outside his window.

He had come not only under the spell of the salubrious Carolina climate and the goodwill of his hosts, but he had also come under the spell of Ruth Jennings Lawton, a woman whose grace and charm lifted her gently but surely above any group she was in. They spoke of Pennsylvania, of Mrs. Lawton's home in Virginia, of the churches my father would find on the island, and the school two miles away. Then Mr. Lawton drew the conversation to a close by snapping open the cover of his vest-pocket watch, saying that if they were to make the milk boat, they would have to leave. He wanted my father to go to Charleston by water and get a "feel" for the place, see the other end of the dairy business, and meet his mother.

Down at the wharf two black men were loading the last milk cans into a flat-bottomed freight boat named the *Palmetto*. The passengers lowered themselves to the boat by a small ladder and took seats under a small canopy in the bow. The one-cylinder make-and-break engine started with a series of bangs, and soon they were cruising around the first bend of James Island Creek. When the *Palmetto* moved out of the creek and into the Ashley River, the entire peninsula lay directly across the water. My father saw for the first time the steeples of St. Michael's and St. Philip's churches. The only modern building breaking the line of housetops was the eight-storied Peoples Building on Broad Street. "That skyline has changed very little over the years," Mr. Lawton said, "and we hope to keep it that way."

The Battery Dairy wharf, built on barnacle-covered piles, extended perhaps seventy-five feet out into the river from Murray Boulevard. The *Palmetto* tied up alongside near a ladder that led to the wharf's floor. The men paused a moment to watch the workers load the milk cans into a horse-drawn wagon on whose sides were written "Oldest Dairy, but Freshest Milk," then made their way across the street to 43 South Battery. When they entered the parlor, a lady, whom my father judged to be in her seventies, rose and greeted them with the remark that her son was much impressed by my father's letters and accomplishments. Cecilia hoped he would like the area, and their plantation in particular.

My father told us later when we were on James Island that she always expressed herself in well-planned sentences and looked straight at you when she spoke. "What did she wear?" my mother would always ask, and my father could never tell her. Cecilia had once taken a beautiful train ride through Pennsylvania and they had followed the Susquehanna River. Yes, my father's town was on that river. Alison brought the reminiscences to a close by suggesting that they inspect the bottling works in the small building behind the house and take the boat to James Island in an hour.

And so the day progressed, Mr. Lawton driving him around the plantation past acres of corn ready to be picked, pasture lands, and vine-covered sweet potato fields. He met the white men who supervised the crops and the dairy, and Peter Brown, who seemed to be Alison's man on call. Then to the milking again, where he gave particular attention to a dozen high-producing cows that were fed a special diet and milked three times a day. It was here that he first met a young black man named Eddie Scott, whose sole responsibility was the care of these cows. My father was, of course, particularly interested in the little "test herd," as it was called, and he wanted to watch Eddie work. He sat up late that night and when, at about twelve o'clock, a lantern appeared in the test barn—a shedlike building that was mostly open windows—he walked across the yard to talk to Eddie while he milked the cows. Halfway to the barn he heard a man singing, a voice of singular beauty, that seemed to float out of the barn and into the sky above him. My father stopped, immobilized. It was Eddie singing to his cows—and to the stars—a voice that my father always said was the sweetest he ever heard. Eddie's tenor voice was so rich and expressive, one that drifted so effortlessly to the highest range, that my father said he did not move for minutes. Some of the tunes he knew—gospel songs that leaped all the state boundaries—and others that may have been spontaneous improvisations on the tunes we call "spirituals." Eddie sang his way into my father's heart, and he would later earn his respect as one of the most able and trusted workers on the plantation.

After we had come down from Pennsylvania in 1921 to live on the Bluff, my father, late one night, asked my mother to walk with him to the dairy barns and stand in the shadows and listen. He must have been deeply moved, because my father spoke of that transcendent experience for the rest of his life—the soft outlines of buildings and trees under the night sky, the yellow glow of a lantern hanging from a post in the test barn, and over it all the sweet, soaring voice of Eddie Scott singing to his cows at midnight.

MY FATHER KNEW Cecilia for a year and a half before she died, and saw her chiefly as an old lady of strong opinions who should long ago have relinquished the control of her business to Alison. I feel sure that he did not know of the memoir she had produced, and so could not see her life whole. Had he known of it, I am certain he would have told us. (I must add here that the information I attribute to my father was not all conveyed to us around the supper table each night while we were on James Island; life on the Lawton plantation continued to occupy a large place in our conversation long after we had returned to Pennsylvania.) His talks with her were formal and mostly about the business of dairying, and from his occasional references to her, I saw her as a problem to be dealt with, not as a remarkable woman whose life had come to an almost triumphant conclusion. How could he know that her family had owned four plantations and hundreds of slaves, of her personal maid, Eleanor, given to her at age five, of those years in a slave cabin on the Old Gillisonville Road? If she had hidden resentment against a northerner, my father never detected it; I do not think such a resentment was present in either her or Alison. A commendable sense of decency kept her from telling a man fresh from the North of the depredations that his forebears had inflicted upon her family. Her memoir was the suitable place for all that; the greatest tragedy of her life, however—the court-martial of her husband for murder—never found its way into words. Only Peter Brown had lived with her and Wallace through it all, and he was not talking. A man as bright as Peter, who had access to everything, surely knew the full story of the shooting in the little cabin near Lawtonville and of the court-martial at Hilton Head.

Fate had been kind to let her play host to the Agricultural Society picnic under the oaks. That illustrious event was the crowning testimonial that she needed; the traditions and aspirations of her upbringing were now fully realized—a beautifully located plantation managed by her son, and a home at the best address (or among the best) in Charleston. Those sturdy forebears, Winborns I and II and Robert Themistocles, could not have asked for more. Only Peter Brown had lived long enough to see Cecilia come full circle.

She had experienced at its darkest moments our greatest national agony with over a million men killed or wounded, and her involvement with the great Cause would never cease while she lived. No wonder that she now devoted much of her later years to veterans' hospitals, care of widows and orphans, and the public recognition of Confederate leaders. This narrative is perhaps overweighted with accounts of the Civil War, but it could hardly have been written otherwise.

On the flyleaf of *Events in the Life of Cecilia Lawton*, she had entered the name of her husband and the date of his death, and below that in her own handwriting is an unfinished sentence "Cecilia Lawton died . . . " In the margin of the page are her instructions: "Please enter here the date and place of my departure and burial place—C.L." Her son, Alison, completed the sentence. In his handwriting are the words "February 27th about 5:30 P.M. at her residence, 43 South Battery; and was laid to rest beside her husband in the church yard of St. James Episcopal Church, James Island, Rev. Cary Beckwith officiating." The year was 1923.

ALISON LAWTON died in 1947. He could never have dreamed that Cecilia's memoirs would fall into the hands of the little boy who stood by the train in the Columbus Street station on that November day when we first arrived in Charleston and received his polite handshake. The kindly man in the cream-colored hat had led us to his car, "the Anderson," and taken our family across the Ashley River over a rattling wooden bridge to a place that he called "the Bluff" and, quite unwittingly, headed us into the spell of history. As he carried us in his quaint sedan over the winding, shaded roads of James Island to his century-old plantation—battered by invading troops, insect pests, and hard times—neither could Alison Lawton have sensed how that old plantation would so enrich the lives of those dazed but expectant travelers from Pennsylvania.

As a child I never escaped the shadow of the war that overhung my growing-up days, and I am not sure that I would have it otherwise. It would be ignoble to forget our heroes, and I grew up believing that. I felt in some strange way that the past was all about me, and that I should somehow make a connection with it. In the intervening years since we first set foot in Charleston and the writing of this book, I have spent more than my share of time exploring the streets, alleys, and cemeteries of the "old part" of the city. I return often to St. Michael's Church, where there is a plaque listing her sons who died in the Confederate War, young lieutenants and captains — youths all — bearing the family names that I still hear in Charleston. Above them is a simple and poignant inscription that evokes the pride and sadness of those years, expunged now of anger and pain, words to close not only a soldier's life, but the lives of people everywhere who endured those embattled years.

> How grand a flame
> this marble watches o'er.
> Their wars behind them,
> God's great peace before.

EPILOGUE

1989

ALISON AND RUTH LAWTON sold the Bluff in 1946 to John R. Jefferies who continued to operate it as a dairy plantation until 1951. The Lawtons moved from the house by the creek to the present Heyward House where Alison died February 14, 1947. Ruth Lawton then took an apartment in Summerville, South Carolina, where she died February 14, 1953.

On the plantation there followed a quiescent period of a few years when the fields produced only truck crops and while the real estate developers were gathering their forces. The magnificent location that Alison had described to my father and that the Lawtons had guarded so jealously was now about to be shared with others. The bulldozers were soon at work. They swept away all the buildings but the Heyward House, leveled the elevations by the creek, and turned the marshy inlets into landscaped lakes and ponds. Harborview Drive now slices the plantation in two and a network of paved roads covers land that used to be known as the graveyard field, the farm, thirty-six, and the Bennetts pasture.

I asked Creighton Frampton, who grew up on a plantation across the creek from the Bluff and whose ancestors had planted on James Island for over a hundred years, to go with me to the cemetery at St. James Episcopal Church. A retired superintendent of Charleston County schools, Creighton had been a rich source of James Island lore for me. As we started down the Folly Road, he said, "Let's take the back road past Stono plantation. It's quieter that way." He was right. The winding, sandy road that used to take me to the plantation was paved now, but the arching trees were still there.

Turning onto Camp Road a few minutes later, we saw the steeple of St. James over the trees—no longer the little Gothic building of pine and cypress presided over by an itinerant preacher every other Sunday, but a church faithfully modeled after St. Michael's in Charleston, its tower a diaphanous white, floating over the treetops, the whole edifice exuding refinement and elegance. The doors were open for a children's service that was then in progress, and mothers in cars were waiting under the trees.

How could this grand building have been fitted between the arms of the cemetery that had nestled close to the sides of the old church that I knew? It did not fit, Creighton told me, and the bones of many had to be reinterred. There was a formal service when it was done, the rector in his ecclesiastical robes standing beside the new earth, prayer book in hand.

The Lawton graves did not have to be moved. They were in the precise plot of land that Winborn had selected nearly a century and a half ago, a rectangle of earth enclosed by an iron fence. Creighton and I stood by the enclosure in silence, our thoughts receding to other days.

The three generations were together at last, I thought, chief players in a story that lasted 160 years. Winborn's stone was the tallest, an eight-foot obelisk mounted on a granite base. Next, the graves of Wallace and Cecilia; for their children who died six days apart, two marble lambs were nestled on a low stone above the inscription "Our Darlings."

"And here are the two we remember," Creighton said, "St. John Alison Lawton, V.M.I.—'91, and Ruth Jennings Lawton, President Regent, U.D.C."

The fence enclosed the graves neatly—no need for extra room, for there are no more Lawtons of that line to join them.

"Alison, you know, had no brothers and sisters who survived infancy and he had no children," Creighton continued. "There have been no Lawtons—at least of that branch of the family—on James Island for many years now. I feel a little bad about that."

This little tract of earth, it occurred to me, is all that remains of the lands of a family who, for a century and a half once owned a goodly portion of James Island—lands brought to fruition by human slavery, fought over by two invading armies, destroyed, restored, and now become city. The forces that were played out on their fields and marshes—forces that once troubled the whole nation—have now subsided. They will be replaced, I thought, by other struggles that future historians will have to name.

We turned away from the little rectangle of earth and monuments, brought abruptly back into the present by the singing of tires on the Folly Island Highway and the laughter and bright faces of children now leaving the church.

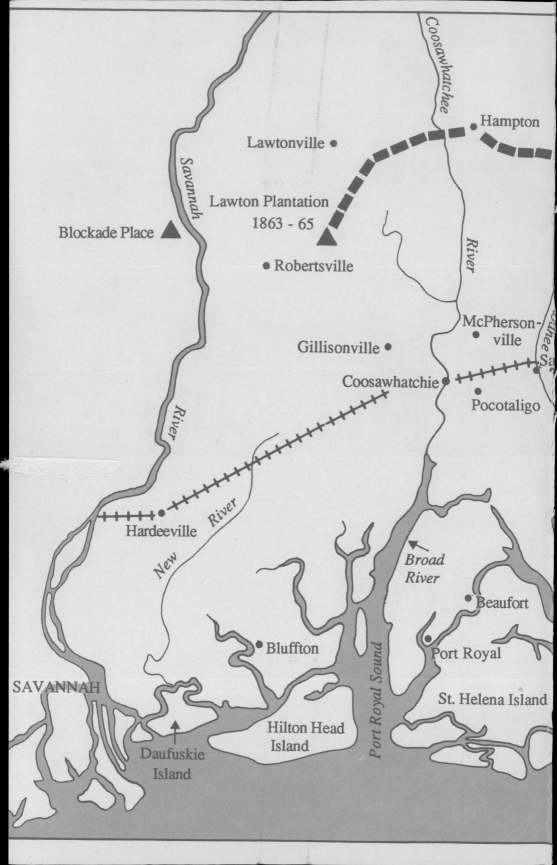